Praise for Leigh Montville's

THE MYSTERIOUS MONTAGUE

"Mr. Montville is as good as the facts he has found and reported—and he has clearly done a thorough job of scouring old newspapers and memoirs. Filled with the kind of jaw-dropping achievements on the fairways and greens that high-handicappers like to repeat with respectful awe."   —*The Wall Street Journal*

"Superb."   —*The Florida Times-Union*

"Montville hits the pin in one with this page-turning account of a long-forgotten golfer. . . . [His] cinematic recounting of the trial and its aftermath will make readers feel like they're right there in the courtroom."   —*Kirkus Reviews*

"Wonderful."   —*The Oregonian*

"Delightful."   —*The Star-Ledger*

"Amusing."   —Leonard Maltin's Movie Crazy

"One of the most intriguing tales of the summer."

—Bloomberg.com

Leigh Montville
THE MYSTERIOUS MONTAGUE

Leigh Montville is a former columnist at *The Boston
Globe* and former senior writer at *Sports Illustrated.* He is
the author of five books, including *The New York Times*
bestsellers *The Big Bam: The Life and Times of Babe Ruth*,
Ted Williams: The Biography of an American Hero, and *At
the Altar of Speed: The Fast Life and Tragic Death of Dale
Earnhardt.* He lives in Boston, Massachusetts.

The Big Bam

Ted Williams

At the Altar of Speed

The

MYSTERIOUS MONTAGUE

A True Tale of Hollywood, Golf, and Armed Robbery

LEIGH MONTVILLE

Anchor Books

A DIVISION OF RANDOM HOUSE, INC.

NEW YORK

The author and publisher gratefully acknowledge the following
for the right to reprint material in this book:

"Mysterious Montague" article. Copyright © Time Inc. Reprinted by permission.
Time is a registered trademark of Time Inc. All rights reserved.

Westbrook Pegler article. Copyright © United Feature Syndicate Inc.
Reprinted by permission.

Material from *Lakeside Golf Club of Hollywood 50th Anniversary Book*.
Copyright © Lakeside Golf Club of Hollywood, California. Reprinted by permission.

Bobby Jones letters. Copyright © United States Golf Association Museum.
Reprinted by permission.

Des Moines Tribune editorial. Copyright © *Des Moines Register*.
Reprinted by permission.

The Library of Congress has cataloged the Doubleday edition as follows:
Montville, Leigh.
The mysterious Montague : a true tale of Hollywood, golf,
and armed robbery / Leigh Montville.
p. cm.
1. Montague, John, 1903–1972. 2. Golfers—California—Los Angeles—Biography.
3. Criminals—New York (State)—Biography. I. Title.
GV964.M543M66 2007
796.352092—dc22
2007037256

Anchor ISBN: 978-0-7679-2650-8

Author photograph © Robin Moleux
Book design by Caroline Cunningham

www.anchorbooks.com

146122990

For Leigh Alan,

For Robin,

For Doug

and Jackson

The Future

Half the people in Hollywood are dying to be discovered and the other half are afraid they will be.

—LIONEL BARRYMORE

CONTENTS

The

MYSTERIOUS
MONTAGUE

A FEW WORDS OF INTRODUCTION

Reports are to hand of a mighty man of sport who would seem to combine the fabulous prowess of Paul Bunyan, John Henry and Popeye the Sailor with the remarkable social knacks of Ivan Petrovsky Skovar, the Muskovite hero of the old college doggerel who could imitate Irving, tell fortunes with cards and sing to a Spanish guitar.

The man's name is given as John Montague and his field of operations is Hollywood, but it seems unlikely that our story is a publicity plant, for he avoids publicity and will not permit anyone to take his picture if he can prevent it....

Westbrook Pegler

United News Syndicate

September 25, 1936

A man who never played in a tournament—not even a modest sectional tournament—is the most discussed golfer in America today. His name is John Montague....

He is at once a myth, a marvel and a monster. On the one hand he is fabulously wealthy. On the other he is just an ordinary person who once in a while turns in an extraordinary round. This legend says he never shoots over 70. That legend insists he frequently struggles to get 90.

A sinister sort of mystery surrounds him. Hundreds of people have met him, no one knows him. His background is a blank wall. He is an Indian, a Mexican, a South American or just a native Californian. You can take your pick. Bull-necked, swarthy, thin-thighed, he has the strength of seven truck horses. No two men can hope to stand up to him. More than one has crumbled under the power of his fists....

Joe Williams
New York Telegram and Sun
March 11, 1937

He is the type of fellow that children like on sight and the ladies trust....

Damon Runyon
New York Daily Mirror
August 24, 1937

He lives in Beverly Hills with Comedian Oliver Hardy (284 lb.) whom he can pick up with one hand. When not in residence with Hardy he is "somewhere in the desert" where he is supposed to own a silver mine or gold mine. He owns two Lincoln Zephyrs and a supercharged Ford, specially geared for high speed. He is about 33, 5 ft. 10 in., 220 lb. He is built like a wrestler, with tremendous hands, bulldog shoulders and biceps half again as big as Jack Dempsey's. His face is handsome, disposition genial. He can consume abnormal quantities of whiskey. He frequently stays up all night and recently did so five nights in a row. He is naturally soft-spoken and dislikes hearing men swear in the presence of ladies.

Time

January 25, 1937

He showed me a golf game that, even in my wildest dreams, I could never equal. He made me feel like a fool, a low, crawling fool, swatting away at a little white ball that hooked this way and sliced that, while, without effort, he sent his screaming down the fairway for 300 yards or more. He let me sock him in the belly. I hurt my knuckles, but not his belly. Then he picked me up with one hand and held me dangling.

Now I reach my point, friends. A guy has charm who can meet you at something at which you think you're pretty good, and show you up as a miserable ass and make you raging mad, but is so damn strong that he can tear you into little squares like a kid fixing the paper for hares and hounds.

You can't lick him at the game and you and a dozen like you couldn't lick him with your fists. You resent it, you resent it plenty, but you can't do anything about it.

So you're charmed no end.

Henry McLemore

United Press

September 8, 1937

It seems John was just as proficient with a pistol as he is with a putter, which just goes to show you shouldn't judge a fellow by his plus
fours.

Jack Miley
New York Daily News
July 12, 1937

Let the tale begin.

CHAPTER ONE

THE ADIRONDACKS

1930

The restaurant sat at the bottom of a large bowl of Adirondack darkness. The surrounding mountains, beautiful during the day, forest green and forest wild, still made their presence known during the night. They shut out all horizons: zipped up, locked down, tucked in the well-scattered population between the New York towns of Au Sable Forks and Jay, under a black and tight blanket. The lights from the restaurant were pinpricks of isolated civilization.

The porch light was still lit.

The inside lights were still lit.

Proprietor Kin Hana and his wife, Elizabeth, and an employee, Paul Poland, finished the work of Monday night in the first hours of Tuesday, August 5, 1930. The last three customers were gone, but money had to be counted, tables cleared, floors washed, stock replenished. A last cup of coffee had to be drunk, a joke told.

The restaurant, simply known as Hana's to the local residents, was a roadhouse on Route 9, the two-lane asphalt highway that meandered down from the Canadian border, fifty-eight miles to the north, then to Glens Falls and Saratoga Springs, then Albany and all the way to New York City, Broadway, 275 miles to the south. Adventure had come to the road in 1920, especially in the dark, with the advent of the Eighteenth Amendment, Prohibition, and an atmosphere of car chases and gunplay as smugglers tried to bring distilled spirits from one country to the thirsty citizens of another.

The restaurant was a modest part of the excitement. A man could buy a drink at Hana's, could also buy a bottle to take home, but this was not unusual. A man could buy a drink at most of the roadhouses along Route 9. The area was awash in alcohol. Farmers rented out their barns and hay wagons to smugglers. Mechanics in Saranac Lake fitted out automobiles for the chase, engines cranked to racetrack speed, false gas tanks and false bottoms installed to convey every possible ounce of hard liquor and beer. Freight trains contained hidden cargo. Boats on Lake Champlain carried more contraband than sightseers. The dance was a decade old, a formalized routine of winks and nods, hide-and-seek, punctuated by occasional murders and publicized court trials. Illegality was the norm.

"I believe that 90 percent of the people in the county were opposed to Prohibition," one Au Sable Forks resident later said. "Not one farmer in twenty-five would not shield, help, or hide a rumrunner. The usual compensation for their help was a bottle of liquor, more highly prized than money."

Kin Hana was Japanese, a relentless bundle of hustle and bustle, always on the job, meticulous about cleanliness. He considered himself a restaurant owner, not a bootlegger. The liquor business was something that had developed by circumstance. He provided good food at modest prices, typical American fare, even set up a roadside stand in the summers to sell hamburgers and hot dogs to travelers who didn't have time for a full meal.

His establishment was run with much attention to detail. All kitchen employees had to wear hairnets. He inspected the waitresses every day from behind his rimless glasses, made the women hold out their hands, checked to see if their fingernails were clean, then looked down to see if their shoes were shined. His children laughed at this fussiness, and maybe the waitresses did, too, but never in front of him. He was not a man surrounded by casual chatter and laughter.

His given last name was Hanada, shortened long ago for easier English consumption. His version of the immigrant success story had started when he was a teenager, a cabin boy on a Japanese ocean liner. Left behind in an Anchorage, Alaska, hospital when he fell ill, he decided to move to the United States. He learned the rudiments of a new language, and then embarked on a new life that eventually led to a position as a houseboy for a wealthy family in Au Sable Forks.

Impressed by his good work, the wealthy family sent him to cooking school in Boston. Cooking school led to the restaurant business. He had edged into his late forties now, a familiar figure in the community, and was long married to Elizabeth, a local girl, a Cobb, quiet and religious. They had five children ranging from nineteen to five, three girls and two boys. The color of Hana's skin sometimes drew comments, obvious and stupid, such as "Ching-Ching Chinaman, sitting on a fence"— there almost certainly was no other Asian entrepreneur, maybe no other Asian resident, in all of the Adirondacks—but he always seemed too busy to be bothered by an overheard insult.

The restaurant on Route 9 constituted his entire empire. It was a long, one-story white building that was not only his business, but also his home. The dining room of the restaurant was the largest rentable room in Au Sable Forks, sometimes used for civic functions. The much smaller illegal barroom was tucked next to the kitchen. A door not far from the restrooms at the other end of the dining room opened into the half of the building that was a four-bedroom apartment.

Four of his five children were sleeping in that apartment at this exact moment, two girls in one bedroom, the youngest boy in another. The third daughter, sick with a cold, was asleep on a couch in the living room. Hana's sixty-seven-year-old divorced father-in-law, Matt Cobb, slept in a third bedroom. Hana himself was in the back of the restaurant, locking the storeroom for the night. Elizabeth and Paul Poland were finishing their work in the well-lit dining room. The chores were almost done, the last dot of activity soon to be extinguished into the darkness.

This was when the three men entered the restaurant.

Elizabeth was the first to see them. She hadn't heard any car; the sound of the front door was what made her turn. The men, a curious sight, were standing by the cigar case. Elizabeth registered at first glance that each of them was wearing a soft felt hat and each had a white cloth mask covering his face. Far from alarmed, she almost laughed. She thought these were friends from the nearby town of Keene playing a late-night joke. She was going to say something funny, had it half composed in her head, but then she saw the three revolvers.

They were pointed at her.

———

The night changed with one blink of recognition. The masked visitors were businesslike, gruff, and efficient. The way they held their revolvers, the sense of authority contained in each slight move, said that these were not kids, half drunk and impulsive, picking a random site for random mischief. These were men who knew exactly where they were and what they were doing. They had a plan.

"Be quiet," one of them said.

Neither Elizabeth nor Paul Poland moved. Neither spoke.

"Where's the little fellow?" the same man then said.

The question showed the extent of the men's knowledge. The little fellow? Kin? Before Elizabeth could answer—before she could make up something or tell the truth, what to do?—her husband came out of the stockroom. A revolver immediately was turned toward him.

The demand now was for everyone to lie facedown on the floor. Elizabeth and Paul Poland complied. Kin Hana resisted, reacted to this intrusion; he asked in his fractured second language what was happening. One of the men quickly threw him onto his back. Kin Hana resisted no more.

While two revolvers were trained on the people on the floor, the third gunman went through the door to the apartment at the end of the dining room. He walked directly into Kin and

Elizabeth's bedroom, as sure as if he had lived in the house all of his life, and yanked a sheet from the bed. He ripped the sheet into strips that were soon used to gag the mouths and bind the hands and feet of the three captives.

The gunmen now turned out all the lights, even the light on the porch, so no strangers would stumble onto the scene. Not even the summer moths would be attracted to any commotion, the dark business conducted under the focus of flashlights the gunmen had brought with them.

First, the men emptied Kin Hana's pockets, taking whatever cash money he had, disregarding any checks. Second, they removed his gag and asked for the combination of the safe in the master bedroom of the apartment. (They knew about the safe?) He said he didn't know the combination; that his wife always took care of the money. The gunmen turned their attention to Elizabeth.

They undid her bindings and walked her back to the apartment and told her to get to work. Stalling for time, chewing on quiet hope that help somehow would arrive, she balked. She said she wasn't sure of the numbers. One of the gunmen said if she didn't remember, he would dynamite the safe and the building and her children would be in peril. Elizabeth said she remembered now.

All of the activity had awakened the oldest daughter, Naomi, who saw her mother and the masked men pass her bedroom door. She started screaming. One of the gunmen quickly grabbed her, and his accomplices soon rounded up the other children and yanked another sheet off one of their beds. The children were bound and stretched on the floor.

The gunmen decided to take care of all possibilities.

"Where's the old man?" one of them asked.

He was directed—why lie?—to the final bedroom, where he was greeted with a surprise. The grandfather, Matt Cobb, also had been awakened by the noise. He was known in the area as powerful and agile for his age, a fighter, and he was out of his bed, waiting. When the gunman entered the room, Cobb jumped him. The old man pulled down the gunman's mask and started flailing. When the gunman landed on his back and feared he was losing, he called for help.

"Verne!" he shouted.

A second gunman joined the fray. Cobb continued to resist, but now was overwhelmed. A hard crack on his head with the butt of the new arrival's revolver ended the struggle. The gunmen ripped up another sheet, tied up the semiconscious grandfather, and left him on his bed.

The attention turned back to the safe. Elizabeth worked the combination at last, opened the door, and one of the men grabbed all the bills he could see, stuffing them into a pillowcase taken from her bed. He worked so fast that he missed some gold coins and bills in the back.

Business completed, the three men now began to leave the restaurant, off to divide their stolen gains in private. Their departure was not without incident.

Matt Cobb had regained consciousness, escaped from his bindings, and climbed out his bedroom window. He had come around to the front of the restaurant and found a fourth gunman guarding the car, making sure no late-night strangers appeared. The fourth gunman ordered him to go back to the other side of the building. As Cobb complied, he ran into the same gunman who had whacked him with the butt of the revolver.

The fight began again. Cobb again was surprisingly resilient, and the gunman yelled for help. One of his partners rushed to hand him a short length of garden hose filled with buckshot and bolts, tape covering both ends to make an improvised blackjack. The first gunman started to hit Cobb on the head.

"Help!" the old man shouted. "Murder! They're trying to kill me!"

A final whack with the garden-hose blackjack silenced the noise. The two men had rolled down an embankment to the edge of the Au Sable River during the tussle. The gunman stood, brushed off his clothes, and climbed back to the restaurant parking lot, where he rejoined his partners. They hurried into their car and drove into the night.

Left behind were Kin and Elizabeth and Paul Poland and the four children, all bound and gagged and terrified as they lay on the restaurant floor. Matt Cobb, bleeding, unconscious, lay at the side of the river. The children wondered if their grandfather was dead.

Sgt. Paul McGinnis and Trooper D. H. Wood from the Malone Barracks of the New York State Police were on patrol for bootleggers on Route 9 at 1:30 in the morning of August 5, 1930. Various measures had been adapted for the perpetual dance with the ever-resourceful opposition—troopers sometimes pulled a six-foot sheet of iron studded with spikes across the road, sometimes tied heavy metal chains to trees a foot off the ground to stop the speeding cars—but the basic element was still the chase.

The state police were the underdogs: overworked, underpaid, and underappreciated. Their average salary was $1,270 a year after eight years of service. They were tempted by the easy money on the other side, and hampered by the indifference of the general population. The smugglers generally had better cars and better public relations. A violent end to the chase, bootleggers shot dead, alcohol confiscated, brought police brutality charges more often than applause. The public liked to drink. The sinners were more popular than the saviors.

All cars on the road at this time of the night in this part of the county were suspicious to the troopers. That was an easy rule. The faster a car was traveling, the more suspicious it became. When McGinnis and Wood saw a Ford roadster hurtling toward them, going south on Route 9, they immediately signaled the car to stop. When it didn't, the chase began.

The driver of the roadster was thirty-five-year-old William Carleton, a veteran of the smuggling wars from Utica. He sometimes used the name William Martin and had been convicted of bootlegging and several other misdemeanors. The passenger was another oft-convicted bootlegger, thirty-two-year-old John Sherry, also of Utica. They were two of the four robbers of the Hana restaurant.

After leaving the scene of the crime in a green Pontiac sedan, the robbers split into pairs when they picked up Carleton's roadster, which had been parked less than a mile down the road. The plan was to meet again in Mechanicville to split up the money. Carleton and Sherry took off first, so they encountered the troopers first.

The chase lasted only a couple of miles. Sergeant McGinnis and Trooper Wood had pulled close, so Carleton and Sherry stopped the Ford roadster in the town of Upper Jay. The troopers also stopped. As McGinnis and Wood stepped from their car, Carleton fired up the Ford's engine, executed a fast U-turn, and steamed north again on Route 9, back toward the Hana restaurant. The troopers returned in a hurry to their own car, made the U-turn, and followed. Somewhere in the new chase, the green Pontiac sedan flew past in the other direction, a fact the troopers noted but were helpless to address. They were already busy.

With a few seconds' lead, Sherry had an idea in the passenger's seat of the Ford. Even though the car was traveling as fast as possible for the road and conditions, maybe fifty miles per hour, he reached across and turned off the headlights. It was an old bootleggers' trick. The idea was that troopers couldn't see the Ford's taillights in the tucked-in mountain dark.

Alas, Carleton, behind the wheel, was not ready for Sherry's idea. While the troopers couldn't see his taillights, he also couldn't see what was in front of him.

Passing the Tobias Homestead, a local landmark, he failed to negotiate a slight bend in the road and crashed through a guardrail over a small culvert off the east branch of the Au Sable River. The Ford roadster flew through the air, landed with a second crash, and rolled over several times.

When Sergeant McGinnis and Trooper Wood arrived, they found the scattered results. Sherry was still in the wrecked car, dead. Carleton had been ejected and lay half conscious on the ground. He had suffered only cuts, bruises, and a sprained ankle. A pillowcase filled with $630 was found in the vicinity. The troopers also found a .38-caliber Colt revolver in the car and another revolver next to Carleton.

The absence of alcohol was an immediate mystery. The troopers weren't sure what exactly had happened. Wasn't this a bit of chase-and-catch business, a part of the nightly game? If it wasn't, then what was it?

———————

The answer arrived soon enough. Elizabeth Hana had freed herself and called the state police barracks in Malone to report the robbery. Sergeant McGinnis and Trooper Wood were notified and took Carleton back to the restaurant, where Elizabeth identified him as the man who had forced her to open the safe. The troopers then took him to the jail in Au Sable Forks and booked him for robbery in the first degree.

The night's excitement became the subject of great conversation the next day. The wrecked Ford was taken to Bola's Garage in Au Sable Forks, where residents gathered and wondered how anyone had survived the crash. ("One of the worst pieces of wreckage ever brought into that establishment," the *Adirondack Record* reported.) A large piece of the guardrail still was crammed through the radiator and into the engine. The body was folded; the wheels that remained on the chassis were bent and misshapen.

"Excitement has been general in Essex County during the past few days over a bold hold-up and the resulting fatality of one of the bandits," the *Essex County Republican* said in its report later in the week, "the story of which savors of metropolitan thrills, and the more fortunate termination of the story than the big cities usually afford, in the fact that the loot was recovered and one bandit caught to answer for his misdeeds. One has answered at the Supreme Bar of Justice."

Carleton, after admitting nothing during two hours of questions at the America House Hotel, was taken to the county jail in Elizabethtown. An ambulance arrived at Bromley Sprague's funeral parlor to take John Sherry's body back to Utica, accompanied by his brother. The district attorney, Thomas McDonald, declared that sufficient evidence had been found to predict that the remaining two gunmen would be arrested in the next two days.

Part of that evidence came from Matt Cobb. The grandfather was battered, had trouble with his hearing, and now was missing several teeth, but certainly was alive. He had recognized one of the gunmen, the one waiting outside with the car, as Roger Norton. The identification was easy. Not only was Norton a distant cousin of Cobb's, the bandit and his wife had eaten at the restaurant only two weeks earlier.

The police put out word that they wanted to question him. He was twenty-nine years old, another character who had been arrested in the past for smuggling activities. He lived in Troy, heard he was wanted, and surrendered to the state police two days after the crime. He said at first that he had no part in what happened, but soon admitted that he had been the driver of the green Pontiac sedan. The state police had also stopped the Pontiac with another patrol near Schroon Lake, but Norton's passenger coolly talked their way out of trouble. The passenger, during the conversation, told Trooper Harry Durand that his name was Lawrence Ryan.

The police now strongly believed that "Lawrence Ryan" was really twenty-six-year-old LaVerne Moore of Syracuse. Two bags of circumstantial evidence, found in the rumble seat of the crashed roadster, led them to that belief. The first, a golf bag, contained LaVerne Moore's golf clubs: thirteen wood-shafted irons, a driver, brassie, and spoon, and a putter. The second bag,

a Gladstone traveling bag, contained clothes plus letters, pictures of girls, LaVerne Moore's driver's license and draft regis-
tration card, plus a package of newspaper clippings detailing his
athletic career.

One of the clippings, from a Buffalo paper, under the headline "Moore Stars as Bisons Win from Ft. Lauderdale Nine," described how he pitched two minor-league innings, struck out
three, walked three, and stroked a double in one at-bat. The
story also noted that he had recovered from an appendicitis attack, which had caused the New York Giants to lose interest in
him.

Two troopers went to Moore's home in Syracuse late on
Sunday night to question him, five days after the robbery. His
mother, Mary, answered the door at 300 Stolp Avenue, a two-
family house, and said that her son was gone. The troopers asked
when he had left. Mrs. Moore replied that he had kissed her and
said good-bye on Wednesday morning. That was the day after
the robbery. She said she had no idea where he was, or when he
might return. A warrant for his arrest was issued on September
25, 1930, but not served. LaVerne Moore could not be found.

He was simply gone.

CHAPTER TWO

HOLLYWOOD

Four Years Later

There was nothing quite like seeing John Montague pick up Oliver Hardy with one hand and place him on the bar in the grill room of the Lakeside Golf Club. No strongman act in the circus was more impressive. No scene in *Sons of the Desert* or *Babes in Toyland* was funnier. This was not some cinematic trick, something out of the nearby Hal Roach Studios in Culver City, California. This was real.

One minute the most famous fat man in America, full name Oliver Norvell (Babe) Hardy, 303 pounds according to *Ripley's Believe It or Not,* would be standing in his plus fours, his over-the-calf stockings, his two-tone shoes, and his cardigan sweater of the day, chatting amiably about the perils and pleasures of eighteen holes of armed combat with a small white ball. The next minute—woops!—the comic actor would be lifted about four feet in the air and deposited, *plunk,* in front of Eddie, the bartender.

"Babe, what'll you have?" John Montague would ask, normal as could be.

The process was so fast and efficient that the various customers in the room, many of them famous Hollywood film celebrities of 1934, would share the same startled reaction no matter what level of insobriety they might have attained. They couldn't believe their eyes. Montague's right-handed grab of Hardy's cardigan or shirt or jacket was so casual. The lift seemed so easy.

Who else in the room could do this?

Who else in the world?

The fat man would sort of teeter precariously on the edge of the bar. His predicament—"Well, this is another fine mess you've gotten me into," he would have said to his comic partner, Stan Laurel, if this were a movie—was compelling. If he teetered the wrong way, he would fall and land with a distressing splat that probably would make international headlines. If he didn't fall, well, the danger of falling still existed. He was an overweight tightrope walker, suddenly very nervous in the middle of the trip. He was Humpty Dumpty, watched by all the king's horses and all the king's men.

What next?

Montague would drain the uncomfortable moment for ten seconds, twenty, maybe more, then offer a hand. The fat man would return to the floor with a semicoordinated jiggle and bounce. Drinking would resume.

Voilà.

If Montague was waiting at the bar, this routine would happen almost every time Hardy came into the grill room at Lakeside. It happened so often that Hardy started sticking his head in the door and asking, "Is Montague around? Is he at the club today?" before he entered. No matter how many times it happened, it was funny. No matter how many times it happened, it was an amazement.

John Montague was an amazement. Every day.

He was a new guy, a member at Lakeside for only a year, but was already the club champion, the most outrageous golfer anyone had ever seen. He was about thirty years old, a big man, but different from Oliver Hardy's version of big. His height was five feet ten, normal, but he weighed as much as 220 pounds, big-boned and powerful, wide across the chest, construction-worker arms; a handshake best to be avoided, always too strong and too long. He was a well-padded isosceles triangle, but built upside down, built as if he were born to break down doors.

Handsome enough, he best resembled an Irish tenor on a world tour, with a round face topped by wavy black hair that always was well trimmed, perfect. He moved with the mixture of menace and mirth that attracts the attention of other men. The mirth mostly was in the foreground, jokes and bets on anything, good cheer, but there was never a doubt that the menace was in his back pocket. John Montague was a better man to have as a friend than an enemy. That was the feeling. He was fun and insurance at the same time.

"We were out one night and somehow or other there was an altercation with the driver of another car," Lakeside member

Johnny Weissmuller, the Olympic swimmer and reigning "Tarzan" in the movies, reported. "Seems like he thought Monty should have stopped and let him ahead of us. The guy started cussing and generally harassing us and walked up to the car and kept it up. Monty didn't say anything, he just got out of the car, walked up to the front of the guy's Lincoln, picked it up about yea high and let it drop. One of the lights fell off and Monty just walked back to the guy and said, 'What did you say?' The smart guy almost fainted as we drove off."

The normal constraints of gravity and distance and the limitations of the human body didn't seem to exist for John Montague. Pick up a car? He could pick up a car. There were dozens of stories about him picking up cars. He supposedly held one up long enough for a friend to fix a flat tire. His strength was a constant subject of conversation.

"One time there was a big 1928 Buick out front of this club where we were playing golf in Whittier," golfer Gene Andrews said. "Montague said he'd move it over three feet to get it out of the way. And, sure enough, he went to the front of the car and picked it up and moved the front three feet. Then he went to the back and moved the back three feet. He moved the whole car three feet."

Exaggeration was part of his daily routine. This was a man who lived in extremes. He seemed to drink more than anyone else, eat more, need less sleep. His wardrobe was flashier. His cars—three of them at last count—were faster. He seemed to do everything louder, bigger, quite often better.

He would walk up to the pool table and bet that he could put all of the balls, including the cue ball, into the far corner pocket on the right with one try. Any takers? He would lift his end of the table, tilt the table to the right, and all the balls would roll into the designated hole. Next? There were reports that three times, playing pool, he had shattered the cue ball with the force of his break shot.

In an oft-described incident, he wrestled with George Bancroft, the character actor, in the Lakeside locker room. Bancroft was noted for playing villains in the movies, people with names like Two-Gun Nolan, Cannonball Casey, Bull Weed, Thunderbolt Jim Lang. He had the size and the face to portray cinematic evil, a graduate of the U.S. Naval Academy who had filtered west from Philadelphia after completing active duty and found a solid level of fame and success.

In one version of the incident, Montague heard Bancroft curse in front of women at Lakeside. Upset and offended, he confronted the actor in the locker room. In another version, the confrontation was friendly, two large men in a contest of strength. In all versions, and there may have been others, the outcome was the same. *Montague picked up Bancroft and stuffed him in a locker. Upside down. And shut the door.* Bancroft had to plead to be released.

"Stuffed him in the locker" was the oft-used phrase around the club. "George Bancroft."

And then, of course, there was the golf. . . .

Montague hit a golf ball farther than anyone who had ever played at Lakeside. The greats of the game, Bobby Jones and Walter Hagen at the top of the list, had all played the course. Bobby Jones had even made a series of instructional films at Lakeside in 1931. But no one had played the way Montague played. He used custom-made, oversize clubs. His driver weighed eighteen ounces, maybe more, almost twice the weight of the average driver of the day. The clubhead was huge, again twice the size of the average driver of the day. Only a very strong man could use such a club. Only Montague, it seemed, could get the desired results.

His drives consistently traveled over three hundred yards at a time when few drives went that far. With these bombs, he carved the course down to a more manageable size. He hit niblicks (nine-irons) and wedges for second shots on par-4s, hit the green in two shots on par-5s. The 13th was the monster hole on the course, 595 yards, the river hole. Montague could reach it in two. Or land somewhere in the vicinity.

He consistently toured the eighteen holes in under 70 shots and had tied the Lakeside record at 63. He won the club championship with ease, beat Bud McCray, a good golfer, 7 and 5 in the 1933 final. The scores—and reports came back about how he had broken course records in Palm Springs, tamed Pebble Beach, played various area layouts in remarkable numbers— were impressive, but his shots were what made him so different.

He did a bunch of things that nobody else even tried. He supposedly hit ten balls from the tee of a 347-yard par-4 one afternoon at the course. He reached the green with seven of them. He supposedly used a putter as a driver and drove the 9th green from the back tees, a distance of 245 yards. (He threw the ball into the air, swung the putter like a baseball bat, and connected with the ball at the exact point where the shaft met the middle of the blade of the putter.) He supposedly said he could drive a ball three-quarters of a mile in five shots. Bets were made. Everyone went to the beach, where the distance was measured out. He made the three-quarters of a mile with room to spare.

Doomed to give strokes to virtually everybody at the club in head-to-head matches, even scratch handicappers, he devised other unique wagers. He would offer to hit every one of his tee shots into the woods and play from there. Or, better yet, he would let his opponent take care of the drive. Montague would hand the opponent his ball. Go ahead, put it where you want. The opponent could pick a spot an inch from the tee. Or deep in a sand trap. Anywhere. Montague, shooting two, would play from there, from the spot.

Every eighteen holes, every idle moment, seemed to feature some new challenge, some wager, some trick. He would step on a ball in a sand trap, completely bury the ball; blast it out, no problem, with a brassie (two-wood). He would hit two balls at once with a mashie (five-iron), sending one of the balls right, the other left. He would ask a caddie to lie down, then place a wooden kitchen match in the caddie's mouth and light the match with a full swing of a cleek (two-iron). He would hit a small box of matches off the head of a patient cocker spaniel. It all seemed to work. The cocker spaniel survived. The caddie survived.

One of his basic tricks took place indoors. In the Lakeside locker room or in a hotel room, anywhere, he would ask someone to open a window slightly and keep it ajar by inserting a glass in the opening. Montague then would begin to chip balls through the small opening. He never would miss, never would break the window or hit the wall. Everyone seemed to have seen him do this. The size of the glass varied as the story was told. A water glass, a cocktail glass, *a shot glass,* the balls always would go through the opening without a problem.

"He practiced that," Lakeside employee Eddie Gannon said. "Everyone else would be gone from the locker room and I'd hear the sound of balls hitting the walls. Montague would be in there by himself, hitting chip shots toward the window. Then he'd bet guys he could chip through the window onto the putting green. He was always doing something like that."

There was a time frame, of course, to the things he did—maybe he hit the box of matches off the cocker spaniel's head on Monday, stuffed George Bancroft into the locker on Tuesday, reached the 13th green in two on Thursday, or maybe in July—but they were all soon lumped in one great ball of chatter. The anecdotes were like comic routines or, better yet, fables, embellished and bent into different shapes by each particular speaker. They spun through did-you-hear-this conversations, wonder stories that didn't need time or date or even attribution.

The story that spun fastest involved the dead bird.

"I was playing in a foursome at the Fox Hills Country Club," Montague eventually told Darsie L. Darsie of the *Los Angeles Herald,* establishing the framework of the tale. "At the 10th tee, which is probably seventy-five yards from Slauson Avenue, we were forced to wait for players ahead to get out of range. As I stood on the tee, I casually said to the others: 'See those birds on that telephone wire? Watch me pick off the farthest one to the right.' I teed up an old ball, took out a brassie and hit a full drive. It hit the bird in the neck, snapping its head off. The bird was perhaps 175 yards from me when I hit the drive."

The magic of that shot—if it really happened—was undeniable. If Babe Ruth could generate national awe and controversy when he pointed (maybe) toward center field and then delivered a home run in that direction to the Wrigley Field bleachers off Chicago Cubs pitcher Charlie Root in the fifth inning of the third game of the 1932 World Series, "the Called Shot," what manner of feat was this? To point out the bird, the particular bird on the right? To deliver a golf ball with such accuracy from such a distance, far longer than the Babe's homer, that the ball not only hit the right bird, but hit the bird in the neck and knocked its head off? Annie Oakley couldn't have done that with a rifle and a bullet. Montague did it with a brassie?

The story, told and retold by Lakeside people, developed its own dramatic life. Grew larger. Multiplied. The site changed from course to course, hole to hole. The playing partners changed, different people claiming to be witnesses. The club changed, from brassie to driver to mashie, depending on the distance of the shot, which also changed. The species of bird changed. Dead crows, pigeons, starlings, *sparrows,* many headless, many not, littered the manicured ground of memory and imagination. Montague kissed the head of his trusty and lethal golf stick after each impossible shot and slid the club back into its holster.

Who wouldn't be impressed with that picture? Added up, Montague apparently had wiped out an entire aviary.

"I remember playing one time at Oakland Hills Country Club, in the valley towards Anaheim," Johnny Weissmuller recalled years later in an interview with Norm Blackburn for the *Lakeside Golf Club of Hollywood 50th Anniversary Book.* "We were playing team matches. The whole telephone wire was full of birds. And he said, 'Let me see if I can knock one of those birds off.' They were very little sparrows, but he hauled off and hit one of those guys right in the nose. He didn't think he ever could do it, but he just had a hunch. He has done so many of those things."

Hit a sparrow right in the nose. There you go.

Who even knew sparrows had noses?

For all the tales about his exploits, few people seemed to know much about the strongman golfer's background. He diverted most conversations away from his past. He never really explained where he earned the money he always seemed to have in large amounts. There were guesses and assumptions, running from son of an old New England family to California-born speculator to former associate of mobster Al Capone, but few facts. Nobody seemed to press Montague on the matter. Nobody seemed to care.

He was, after all, in a sun-splashed environment that was filled with transplanted characters, people who had arrived without personal histories tucked into their suitcases. Names had been changed. Résumés had been forged. Humdrum pasts routinely had been forgotten, shoes shined, and makeup applied in large amounts. Tomorrow always was more important than yesterday in Hollywood, California. The one important fact was that daydreams and promise hung in the scented air of another perfect morning.

John Montague was part of a crowd.

"Hollywood probably attracts more types and nationalities than any city of its size," Carl Foreman wrote in *The WPA Guide to California,* a chronicle of the time. "Here are the nobility, the ex-nobility, and pseudo nobility of a dozen countries: the artistically inclined from every corner of the world who aspire to movie jobs; and average Americans who like the climate, or who were born here. Precocious children from all over the country are brought to Hollywood in hope of breaking into motion pictures. Dozens of dance studios and dramatic schools attempt to train children and adults for screen careers. About 75 per cent of the population is connected in some way with the motion picture industry."

The small city—population 153,294, actually part of the larger city, Los Angeles, official name the Hollywood District of Los Angeles—increasingly had become a glamour destination in the past twenty years. Eight miles west of downtown L.A., twelve miles from the Pacific Ocean, it had been a small and sleepy place, population under four thousand, until David Horsley's Nestor Motion Picture Company arrived in 1911 from New Jersey in search of better weather, lower rents, and fewer legal entanglements. One company after another had followed. (Cecil B. DeMille had stopped in Flagstaff, Arizona, didn't like it, and kept heading west.) The growth of the movie industry had also been the growth of Hollywood.

Everything had happened in a stunning upward slash across any sheet of graph paper. Silent films had captured the country's attention and then, in an instant, been replaced by talking films. Movie palaces with names like Dreamland and Fairyland, Bijou, and, well, the Palace, had been built across the country. Vaudeville had been eclipsed by flickering fantasy. The industry now generated a billion dollars a year. That money flowed through Hollywood.

Who didn't want a part of it?

"Will you accept 300 per week to work for Paramount Pictures?" producer Herman Mankiewicz asked in a cable to New York writer Ben Hecht in 1926. "All expenses paid. 300 is peanuts. Millions are to be made out here and your only competition is idiots. Don't let this get around."

That was still the thinking in 1934. Hollywood not only was

a place to make a buck, but to make an easy, exciting buck. The rest of the country was hemorrhaging as it moved into the fifth year of the Depression, which started with the stock market crash of Black Friday, October 25, 1929. The rest of California was hemorrhaging, filling up with refugees from the Dust Bowl in Oklahoma, families arriving in battered trucks packed with all of their possessions, hoboes jumping off boxcars at their final stop, one out of every four citizens in the state unemployed. Hollywood was thriving.

There had been a slight stall in the upward progression in the first few years of the thirties as the economy faded at the exact same time the studios were spending money to adapt to the new technology of sound, but by 1934 the movie business had rebounded with vigor. Attendance had jumped by 15 percent, with profits even higher. Most studios would make twice the money in 1934 than they had in 1933. The theory was that people, no matter how troubled their financial conditions might be, still would find a way to watch a movie, to escape their worries by watching a story. More than 70 million customers saw a movie each week, giving the industry a weekly income of over $20 million.

To churn out product to meet this demand, the studios had built more and more fake mountains and fake apartment houses, fake Main Streets and deserts and ocean liners and skating rinks on their enormous back lots. The architecture of invention had spilled over to the streets with "drive-in barbecue stands, restaurants and bars built of papier-mâché to represent fairy-tale castles, tumble-down houses, gargantuan fish, ice cream cones and lop-eared puppies. Each stands on a large parking area and waitresses in slacks and brass-buttoned jackets hook trays over open car windows to serve customers in their automobiles" (*The WPA Guide to California*). Elaborate mansions had been built for Hollywood people in Beverly Hills, Bel Air, Brentwood, gates at the front, swimming pools in the back. Men wore polo shirts and women wore halter tops during the day, walking down streets lined with palm trees and closely cropped lawns. A bridle path ran straight down the middle of Sunset Boulevard, former silent movie star Hobart Bosworth riding through his former public, his long white hair flowing in the wind as his large white horse galloped the route every afternoon. Klieg lights flashed through the night, announcing supposedly great and supposedly important events.

"Strip away the phony tinsel of Hollywood," composer and pundit Oscar Levant said, "and you'll find the real tinsel underneath."

The producers had decided early that Americans liked stars, familiar faces, and real millionaires had been created out of normal people like a former worker in a tire factory in Akron, Ohio (Clark Gable), a former store clerk from Stockholm (Greta Garbo), and the five singing sons of Minnie and Frenchie Marrix from the Upper East Side of New York City (the Marx Brothers). A six-year-old girl from Santa Monica, Shirley Jane Temple, discovered at Meglin's Dance School, already made more money than the heads of many corporations. Directors had been imported from Europe, writers from the best-seller lists, extras from Central Casting, where more than ten thousand people had filed applications for employment.

The effect of all this was dizzying. Nothing like Hollywood existed anywhere else, "a town that has to be seen to be disbelieved," as newsman Walter Winchell told his radio listeners, "a place where a man can get stabbed in the back while climbing a ladder," according to novelist William Faulkner. Hollywood was the great lottery ticket. Nowhere else could fortunes be earned or lost quicker. Nowhere else were the fake and the real matched together so closely, overlapping, side by side, sometimes virtually indistinguishable.

Ben Hecht, the writer, eventually took Mankiewicz's advice. He headed west and became a successful screenwriter, *Scarface* and *The Front Page* and *Viva Villa* among his credits. He learned how everything worked.

"Many ironic things happen in Hollywood," Hecht wrote. "Overnight, idiots become geniuses and geniuses become idiots, waitresses turn into duchesses and what duchesses turn into won't bear mentioning. Overnight in Hollywood, panhandling hams bloom into Colequins and Lorenzos and vice versa. The boulevards are crowded with royal coaches turning into pumpkins before your eye. It's an Aladdin's Lamp of a town, and whichever way you rub it, genii jump out and make sport of the laws of gravity and sanity."

The idea that a golfer would join that line of hopefuls around Mr. Aladdin's lamp was not strange. If the redheaded son of a bartender from New York, Jimmy Cagney, could become America's favorite villain, and if the former manager of a tobacco farm from Hobart, Tasmania, Errol Flynn, could become Captain Blood, if a twenty-two-year-old virgin could arrive from Lowell, Massachusetts, with her mother, lie on a couch, and passionately kiss fifteen strange men in a screen test and become Bette Davis, sex symbol, and if Charlie Chaplin, poor kid from London, could put on baggy pants and a false mustache and make the world laugh, and if ambitious, semiliterate immigrants and sons of immigrants, people like Louis B. Mayer, Sam Goldwyn, Jack Warner, and Harry Cohn, could leave the hurly-burly of fashion and retail in New York and become the heads of studios, the kings of Hollywood, then anyone from anywhere had a chance.

Montague didn't bill himself as a golfer, anyway. He was an *amateur* golfer, a man with a real business, a real job. He would never spell out what that real business was, though he did allude every now and then to "mining interests in Nevada" and sometimes extolled the virtues of superchargers to make automobiles faster. He was adamant that he wasn't a professional golfer. He played the game for fun. Golf was his passion, not his work.

He mostly had just shown up around Hollywood, more than arrived. There were no stories about a small-time life left behind, a bad job in a widget factory, an overbearing wife or girlfriend, a trip from farmland or tenement poverty across the country in a car with no second gear. He had just shown up, the way a new kid will show up at the playground, looking to play with everyone else. He was just there, definitely by 1932, maybe before that. He explained nothing. No dates. No stories. Just there.

Golf was his entrée. The value of the game as a social and business tool always had been part of its attraction. New and often influential friends could be made in a morning or afternoon in the sun. If a man showed up at the starter's booth and asked, "Does anybody need a fourth?" the chances were quite good that after eighteen holes he would know three strangers much better than if he had met them at a half dozen lunches or any number of cocktail parties. If he played good golf, great golf, fabulous golf, the strangers would be interested in him even more, no matter where he was from, what else he had done, or how fat or lean his bank account might be.

Montague followed that routine. He showed up at a number of courses around Hollywood, around L.A., mostly public courses like Rancho and Sunset Fields and even Western Avenue, where mostly black golfers played. He was a gentleman, funny and likable. He had his big clubs and his big game and, pretty soon, a big reputation. The trick bag would be opened and he would hit carom shots off trees—planned, announced carom shots—bend shots left and right around stationary objects, and chip like a demon, strangely graceful for such a big man. He had a betting proposition where he would allow his opponent to retake missed shots. The opponent could take the same shot as many times as he wanted until he got a shot he liked. Who could resist an offer like that? By the end of a round, maybe two hundred swings later, maybe more, the opponent couldn't lift his arms. Except, of course, to pull out his wallet.

The word spread, as it will in these situations, about this big guy and the things he could do with a golf ball. Throw in an extracurricular report or two about feats of strength—"And then he ripped off the steering wheel and handed it to the driver and told him where to go with it"—and people were lining up to meet this new addition to the golf culture of L.A.

Richard Arlen, the actor, was one of the first members of the movie community to discover Montague. Arlen's success story was an Aladdin's lamp classic, so good that half of Hollywood thought it had been invented by a publicist, which maybe it was or maybe it wasn't. Born in Charlottesville, Virginia, real name Cornelius Richard Van Mattimore, raised in St. Paul, Minnesota, Arlen was a pilot in the Royal Canadian Air Force in the world war, a sportswriter in Duluth, and a roustabout in the oil fields of Texas before he arrived in Hollywood, thinking about becoming an actor.

He found a job as a motorcycle messenger servicing the studios. A malfunctioning gate at what is now Paramount Pictures knocked him from his motorcycle on one delivery. He wound up in the hospital. After recovering from his injuries, he visited the studio to thank the appropriate people for paying for his medical care. In the process, some director noticed Arlen's good looks and thought they might carry over to the large screen. A series of bit parts plus his air force background led to a larger role in the silent classic *Wings,* which won the first Academy Award for Best Picture, in 1927. He now made over $200,000 per year, a certified leading man.

"Your father always had one thing in mind," his ex-wife, Jobyna, told his daughter, Rose, when *Wings* debuted. "He wanted to see his name in lights and make a million dollars. Well, I have to give him credit. He did it."

Arlen was one of Hollywood's best movie-star golfers, playing at a four handicap. He played everywhere around Los Angeles, and often, which was how he soon heard of Montague. They became friends at the public courses and soon were playing at the private courses at Arlen's invitation. They made money together as partners.

"I think I met him the first time at Palm Springs," Arlen said. "We played at the only course [O'Donnell Golf Club] there was at the time. Par [for 18 holes] was either 68 or 70. The latter I think. O'Donnell was a nine-hole course that put a premium on accuracy. This always was one of Monty's strong points. His four rounds were 61-61-61-59! The fairway on the 525-yard

8th hole is so narrow I've seen top players hit as many as four shots out of bounds there."

Who wouldn't want to be partners in a dollar, five-dollar, five-hundred-dollar Nassau with a player who could shoot 61-61-61-59? That was another part of Montague's attractiveness. Men wanted to pair up with him on a golf course, be partners, make money. He was a good partner to have.

"My brother Bob first met Montague when he was playing out at Sunset Fields," Bud McCray, a friend of both Arlen's and Montague's, said. "Bob used to tell me about this fantastic golfer and I couldn't believe it. There is a dogleg where the city of Beverly Hills turns into the city of Los Angeles on Wilshire Boulevard. At two o'clock in the morning, Montague used to stand there and hit golf balls down Wilshire Boulevard."

Who wouldn't want to team up with someone who hit golf balls down Wilshire Boulevard at two in the morning? The brothers brought Montague to their home club. They set up a match that included a fellow named J. C. Earle.

In the prematch arranging of handicaps, Montague said he was a ten. He then proceeded to unload a couple of three-hundred-yard drives, knock down a couple of birdies, fill in with a couple of pars, and J. C. Earle was a bit distressed by the 5th hole.

"Bud," he said, "who'd you ring on me this time?"

Everybody laughed. Montague called off all bets.

"Actually," he said, "I'm a scratch handicap."

The course was the Lakeside Golf Club. Richard Arlen also was a member of the Lakeside Golf Club. The inevitable happened. John Montague in 1933 became another of Lakeside Golf Club's six hundred members.

He was on the inside.

The Lakeside Golf Club was one of the rewards for Hollywood success, one of the payoffs. Golf courses everywhere were having problems with the Depression, the number of private clubs belonging to the United States Golf Association dropping from 1,155 to 763 between 1929 and 1936, as many as a million members lost, many clubs now operating on a daily fee basis, but this one was vibrant, thriving. It could have been an eighteen-hole creation of some movie fan's overactive mind. If you took the publicity pictures of some of the most recognized film characters of the day, then shuffled them together, Lakeside would have been the grand, incongruous result. A famous cowboy (Randolph Scott) could be found in the grill room next to a famous comedian (Oliver Hardy), who was next to the King of the Jungle (Johnny Weissmuller), who was next to, oh, the dapper Douglas Fairbanks or his estranged wife, beautiful Mary Pickford, or a blustering Charles Coburn or a continental Adolphe Menjou.

Howard Hughes, arguably the richest man in the world, was on the practice tee as often as he was on the course, three of his cameramen often surrounding him to record swing after swing for film analysis back at the studio (something few people did). Humphrey Bogart played here. John Barrymore. Leon Errol. Walter Lantz. Buddy Rogers. Jack Oakie. Walter Huston. Basil Rathbone. Don Ameche. More than half of the membership was associated with the film industry, and more than half of that half seemed to be stars. The first female member was silent film actress Anna Q. Nilsson, the first Scandinavian sex goddess.

Opened nine years earlier in 1925, one of five country clubs built in Los Angeles during the boom times of the twenties, Lakeside offered both golf and convenience to the movie colony. It was stuck in the middle of the studio lots for Paramount and First National (which soon became Warner Bros.), and so close to Universal that it bordered the studio zoo, so close that golfers were able to hear the sounds of the lions, tigers, and elephants kept on the premises for jungle movies. The Los Angeles River ran through the property, and Toluca Lake, a small body of water that soon became a fashionable Hollywood address, was on the northern edge.

Richard Arlen lived on Toluca Lake. Amelia Earhart, the famous aviatrix, lived on Toluca Lake. W. C. Fields lived on the lake. The millionaire comedian's house was on the shore, water view, his backyard visible from the club. One of the Lakeside pastimes was to sit by the pool on Sunday mornings and watch for W.C. to come out of the house in his pajamas to try to shoo away the quacking ducks that apparently had an attraction to his property. It was a constant battle, Fields and the ducks. He'd swing the cane and chase them, cursing, hilarious, always to no avail. The scene, if filmed, could have filled theaters.

"One day the sliding doors opened and he came out and he didn't have the cane; he had a damn shotgun," one Lakeside member said. "We all thought he was going to try to scare the ducks. He shot every one of them. He said, 'That will teach you.' "

Fields, a member, had a rowboat and lived so close he sometimes rowed to the course. He always played a round of golf with a bottle stuffed somewhere in his pockets, and the bottle usually contained gin. His love of gin—"I exercise extreme self-control; I never drink anything stronger than gin before breakfast"—worked well with his love of golf. Well fortified with his favorite liquid on one certain afternoon, he whiffed on his tee shot but thought he had hit the ball. His caddie dutifully followed him down the fairway, and when Fields started looking for the ball, the caddie quietly dropped one. Ahhhhhh, a very good drive. If I say so myself. Fields never knew the difference. He scored a 5 on the hole.

Matches were played for large money, small money, and no money at the club. Any wagers involving Hughes, wealthy as he was, were noticed. He played as hard for a dollar as he did for a thousand, passionate, pretty much addicted to the game. He would stop talking on the back nine if he was losing, move straight to the practice tee if the match was lost and done.

He played often with George Von Elm, a member who had won the 1926 U.S. Amateur in a 2 and 1 final over Bobby Jones and lost a 36-hole play-off to Billy Burke for the 1931 U.S. Open. The thirty-one-year-old Von Elm, a smallish blond-haired man, called himself "a businessman golfer" rather than a professional. He routinely would win the high-stakes matches against Hughes, piling up a bunch of money, but Hughes finally beat him one afternoon for five hundred dollars. When the former amateur champion groused about his fate, Hughes ended the argument. He tore up Von Elm's check.

"In that case, here's your check," he said. "We're through."

They never played again. Von Elm, everyone said, probably lost thousands of potential dollars in the affair, bad business for a businessman golfer.

"Howard probably was as good a golfer as Von Elm," the director Henry King said. "I played with Howard once a week, maybe twice a week, for about a year.... I'd arrive here to play at 9:00 A.M. on a Sunday and Howard already would have been out practicing for one hour, driving, pitching and putting, etc. . . . I played with him when he was one over on the first nine and even on the second nine, many times, and I saw him play two under a number of times."

The golf was important—a number of fine golfers belonged to the club, a group that included the fifty-four-year-old Fields as well as the twenty-eight-year-old Hughes—but the fun was more important. A quick wit was more valuable than a good putter. What would be remembered longer, someone's par-busting round or the following exchange between comedian Guy Kibbee, a member, and Jones, the grill room waiter?

Kibbee: "Jones, these pork chops are ghastly. You take 'em back and you know what you can do with 'em."

Jones: "Yes, sir, Mr. Kibbee, but I've got two steaks and a roast beef ahead of them."

A fact that said more about Lakeside than anything was that the most celebrated match in club history was for the championship of the eighth flight one year between Hardy and Menjou, the fat and funny man against the suave big-screen lover. Neither of them was a good golfer. (Hardy once showed up with a radically different, newly invented club called a "sand wedge," first time anyone ever had seen one. Fields, outraged, said, "Any man who would use an illegal club like that would strangle his mother.") The ballyhoo for the final match of the eighth flight continued for weeks, the event scheduled and rescheduled. Hardy and Menjou each declared that his opponent was "duck-ing" him. When the match finally was played, there was a large gallery, with thousands of dollars in side bets. Menjou won on the 18th green, and the fact was noted that neither golfer broke 120.

Lakeside was an everyday celebration of good fortune, a per
petual boys' night out. The members, at least the ones in the
movie business, were the winners in the big rush to California,
most of them far removed from their modest small-town be-
ginnings in Darby, Pennsylvania (Fields), or Freidorf, Austria-
Hungary (Weissmuller), or Kenosha, Wisconsin (Don Ameche).
Money was not a problem, not even in 1934; the Depression
was being lived by other people. Prohibition was dead, repealed
on December 5, 1933, when President Franklin Roosevelt signed
the Twenty-first Amendment. The fame of everyone was ridiculous, a new concept, this accrued celebrity for speaking a few
words in front of a camera and somehow becoming a familiar
member of families across the entire country.

The men's grill was as packed at midnight—or at one or two
in the morning or even later—as it was at sunset. Big-money
card games were constant. Dice games were held in the locker
room. Liquor ran through everyone. Late-night decisions would
be made to go to the Brown Derby or the Trocadero or Musso
& Frank Steakhouse. Or maybe a group would head straight to
Catalina on somebody's yacht. Or drive to Palm Springs. Or fly
to Mexico.

Anything was possible. Anything was okay. The members at
Lakeside stormed through marriages, trading one beautiful
woman for another and then another. After they drank to grand
excess, they drove, the roadways open, the few police friendly
toward movie stars. (Weissmuller, friends said, had driven his
car into Toluca Lake at least four times.) The members were bul-
letproof. Nothing they did could be wrong. They had all of
America behind them.

Richard Arlen would land a small plane on the 18th fairway.

It seemed like a good thing to do. Humphrey Bogart, kidded all the time by a caddie for his gangster roles, the caddie pointing his fingers like a machine gun and shouting "Rat-a-tat-tat," would arrive on a bicycle one day with a real machine gun and fire rounds at the terrified caddie. Blank rounds. Studio head Jack Warner would try to put the club off-limits during the workday, as too much of his talent would return too tired to work after a long and convivial lunch.

"Lakeside Golf Club was unlike any other country club that ever existed," Allene Gates, one of Johnny Weissmuller's former wives, said years later. "There'll never be anything like it again. It wasn't a country club, it was family."

One of the many characters at the club was Vince Barnett, a member and sometimes actor, who would pose as a caddie for visiting dignitaries at the course, driving them crazy when he misclubbed them and admonished them for their bad shots. He also posed as a bumbling waiter at Hollywood dinners, dropping forks and pouring water into famous laps. Once, at a dinner for Winston Churchill, he noticed that the respected British statesman at the head table had his arm around the back of the chair of actress Marion Davies, mistress of William Randolph Hearst.

"I beg your pardon, please," Barnett the Waiter advised, "we've got rooms upstairs for that."

Lakeside was a lot of fun.

———

John Montague fit perfectly into this scene with its equal parts alcohol, golf, testosterone, and madcap bravado. His talents were talents that all of the otherwise talented men secretly wanted to have. Everyone at Lakeside wanted to do the things on a golf course that he did. Everyone wanted to be strong, to be able to walk into any room and know, absolutely know, that he could handle any difficulty that might arise. Not in a movie role, but in life. Men everywhere wanted to do that.

Montague entertained the entertainers. If they lost money to him on the golf course, well, they really didn't mind. They enjoyed the show. He was part of the fun. He didn't push himself on other people, simply molded into the active mix and hit golf balls a long distance. He drank with the drinkers, gambled with the gamblers, though not so much at the card tables, charged with the late-night chargers. One thing he didn't do was chase other men's women, a notable quality of Hollywood discretion.

Arlen was a friend. Weissmuller, the Olympic champion, was a friend, two hard-drinking athletes who could talk about the things that hard-drinking athletes talk about. Guy Kibbee, the comedian with the pop-eyed, daffy look, was a hilarious friend. Oliver (Babe) Hardy was a best friend.

The two men made an interesting pair. Hardy forever was the fat kid from Milledgeville, Georgia, always battling his weight while at the same time knowing that it was a prime ingredient in his success with the American public. Doomed by his size, stuck with the blunt early nickname of Fatty, he had been a fifteen-year-old umpire, not the star center fielder in Milledgeville, part of his early theatrical start, calling the balls and strikes with elaborate gestures. He always loved sports.

"There's very little to write about me," he told biographer John McCabe. "I don't do very much outside of doing a lot of gags before a camera and play golf the rest of the time."

Montague was the athlete Hardy always wanted to be, the

sure-handed, coordinated character who lurked inside Hardy's lumpy body, the character who could never climb out. The golfer's size, combined with his grace, was an asset, not a liability. He could whack a ball. He could answer an insult with force. He was a physical wonder. No matter how much fame or wealth Hardy acquired, he could never make people look at him the same way they looked at John Montague.

The two men became buddies, even though Montague was twelve years younger. There would even be a stretch when they lived together. Hardy, bruised by a final separation from his second wife, Myrtle, a woman with alcoholic and psychological problems, invited Montague to move into his house in Beverly Hills. (Both Laurel and Hardy had bad luck with women. Laurel was married four times, Hardy three.) Montague accepted. The two big men spent a lot of time together, no doubt shared some impressive nightly dinners.

Hardy loved to tell the wonder story about the night he and Montague went to an exclusive restaurant. Montague was dressed in appropriate dinner clothes. Hardy wore a flowing silk bolero shirt, very expensive. The maître d' informed him that he could not enter the restaurant because he was not wearing a tie. Montague was fine, but Hardy, I'm sorry, sir, was not. Montague was not amused.

"Without a smile he removed his black silk tie, tore it neatly in half, gave me one half and retied the other around his wing bat collar," Hardy said. "I tied the half a tie about my throat and we had dinner."

Tore the tie in half. Simple as that.

The wonder stories continued to accumulate.

"Four of us, including Monty, went on a fishing trip to Henshaw Dam Lake near San Diego and crowded into a small rowboat," Guy Kibbee reported. "It was almost dark when we heard a faint scream.

"We rowed across the little lake and found a woman, just losing consciousness, hanging to an overturned boat. She gasped that she had been there for hours and her husband already had drowned. Our boat was so small it was a problem to lift her in without capsizing it.

"Montague sat far back to counterbalance the new weight, reached over the side and holding the woman, who weighed more than 160 pounds, at arm's length lifted her from the water and into the boat. It was the greatest exhibition of strength I ever saw."

On the same trip there was another problem. Kibbee had a steel camping trailer. At the rear of the trailer was a filled 175-pound icebox. One of the fishermen's rods got caught under the trailer. After not being able to find a jack to lift the trailer, Montague put his back to the far end, grabbed hold, and lifted. The fisherman removed the rod.

"It was a straight lift of more than five hundred pounds," Kibbee said.

Peter DePaolo, the Indianapolis 500 driver, the first man to average over one hundred miles per hour when he won the race in 1925, was another Lakeside member. He and his brother Danny stopped for gas one day. Montague was with them. As the car was being serviced, Montague pulled out a niblick and a golf ball. He placed the golf ball on the cement sidewalk.

"You see that little balcony on the apartment house across

the street?" he asked. "It's about six or eight feet off the ground. What will you bet that I can't play a niblick shot off the sidewalk into the hammock on that balcony?"

Danny DePaolo bet the price of the gas. Montague got into his stance and swung naturally. The ball traveled a straight, parabolic course, hit the railing of the balcony, and bounced, *plop,* into the hammock. Danny DePaolo paid for the gas.

The action on the golf course continued to be just as memorable. Montague supposedly bet two thousand dollars that he could break the record on both the east course and the west course at Fox Hills Country Club in the same day. He supposedly shot 64 in the morning, 63 in the afternoon. He supposedly posted eight birdies in eleven holes at Riviera. George Von Elm said he went with Montague to Palm Springs for a month and Montague never shot a round of golf over 68.

In Palm Springs he often stayed with Bert Wheeler, half of the comedy team of Wheeler and Woolsey, who made a series of successful movies for RKO Studios. Wheeler, a Lakeside member, played with Montague a bunch of times in Palm Springs. The comedian came back with the appropriate astonishment.

"The second hole at that little desert course is 386 yards in length, and some 30 yards from the green a palm tree–bordered road crosses the course," Wheeler reported. "Here, last winter, I saw Ralph Guldahl [who finished second by a stroke in the 1933 U.S. Open and would go on to win it in 1937 and '38] repeatedly try to drive the road. I never saw him within fifteen yards of it. Yet I have seen Monty drive the road half a dozen times."

One of the most relentless golfers at Lakeside was Bing Crosby. He had joined the club in 1929 as an associate member for five hundred dollars when he was part of a trio called the Rhythm Boys in bandleader Paul Whiteman's orchestra. He was from Spokane, Washington, another transient dreamer who had quit Gonzaga University in Spokane in the middle of his senior year to find a Hollywood career as a singer, an actor, whatever would make him into a wealthy household name.

By 1934, all of that had come true. He was in movies, on the radio, churning out hit records, well on a course that would make him as famous as anyone in the country, his voice recorded more often than any man's on earth. He already was having a grand mansion built on six acres at 10500 Camarillo Street, right at Toluca Lake, bordering the course. Lakeside was a place he loved, a place where some of the good things had begun.

This was where he met producer-director Mack Sennett, who put him in the movies. The son of immigrant farmers in Danville, Quebec, Sennett had built a movie empire in Hollywood on comic foundations, discovering Fields, Charlie Chaplin, Gloria Swanson, and the Keystone Kops. He was the man who had found the humor in a well-placed custard pie.

"Bing's success would have happened anyway, but this is how it started," Willie Low, the pro at Lakeside, said. "In the fall of 1930, early one morning, I was giving Mack Sennett a playing lesson. Bing was playing alone and caught up with us on the second hole. I had seen him coming and asked Mack Sennett if he minded if Bing joined us. He wanted to know who he was and I told him that he was the rage of Coconut Grove, and that all the women were wild about him. Bing joined us and after we finished we were having a beverage. Mr. Sennett said, 'Bing, Willie tells me you sing.' Bing replied, 'Yes, they call me a crooner,' and Sennett asked him over to the studio. That's how it happened because I was there."

Crosby played as much golf as anyone. He would play in the morning with caddies who had names like Scorpy Doyle, Side Hill Henry, Staggering Haggerty, Phone Booth, and Louie the Lug, more transient characters who had left long-ago pasts and found jobs in California carrying golf bags. He would play in the afternoons with members. He would sneak out in the middle of movies being filmed at Paramount to play. He played 36 holes and 54 and 72 holes a day, sometimes finishing in darkness, everybody lighting matches to find one another. He would play with Montague.

They were about the same age—Bing was thirty-one—and Crosby was good enough to give him a match. Not good enough to beat him most days, but good enough to come close. Crosby was playing at a three or four handicap, and Montague would give him five or six shots and still usually win at the end.

"He was a great golfer," Crosby said. "He could play very, very, very good golf. He was very strong. He was a good trouble player. He could play out of trouble with his strength on a long drive, and was a good putter. He had a good eye. He was a big, jovial, good-natured guy the way I found him."

At the end of one of their matches, the result another Montague win, Crosby complained in the grill room over beverages about whatever the handicap situation had been. He said Montague should have given him more strokes. This was typical grill room talk. Montague bantered back. Crosby persisted. Montague eventually came up with a proposition.

"I'll tell you what," he said. "I could beat you with a shovel, a baseball bat, and a rake. You use your own clubs."

"For how much?" Crosby asked.

"Five bucks a hole."

"You're on."

Montague went to his car and returned with the necessary implements to the 10th tee. Every man just happens to have a shovel, fungo bat, and a rake in his car. The hole was a straight par-4, 366 yards. Montague tossed the golf ball into the air, swung the fungo bat, and hit a shot that landed in a greenside bunker. (Oh, my.) Crosby hit a solid drive, maybe 250 yards down the middle of the fairway. He then hit an iron to the middle of the green, maybe thirty feet from the pin. Montague shoveled his ball from the trap to within twelve feet. (Oh, my.)

Crosby's birdie putt went two feet past the hole. Montague told him the par putt was good. The big man then approached his ball with his ordinary garden rake. This had become very interesting.

Instead of trying to sweep the ball forward, he dropped to his knees, turned the garden rake the wrong way, and used the handle as a pool cue. He calmly sank the golf ball into the only pocket in the grass for a birdie. (Oh, my. Oh, my. Oh, my.) The story eclipsed all of the other wonder stories before the ball hit the bottom of the cup.

A fungo bat?

A shovel?

And a rake?

No one had ever heard of such a thing. A birdie? On a par-4? The size of the wager would grow from $5 to $500 to $5,000 as the story was repeated. The length and difficulty of the putt, the rake used as a pool cue, would grow. Montague would be seen as canny, wise, biding his time for the proper moment. He surely had this all planned. Didn't he? He surely had practiced for hours, days. The trap had been set; then it had been sprung. Exquisitely.

The story would be told any time his name was mentioned in conversation for the rest of his life.

"John Montague..."

"The guy who beat Crosby with a baseball bat, a shovel, and a rake..."

"Yes, the guy who beat Crosby with a baseball bat, a shovel, and a rake..."

This was his masterpiece. This was his *Mona Lisa*.

The most curious part of this curious man was that he apparently had no ambition. He was happy where he was. That didn't seem to fit. Secrecy was fine, hell, pastors and altar boys, caddies, and national idols all had their secrets in Hollywood, California, things they didn't want to discuss, but lack of ambition was startling. Everybody wanted more in Hollywood, even the people who had everything. Montague simply refused to pursue his talent. Why?

It was understandable, perhaps, that he didn't want to take a shot at the professional golf tour. The tour was an itinerant life without a lot of compensation. The PGA money leader for 1934, Paul Runyan, made only $6,767 for the year. Horton Smith, who in 1934 won the first edition of the Augusta National Invitational, later to be renamed "the Masters," received only $1,500 for a prize. The entire purse was $5,000.

The alternative to the PGA circuit, the other way to earn a professional golf living, was to give exhibitions. These were more lucrative endeavors, especially for a golfer with the showmanship that Montague possessed. They paid as much for one day as first place in some PGA event. Walter Hagen, who virtually invented the exhibition circuit and took it around the world, usually with trick-shot artist Joe Kirkwood, would play an estimated two thousand exhibitions in his career.

The exhibition circuit had dried up, though, with the Depression. Hagen and Kirkwood had reacted by taking their show to places like South Africa, Australia, and Japan. Again, that was a gypsy life. If a man like Montague didn't want to travel the world, that was understandable, too.

Why, though, wouldn't someone who played golf the way he did want to show it off somewhere? Why didn't he want the challenge? Why would he refuse to enter any tournament at all beside the Lakeside club championship? Why wouldn't he play in a state amateur tournament, the U.S. Amateur, the U.S. Open, the Bakersfield Open? Montague was ready, willing, primed to play any opponent in seclusion, head to head, bets all around, but refused all chances at the public stage.

"I don't play golf for records and trophies and championships," he said every time the question was raised. "I play for other reasons."

He was an enigma with great talent. What could his reasons be? Doesn't everyone, in the end, want to win, to be the best? Montague, who obviously loved the everyday attention at his own club, cringed at any mention of the outside spotlight. He even refused to have his picture taken, and confronted photographers who tried, handing them money and requesting their undeveloped film. He seemed to enjoy fame, but fought hard against it.

The laws of human nature did not seem to apply here.

None of the wonder stories, even the bat-shovel-rake conquest of Crosby, ever made the newspapers as the magic accumulated in a fat pile. They were oral legend, meaty sports gossip on a par with tales of the romantic peccadilloes or drunken hijinks of the stars. They were intramural, insider stuff. With Montague's aversion to publicity, they seemed destined to stay that way.

Every country club in the land had its character, its scratch golfer, a club champ who could shoot out the available lights and make that small dimpled ball do tricks that no one else in the club could make it do. Montague seemed destined to be an extreme version of this local hero, different mostly because his witnesses, bug-eyed and whispering about his exploits, were so famous for their own exploits, their work splashed across the movie screen. Okay, maybe he was better than most other local heroes—hit the ball farther, was much stronger, performed these amazing and wacky feats no one else would even consider—but this seemed to be his role.

He seemed comfortable being the big man at the country club. There was a very good chance that he forever would be a local character, local knowledge. That would be the far limit of his story.

Except the country club was Lakeside. Grantland Rice, the most famous sportswriter in America, was also a member of the Lakeside Golf Club.

CHAPTER THREE

EVERYWHERE

1935–37

Grantland Rice was fifty-five years old. He was as famous across the country as the rest of the Lakeside roster of celebrities. The term "sportswriter" somehow seemed too small for what he did, carrying with it the image of sweat and locker rooms and a bit of pandering, trying to persuade the great athletic man of the great athletic moment to share a word or two with the insignificant mortals who had been privileged to watch his exploits. Grantland Rice might have sweated and might have visited a few locker rooms after games—though not many—but certainly had no need to pander.

He not only was better known, larger in the public mind than almost any athlete he might cover, he also brought home a larger paycheck. His biographer Charles Fountain estimated in

Sportswriter: The Life and Times of Grantland Rice that Rice made more money than any sports figure of the twenties with the exception of Jack Dempsey. Rice was the common man's Ernest Hemingway, an everyday literary star. His contract with the *New York Herald Tribune* in 1925 paid him $1,000 per week, $52,000 per year, exactly the same as Babe Ruth.

On top of that salary, he edited *American Golfer* magazine for eight years, did the play-by-play (and color) for the first World Series game ever broadcast on radio (in 1922), produced and narrated an ongoing series of short sports films for theaters to show before feature attractions, wrote a few books and one play, plus contributed a stream of freelance articles to assorted publications. He was a one-man industry, appearing in more than one hundred newspapers across the country, his words digested by more than 10 million readers.

Six feet tall, mannerly, loquacious, and friendly—"courteous" was a word often used in descriptions of him—Rice brought dignity to the rough-and-tumble games and people he covered. He was a Southerner, born in Murfreesboro, Tennessee, raised in Nashville, a Phi Beta Kappa graduate of Vanderbilt University, class of 1901. He had a classical education, a double major in Greek and Latin, but also knew his sports. He played football, basketball, and baseball in college, turn-of-the-century athletics, crude physical contests that helped determine by each broken clavicle, each ruptured disk, indeed, each fatality, what future rules for safety should be.

Unlike a lot of sportswriters, he had a true passion for the games. Rice, the former player, could talk with knowledge with the people he covered, seemed almost to be one of them. As the captain and shortstop of the Vanderbilt varsity baseball team in his senior year, hitting .304, he barnstormed against minor-league teams in the South and was tempted to sign a contract, just to see how good he could be. His parents, citing the small paychecks and lack of a business future in the game, talked him out of it.

His father found him a job in a dry goods store, which lasted less than one dull month. A new newspaper, the *Nashville Daily News,* had opened for business, and Rice applied to be the sports editor. He got the job and began a decadelong rise in the profession, with stops in Atlanta, Cleveland, and back in Nashville with the more solvent *Nashville Tennessean.*

(His time at the *Atlanta Journal* was memorable for a string of telegrams and postcards he received in 1904 that detailed the exploits of a young minor-league outfielder from Royston, Georgia, named Ty Cobb. The postcards were sent from different stops along the Southeastern League itinerary. The messages had different signatures at the bottom, names like "Smith" and "Brown" and "Jones," but were consistent in their praise of Mr. Cobb. It wasn't until many years later that Cobb admitted to Rice that he had been the one sending the messages, an early indication of the power thought to exist in Rice's typewriter.)

In 1911, Rice made the big jump of his career when he took a job at the *New York Mail* at a salary one-third less than what he was making in Nashville. New York, with its fourteen daily newspapers, its three baseball teams, its importance in all areas of commerce, was the only place to become truly famous in his profession. The *Mail* was one of the weaker competitors in the fight for readers, but it brought Rice into the action. He covered the New York Giants of John McGraw and Christy Mathewson. He covered Jim Thorpe, covered the range of sports, wrote a column, and did well. Four years after his arrival in the city, he moved with great fanfare to the more established *New York Tribune* with its much larger circulation and, more important, its far-flung syndicate, which now dispatched his words across the country to other newspapers.

"The Tribune has been speeding up its pace in all departments and the Sporting Pages must necessarily swing into the fast-traveling lane," his new paper announced on his arrival in a full-page ad filled with tributes from fellow writers and athletes like Damon Runyon, Bozeman Bulger, Walter Johnson, and Connie Mack. "GRANTLAND RICE is just the man to give the desired momentum. He has done great work in the past. With the 'atmosphere' and the opportunities that he will find here we feel this young genius will do the best work of his career."

The young genius fulfilled all expectations. He soon was in the midst of any debate about who was the nation's top sportswriter. There was a manly quality to him despite his stodgy-sounding name and Southern charm. He was no prude. He smoked; he drank. He loved to gamble and stay up late. People simply liked him.

When he was thirty-eight years old, married, and the father of a ten-year-old girl, he called a temporary halt to his career, even as his largest dreams were materializing one by one. Exempt from the military draft due to his age and family status, he nevertheless enlisted in the army for the world war in 1917. He slogged across France as an artillery officer, saw things he wished he had never seen, and finished in Germany. He came back fourteen months after he had left and was bigger than ever.

His voice was perfect as spectator sports took hold in the twenties. As great concrete bowls popped up across the country   every university suddenly had to have one—as Babe Ruth changed baseball forever by sending long fly balls over assorted fences, as Dempsey dropped opponents to the canvas and Man of War ran free, Rice applauded with enthusiastic eloquence. He composed poems about the people and events he had seen. He found florid, heroic similes. He didn't simply write about athletic legends, he helped create them.

When he typed the words "Outlined against a blue-gray October sky, the Four Horsemen rode again. In dramatic lore they are known as Famine, Pestilence, Destruction and Death. These are only aliases. Their real names are Stuhldreher, Miller, Crowley and Layden..." to open his story of Notre Dame's 13–7 win over Army in 1924, he gave the Fighting Irish backfield a grand, mythic afterlife. When he called Illinois halfback Red Grange "the Galloping Ghost of the Gridiron" only six days later, well, Red Grange also had a nickname that never would leave. When, starting in 1925, *any* college football player was selected as an All-American, well, he became a member of Grantland Rice's All-American Football Team in *Collier's* magazine. This was the most prestigious all-star team of all.

Rice's style had grown a bit tired in the thirties as a more cynical group of sportswriters began to evolve under the new economic realities. He now was "the dean," a term bestowed on him by writer Gene Fowler, not the "young genius." His optimism suddenly seemed dated, attached to other people, other times, but he still had great power. He was still the preeminent sportswriter in the country by a solid margin. His opinions still counted.

"He was far and away the one I admired the most," sportswriter Fred Russell, a Vanderbilt grad who followed Rice at the

Nashville Banner, said. "He had such a grace of writing, such a feel as both a writer and person. The toughest thing in the world is to have a following and still be entertaining and be read and not be controversial. The easiest thing was to be real negative and sensational, which he never did and still had a tremendous following."

Rice's only child, his daughter, Florence, called Floncy, had become an actress. After a modest start on Broadway, highlighted by a role in her first play, *June Moon,* written by her father's friends Ring Lardner and George S. Kaufman, she had migrated to Hollywood in search of a film career. Rice and his wife, Katie, did what any good parents would do: they followed the migration when possible.

The quiet time in a sportswriter's schedule in the thirties came in December, January, and February. With the college football season completed, except for the bowl games, and with few major events scheduled before the start of spring training, Rice and his wife now traveled from New York and checked into the Beverly Wilshire in late December and spent Christmas and the first two months of the new year with Floncy. They were able to give her advice and consolation on her professional life, which reached a certain B-movie level of success, and on a tumultuous personal life that roared through five marriages.

Floncy joined Lakeside in 1934. Her father joined a year later and could be found many afternoons on the course. He always loved golf.

———

"Golf is like no other game," Rice wrote in his autobiography, *The Tumult and the Shouting,* years later.

You are attacking an inert ball. Also, you are on your own. You are the referee. Nine times out of ten you must call the penalty on yourself—if a penalty is to be called. You can play the game by the rules or you can cheat. You are meant to play the ball as it lies, a fact that may help to toughen your own objective approach to life.

Golf gives you an insight into human nature, your own as well as your opponent's. Eighteen holes of match or medal play will teach you more about your foe than will 18 years of dealing with him across a desk. A man's true colors will surface quicker in a five-dollar 'Nassau' than in any other form of peacetime diversion I can name.

Golf lends itself nicely to the 19th hole, a period of re-freshment, happy talk and commiseration. I've got a host of columns from the locker room . . . not only about and with name golfers, but about and with headliners of every sport and business. Peeled down to his shorts, a highball in one hand, an attested score card in the other, it's hard for a man to be anything but himself.

Rice wrote about golf all the time. Not only did he write about the important tournaments and personalities, he wrote about the mechanics of the game. Looking for the odd column, the fallback, nothing else on the schedule, he would tap out nine hundred words about the importance of the left arm in a golfer's swing or the significance of a good grip before all else. He often wrote instructional columns in *The American Golfer.*

Late to the game at age twenty-nine, a year before he moved to New York, he took to it quickly. He had a natural, easy swing. Hard work brought him all the way down to a zero handicap at one point. He could play with the best professionals and not feel foolish, could play the hardest courses at championship back-tee distances. He became best friends with Bobby Jones, whom he first covered when Jones was fourteen years old. It was his suggestion to Jones and Clifford Roberts in 1932, when they scheduled their first tournament (soon to be renamed the Masters) at their new Augusta National Golf Course, to move the dates back a week to make the event a stop for baseball writers returning from spring training. That would bring more publicity.

Golfers always were athletes to Grantland Rice, maybe the best athletes of all. The game, which he had watched rise to prominence in the United States during his sportswriting career, which he helped promote from the society pages onto the same page as baseball, boxing, and football, was one of his great joys. It was important. He played every day if he could. He brought his clubs with him wherever he traveled.

"Golf is twenty per cent mechanics and technique," he once wrote. "The other eighty per cent is philosophy, humor, tragedy, romance, melodrama, companionship, camaraderie, cussedness and conversation."

It was with all of this background—he belonged to four country clubs: Englewood in New Jersey, Maidstone Links on Long Island, Augusta National, and Lakeside—that he met John Montague. Rice's partner in most matches at Lakeside was Guy Kibbee, the comedian, and they journeyed one afternoon to the Riviera Country Club in Pacific Palisades to play in a sixsome with actor Frank Craven, Northwestern football coach Dick Hanley, Oliver Hardy, and Montague.

The round of golf was a revelation. Rice quickly decided he had never seen anyone play the way Montague did. The big man with the big clubs changed the game in the same way Babe Ruth changed baseball. His strength altered the dimensions, his drives the shocking equivalent of Ruth's home runs. The middle irons in Montague's bag were unnecessary. The course was squeezed to a different size, Montague always with a short iron or a chip to the green. No one else in the country did this.

When the sixsome reached the 18th tee, Montague needed only a par for a round of 61, which would break the course record. He then did the strangest thing. He purposely hit a drive deep into the woods and told his caddie to pick up the ball. This was the end of his day. He explained that he didn't want the notoriety of setting the course record.

Rice was amazed. Again, he never had seen anything like this. Never had heard of anything like this. In the coming weeks during his California stay, he arranged to play a number of rounds with Montague. Nothing changed Rice's feelings. He was in a sevensome one day, Montague in the group, and everyone tried to hit with Montague's oversize, overweight driver. Only Gene Tunney, the former heavyweight champion, did not slice. Only Montague could control the club.

The thought occurred to Rice—absurd, ridiculous, but loud and convincing—that the greatest golfer in the world was someone no one else had ever heard about, someone who never had played a round of tournament golf. Could this be? Rice had certainly heard all of the wonder stories about the baseball bat, shovel, and rake, the bird on the wire, and the chip shot into the hammock. He no doubt saw one or two of Montague's tricks. He continued to play with the big man, continued to be impressed.

Writing his column for January 18, 1935, the sportswriter could not contain himself any longer. He spelled Montague's name a curious way, the same way John Montagu, the Earl of Sandwich, the sixteenth-century English lord immortalized for his revolutionary luncheon request for a piece of dried beef between two slices of bread, had spelled it:

LOS ANGELES, Jan. 18—When you bat around in this sporting game for more than thirty years, you stumble over stories beyond belief.

I have just come upon one of these rare episodes in the person of John Montagu, an amateur golfer who never plays in tournaments of any sort—and yet he is a golfer who would be a wrecking whirlwind in any amateur championship and on a par with almost any pro.

In the first place, John Montagu runs neck and neck with Jimmy Thomson of Long Beach as the longest consistent hitter in the world. He has all the backing any one wants that he will out hit Thomson, one of the mightiest maulers of all times.

In addition to this, he can play any type of shot the game calls for—from a full iron to a short pitch—and there are few better putters.

He is more likely to break 70 than go over 70 on any championship course you give him—under pressure, where he is at his best—and with all his blasting power, he is one of the finest golf stylists you will see in a long time. He broke 70 ten consecutive times on one of the most difficult scoring courses around Los Angeles.

Only a year or so ago he played a U.S. Open champion who shot a 67 over his home course. Yet Montagu beat him 2 and 1 with a 65.

He has played many of the hardest courses in California in 63 to 66—and yet you probably never heard his name. Once, on nine holes, Leo Diegel shot a 33 against him and was 2 down.

"You can have him," Leo said to me.

He is ten to fifteen yards beyond Lawson Little in distance and one of the best irons players in golf—but he is still nationally unknown. For one thing, Montagu swings a 17-ounce driver as if it were a feather duster.

I have played several rounds with John Montagu in California and I'll take him as an even bet against any golfer you can name—over a championship course.

In the first place, he is around 30 years old. He is 5 feet 10 inches in height and he weighs 205 pounds.

His physical power is amazing; a strength that is combined with litheness and physical looseness. He is built like [wrestler] Jim Londos and just about as strong.

I played with him at Lakeside, Riviera and other hard courses around Los Angeles and he handled most of the long par 4 holes, from 430 to 450 yards, with a drive and a niblick over soft fairways.

He has the grip of doom in his hands, which are like active steel.

He has the ability to concentrate with a keen, alert mind.

He would be murder in an amateur championship—here or in Great Britain—and a distinct threat in any open.

"Why don't you enter one of these championships?" I asked him.

"I'm not interested in championships," he said. "I like golf for other things."

Montagu comes from the East—he has mining interests in Arizona—and he is one of the most pleasant golfing companions you will meet, a square shooter who will at least try to give you the best of it.

Here is a peculiar angle of Montagu's game. Built something like Bobby Jones and Gene Sarazen, he is far more powerful than either. He has every physical attribute. On a rainy day at Riviera, against a slight wind, I saw him drive into a barranca at the twelfth hole, which happened to be 305 yards from the tee.

"To me," he said, "golf is played with the head, mind or brain—whatever you want to call it. Of course, there are fundamentals of stance, grip and swing. But I must have a clear, clean picture of what I am doing before I play the shot. The mental picture takes charge of the muscular reaction. If there is no mental picture, the rest of course is a mere guess. This means almost endless concentration, if you are under pressure. And there is no thrill in any game unless you are under pressure."

"You mean the test of form, style and fundamentals in general comes from pressure?" I asked.

"In any game," he said, "brains, courage, nerve can only go so far. They must be backed up by skill on the job—or they may mean little."

Which is 100 per cent true.

"Of course," he added, "if mechanical skill isn't supported by brains and courage you may never get the same result. That is why we have so few real champions."

Which is also true.

One remarkable feature of Montagu's game is his combination of accuracy and power. He is rarely off the line. After his tee shot there is little left to do—yet his short pitching, his chip shots and his putting are on a par with the rest of his game.

He uses practically the same grip that Bobby Jones and Tommy Armour use, left-handed power and control.

"But at the finish," he says, "I hit against that left hand and left side."

"When will you play in an open or amateur championship?" I asked.

"Maybe never," he said. "I don't know. I'm still not interested. I have other things in mind."

But any golfer in the world, amateur or pro, who wants to lay his own dough on the line will find Mr. Montagu in a receptive mood. And that bars nobody.

A door to the outside had been opened. The words spoken around Lakeside and Hollywood about John Montague had been written for the first time, written by the most famous sportswriter in the country.

No great rush of attention followed, no instant celebrity. Rice mentioned his discovery again in print during 1935, said that the U.S. Amateur champion of 1936, whoever it was, would not be the best amateur golfer in the country because John Montague was not entered, but again nothing happened. Montague was in California, far from the eyes and attention of the all-important New York press. He wasn't appearing anywhere, wasn't doing anything that would be recorded in public. He wasn't selling any product, especially himself.

More than twenty months passed after Rice's first column, nothing, and then in September 1936, Westbrook Pegler revisited the story. Pegler, forty-two years old, was probably the most controversial syndicated columnist in the country, not a sportswriter but an out-in-the-world, right-wing saber rattler who battled daily on the editorial page with Franklin Delano Roosevelt, the New Deal, labor unions, and whomever else caused him displeasure. He once wrote a column applauding a lynching.

"My hates have always occupied my mind much more actively and have given greater spiritual satisfactions than my friendships," he wrote in a description of his basic viewpoint. "The wish to favor a friend is not as active as the instinct to annoy some person or institution I detest."

"I claim authority to speak for the rabble," he also wrote, "because I am a member of the rabble in good standing."

The son of a newspaper editor from Excelsior, Minnesota, Pegler had started his career on the sports page. That was where he became one of Grantland Rice's many good friends. They played bridge together, drank together, rode trains together, covered ball games and events together throughout the twenties, a decade Pegler categorized as "the Era of Wonderful Nonsense." Pegler's most famous sports page line, after watching the cheering Yale football fans in their fur coats, was "they rose as one raccoon."

He now pounded out six columns a week for the Scripps-Howard syndicate, his words—some said venom—in 174 newspapers reaching more than 10 million readers. His appearance in the midst of the turbulent California gubernatorial campaign in 1934 between Republican incumbent Frank Merriam and Upton Sinclair, the author and socialist running on the Democratic side, had been credited as one of the reasons for Merriam's win and Sinclair's demise. Pegler was a perpetually provocative man.

On Friday, September 26, 1936, his column "Fair Enough" was about John Montague. Vituperation is hard to sustain six days a week. Pegler needed a sports break. There was little doubt that old friend Grantland Rice was a major source, maybe the only source, in the effort:

> Reports are to hand of a mighty man of sport who would seem to combine the fabulous prowess of Paul Bunyan, John Henry and Popeye the Sailor with the remarkable social knacks of Ivan Petrovsky Skovar, the Muscovite hero of the old college doggerel who could imitate Irving, tell fortunes with cards and sing to a Spanish guitar.
>
> The man's name is given as John Montague and his field of operations is Hollywood, but it seems unlikely that our story is a publicity plant, for he avoids publicity and will not permit anyone to take his picture if he can prevent it. Grantland Rice, the greatest American authority on athletes, has played golf with Montague many times and declares that his equal as a shot maker never lived.
>
> A man who often has seen Montague in action at the Lakeside Club, in Los Angeles, reports that his drives average from 40 to 60 yards longer than Bobby Jones' and will almost equal those of Jimmy Thomson, the pro, whose spe-

cialty is distance off the tee. That would be nigh on to 355 or 360 yards. Yet although Montague has lived in Hollywood several years, an inquirer who made investigation on the ground says: "Nobody knows where he came from. He refuses to play tournaments in which his prowess would attract publicity. He is about 30 years old, five feet ten, weighs about 210 pounds and could toss Jim Londos out of the ring."

This part of our report is received from a man who is an authority on athletes and gazed on the mysterious prodigy with the eye of an expert.

There was a fellow in our office the other day, telling about this Montague, and on the strength of his report we sent a wire to the coast asking for details. The reply says, in part, as follows:

"Scotty Chisholm, the dean of golf writers on the coast, knows Montague as well as the next one, but hardly knows him at all. One report says he is a member of a prominent Boston family. A photographer took three shots of him one day, but Montague flatly refused to let him print the pictures. He is such a formidable guy that the photographers are afraid to sneak shots of him. He has a chest like an apple barrel but doesn't carry an ounce of fat. In a fight he is said to have picked up a 250-pounder and thrown him over the bar.

"The only tournament he ever played was the Lakeside championship of [sic] 1935, which he won easily. He is reported that with a driver he can hit thrown golf balls as in batting practice in baseball, but his golf style is unorthodox. He refuses to enter driving contests but played Gene

Sarazen once and lost with a 70 to Gene's 69. However, Montague already had played 18 holes. He beat Olin Dutra with either a 64 or 65 to Dutra's 67, and has played all but two holes at Lakeside, a long course, using only a driver and a niblick to reach the greens.

"I confirmed the story of his bet with Bing Crosby. Montague bet Crosby he could beat him with a ball bat, a shovel and a rake. They played one hole for $50. Montague hit two fungoes, landing in a trap near the green, shoveled out and went down with one putt from his rake. Crosby took a five with golf clubs and paid off.

"He can take a dozen balls and bet $100 on each one that he can land within 10 feet of the pin from 200 yards and collect most of his bets. He bet a fellow he could drive a golf ball from the first tee at Lakeside across Dark Canyon Road in five shots. This is a distance of about three-quarters of a mile. He did it with distance to spare.

"He is a whale of a man at cards; no magician, mind you, but an expert at cards, as in athletics. I hear he can flip a card and make it stick in the crack of a door from five feet, but can't verify that. The caddies at Lakeside won't talk about him, even for money.

"For a couple of years he has lived with Babe Hardy, the movie comedian, but now and again he will disappear for a few months, and they say he goes out into the desert some-where. At trick shots, he is the only man who ever excelled Joe Kirkwood, the Australian wizard."

I have been unable to take the readers of these pieces entirely into my confidence regarding the authorities for the foregoing mixture of information, opinion and report. Several men are represented, but none of them is willing to be quoted.

They are prominent and reliable.

"Can he make toast?" I asked one of the men who have peered at the fabulous Mr. Montague in person.

"Can he make toast?" my friend exclaimed. "Give him an egg and he will churn you up the best fried chicken you ever tasted in your life."

Pegler's column tapped the wackiness of the oft-told Hollywood wonder stories. Rice had stayed mainly on the golf course, birdies and bogeys, captured by Montague's ability. Pegler was captured by the mystery. The guy didn't want to have his picture taken? He wouldn't play in tournaments? What's the deal? Intrigue entered the picture. The subject of the column, Montague, became far more interesting than he did as a simple golfer. Intrigue is a better seller than great golf any day.

This caught the attention of the editors of *Time* magazine. Now thirteen years old, the inspired creation of Henry Luce and Briton Hadden had supplanted *American Mercury* and the *Literary Digest* as the leading weekly magazine in the country. It had developed a lively, punchy style of writing, heavy on detail and description. The favorite *Time* stories involved personalities, "newsmakers," characters who would interest a fine, middle-class family in Appleton, Wisconsin, after an uninteresting workday.

Montague seemed to fit the requirements. *Time* hired a photographer to take his picture, whether he liked it or not. The photographer succeeded. In its issue of January 25, 1937, *Time* picked up the tale of Montague. Part of the magazine's style was to put an identifying title in front of every name, like "Aviator Lindbergh" or "Automaker Chrysler" or "Cinemactor Gable."

The headline in that week's Sport section was "Mysterious Montague":

He drove a golf ball 50 yards farther than Bobby Jones. He could put an approach shot within ten feet of the pin from any distance up to 200 yards. He bet he could knock a ball three-quarters of a mile in five shots and won easily. He said he could beat Bing Crosby at golf using a shovel, a rake and a baseball bat, and he did it.

These, last summer, were a few of the wild rumors that were going the rounds about a mysterious denizen of Hollywood who called himself John Montague, refused to let himself be photographed, told no one where he came from or how he made his living, and never entered tournaments where he might attract publicity. The rumors were so wild that even when benign Sportswriter Grantland Rice, who is too serious about sport to hoax his public and much too wise to be beguiled by Hollywood hoaxers, wrote a column in which he called Montague one of the world's greatest golfers, no one took him seriously. When Westbrook Pegler labeled Montague a combination of Paul Bunyan, Popeye the Sailor and Ivan Petrovsky Skovar, it gave the story more color than credibility.

Last week Mysterious Montague descended abruptly from fiction to reality. At Los Angeles's Lakeside Club, free-lance Photographer Bob Wallace trailed him onto the golf course, hid in a clump of bushes, snapped him twice with a telephoto lens, as he was putting and as he was marching down the fairway, niblick in hand. After taking the pictures, Photographer Wallace handed the film to his brother, popped a dummy magazine into his camera. Golfer Montague, who had heard the shutter click, ran over to Photographer Wallace, took the camera away, removed the dummy magazine, destroyed it.

With the existence of Golfer Montague proved, there remained last week the glamour of legend about most of his doing: Since he never appears publicly, all accounts of his prowess come from his friends. If available reports about Golfer Montague are accurate, Columnist Pegler was last summer guilty of serious belittlement. Montague lore:

When he bet Actor Bing Crosby that he could beat him with a baseball bat, shovel and garden rake, the match ended after one hole because Montague started off with a birdie, using the rake as a putter. With golf clubs, he almost never scores above the 60s. Two years ago, Golfer George Von Elm said he had played golf with Mysterious Montague for a month without seeing him score above 66.

Mysterious Montague's private life is modeled on his golf game. He lives in Beverly Hills with Comedian Oliver Hardy (284 lb.) whom he can pick up with one hand. When not with Hardy, he is "somewhere in the desert" where he is supposed to own a silver mine or gold mine. He has two Lincoln Zephyrs and a supercharged Ford, specially geared for high speed. He is about 33, 5 ft. 10 in., 220 lb. He is built like a wrestler, with tremendous hands, bulldog shoulders and biceps half again as big as Jack Dempsey's. His face is handsome, disposition genial. He can consume abnormal

amounts of whiskey. He frequently stays up all night and recently did so five nights in a row. He is naturally soft-spoken
and dislikes hearing men swear in the presence of ladies.

In Hollywood last week, Crooner Crosby, who also
maintains a prizefighter, a girls' softball team and a stable of
race horses, one of which, Fight On, last week won its
maiden race at odds of 80–1, announced that he would run
a $3,000 invitation golf tournament at Rancho Santa Fe,
near San Diego, on Feb. 6–7. Golfers wondered whether
Mysterious Montague would be invited to compete and, if
so whether he would oblige his friend and the public by accepting.

The two pictures, taken with such subterfuge, revealed little.
Neither showed Mysterious Montague's face. In the first shot,
he was caught in the finish of a putting stroke, head down. The
second was a picture of him walking down the fairway, brassie
in hand, bent halfway, his head turned three-quarters of the way
from the camera. He was wearing a little golf cap in both pictures. His mother wouldn't have recognized him.

The story ran on page 22, jumping to 24. A pen-and-ink
drawing of Leon Trotsky was on the cover of the magazine,
framed by the familiar red *Time* border. The caption was "World
Revolutionist Leon Trotsky" and "He Wants to Go to NY." The
back cover was an ad for Lucky Strike cigarettes, "A fine
smoke . . . only Lucky Strike gives you such fine tobacco plus the
priceless throat protection of the 'Toasting' Process." Eight
pages in front of "Mysterious Montague," an article in Foreign
Affairs described the first meeting between Hermann Göring

and Benito Mussolini. They declared in a joint press conference that "democracy is finished."

The man, John Montague, the Mysterious Montague, was out in the world. There was no stopping now.

———

A vacuum had developed on the American sports scene. With the sad finish of Babe Ruth in a Boston Braves uniform in 1935, the heroes of the twenties whom Grantland Rice and his contemporaries had helped create, people like Dempsey and Tunney and Red Grange, had left the scene. The rookie center fielder for the New York Yankees, Joe DiMaggio, looked pretty good, and the heavyweight boxer Joe Louis, the Brown Bomber, might be something if he could avenge that loss to Max Schmeling, but they were candidates for greatness, not certified stars.

The situation was the same in golf. Some promising youngsters had joined the tour, players like Snead, Ben Hogan, and Byron Nelson, but none of them had won a major event. The departure of Bobby Jones with his bad back and medical problems after he completed his 1930 Grand Slam of winning the British Amateur, British Open, U.S. Open, and U.S. Amateur left the sport looking decidedly unglamorous. Hagen was still around, flamboyant as ever, soon to appear in a town near you, especially if you lived in South Africa, Fiji, or Australia, but was into his forties and hadn't won a major championship since 1929. The predominant golfers, the biggest names, like Horton Smith, Ralph Guldahl, even Gene Sarazen, lacked the talent and charisma of their predecessors.

This mystery man of California, this Paul Bunyan strongman with his baseball bat, shovel, and rake and his Hollywood connections, was a welcome literary addition, a needed splash of color on a gray landscape. The words of Rice and Pegler and now *Time* gave him credibility, validation. He was a new and different character, best of all a challenge, someone whose story still contained large gaps to fill and interesting questions to answer.

Three weeks after the *Time* story appeared, Montague saw firsthand how his life had changed. As a favor to Bing Crosby, he had entered his name on the list of amateurs scheduled to play in the inaugural Crosby Pro-Am tournament at Rancho Santa Fe, outside San Diego. The tournament was a new, favorite project of Crosby's, a matchup of Hollywood and the pros, fun and good golf, an entertaining event that would later be moved north to Pebble Beach.

Despite all of the star power that was gathered from both the movie sets and the PGA Tour for this first tournament, Montague was the story. Would he play? Wouldn't he? His name was on the pairing sheets and he was on the premises. Speculation followed his every move.

"Bing lined up at the first tee with his distinguished guests (for practice), but chief interest in the tourney was centered upon John (Paul Bunyan) Montague, the legendary mystery man from Hollywood and whether he would 'choose to play' today," the United Press reported. "Montague was lured to the course by Crosby after Montague used a shovel, rake and hoe [*sic*] to defeat the singer in golf. The powerful Lakeside amateur is credited with drives past 300 yards, spectacular approach shots and the feat of killing a bird on a telephone wire with a brassie shot...."

Montague remained noncommittal throughout the day before the tournament about whether or not he would play. The weather was wet, and many of the participants and the press gathered early in the afternoon in the room of 1934 U.S. and British Amateur champion Lawson Little at the DelMar Hotel for a cocktail party. Montague was in the group. He continued to refuse to say, yes or no.

One of the people in the room was Bob Myers, the sports editor in Los Angeles for the Associated Press. His bosses in New York kept pressing him for an answer about Montague. Myers kept asking. Montague kept refusing to reveal his intentions. Cocktails were served in between these questions and refusals. Myers, frustrated, kept drinking.

He had been an amateur boxing champion as a young man in Texas and retained a boxer's disposition. He was a small man, however, his championship won in a lower weight class. As his deadline approached and the cocktails piled up, he confronted Montague. The golfer was calm. The little man was well oiled and agitated. Nose to nose, he told Montague to put up or shut up. The AP needed to know his intentions.

Lawson Little, seeing the prospects for trouble, fearing for little Bob Myers's health, grabbed Montague from behind, pinning down his arms. At this moment Myers unloaded with a left cross.

Montague dodged the punch easily.

Lawson Little, behind him, did not.

Little wound up with a black eye. Myers immediately began apologizing to his victim, to Montague, to everyone in the room. Montague accepted the apology, but still said nothing. The stories the next day talked about Montague playing pool at DelMar with bridge champion P. Hal Sims, sinking the 9, 11,

and 14 balls on a single shot to win the match, but his participation in the tournament was still in doubt.

"I'll see in the morning if I choose to play" was all he said.

He chose not. The day turned up rainy again and the tournament was shortened to 18 holes from 36. The five-hundred-
dollar first prize was won by Sam Snead, the twenty-four-year-old
professional from White Sulphur Springs, West Virginia, who
shot a 68. George Von Elm finished second. Richard Arlen was
part of a team that finished second in the pro-am portion of the
tournament.

Montague's refusal to play did nothing to stem the buzz of
interest that now surrounded him. If anything, it helped.

"John Montague, amateur trick shot artist, who experts
contend is the country's best at match play, watched the soggy
proceedings from the gallery," the *San Mateo Times and News-
Herald* reported in the fifth paragraph of its story on the Crosby.
"Although entered in the tournament, he did not play."

The typed-out reconstruction of the oral legend of Lakeside
was well under way. He would become not only "Mysterious
Montague," but "the Sphinx of the Links," "the Garbo of Golf,"
"the Phantom of the Fairways," and whatever other catchy
phrases could be invented. With no facts to get in the way, no
empirical evidence to be presented, imaginations could go to
work. This was fun.

"Hollywood's mysterious 'miracle man' golfer, John Montague, bosom golfing buddy of O. N. Hardy, and phenomenally
lucky bet winner—on any subject, whether it be a horse race or
the length of a prayer at a funeral—is reportedly 'hot under the
collar' over the article appearing about him in a current news
magazine, an article which doesn't begin to tell the story of the

man," Darsie L. Darsie wrote in the *Los Angeles Herald*. "Not that he isn't news! He is. Whether it be in the locker room, hotel lobby or barber shop a leading subject of any conversation is 'Have you heard about Monty?' "

The wonder stories were unfolded, sometimes mounted and polished with exaggeration. Montague beat Bing Crosby again and again with the baseball bat, shovel, and rake. Birds dropped in astonishing numbers from telephone wires after being hit by Montague's uncanny shots. Every now and then a new story would emerge. Montague pulled down comedian Jack Oakie's pants with one tug! Oakie didn't know what to do! S. F. B. Morse, president of Del Monte Properties, reported that Montague had reached the 550-yard 18th hole of the Del Monte course in two! Never had been done before! These would be added to the pile.

"I was in a gas station when Monty drove in," Fred Murphy, caddie master at Lakeside, said. "He strolled over to a twelve-cylinder sedan, casually said, 'How do these cars feel?' and lifted one of the rear wheels six or eight inches from the ground without drawing a deep breath."

Cars were lifted and examined and moved with regularity. Famous names from Lakeside were dropped into paragraphs as often as possible. One report had Montague lifting Oliver Hardy and holding him over his head. A witness said he had seen Montague bet that he could chip a golf ball into an old-fashioned glass on the mantel in three tries and had done it in two. George Von Elm called him "the best golfer in the world."

"Each time a Montague story is told, it picks up additional color, just like a snowball rolling down a hill grows larger and larger," Darsie L. Darsie wrote. "Stories originally based on fact have stretched far from the truth...."

The contrarians soon appeared. Logic said that if a story was too good to be true, then it probably wasn't true. Reporters made calls to find voices that would debunk the myth that was being built, exclamation point by exclamation point, adjective by adjective, across the land. Voices were found.

Joe Williams, columnist at the *New York Telegram and Sun*, talked with Jimmy Thomson, the twenty-three-year-old professional who was known as the longest driver on the Tour. Montague supposedly could outdrive Thomson with ease. Had the two men ever played each other? Thomson said they had. Once. And the drives? Thomson said he had outdriven Montague on every hole.

Williams also talked with Ed Dudley, the winter pro at Augusta National Golf Club. Dudley said he had played Montague at Lakeside once and shot a 63. It was one of the best rounds of golf he ever shot. Montague shot a 73, a difference of ten strokes. A final call went to Gene Sarazen. Had he ever played Montague? Yes. He had beaten Montague, 4 and 3 in match play.

"I think I have shown by authenticated evidence that Mr. Montague is (1) neither an incredibly long hitter (2) That he is anything but invincible and (3) That at least on one occasion—his match with Dudley—he couldn't even break par on his own course," Williams concluded. "What then is the verdict? I should say the jury would be justified in accepting him as just a top notch club player and nothing else."

An even tougher appraisal came in a new magazine called

Sports Illustrated. The Depression economy, revenues disappearing monthly, had forced *The American Golfer,* the magazine Grantland Rice had edited for years, to morph into this new publication in hopes of broadening its advertising base. The *American Golfer* name was still used to top the golf section, but Rice was no longer involved.

Writer John Escher, the magazine's managing editor, found an unnamed source who claimed he had played with Montague at Westwood Hills "dozens of times." The source said they played for dimes at the public course and that he won most of the bets. He also said he was not a great golfer.

"Never broke 80 in my life," the unnamed golfer said. "As a matter of fact I only saw Monty get under that figure a few times. Lowest score he ever had playing with me—and we played nearly every day all summer—was 76. Of course that was two or three years ago and he may have improved. He certainly did hit a tremendous ball off the tee in spite of his unorthodox form, but his short game was pretty bad in those days."

The debunkers, of course, soon had debunkers. Braven Dyer, columnist at the *Los Angeles Times,* fired back at Escher and any other skeptics.

"As a matter of fact, Monty could not shoot an 86, no matter how hard he tried, provided he made an honest effort to hit the ball," Dyer wrote. "The East always has been reluctant to believe anything that came out of the West unless it be reports of earthquakes or floods. Having played with Montague myself I know full well he can shoot par any time he desires. . . ."

The buzz grew so loud that Frank Finch of the *Los Angeles Times* put his hands over his ears:

"Montague?" inquires your barber, lacerating your chin with a wild swipe of the blade as he extols the virtues of the wonder man. "Montague, did you say? Did you hear about the time he pointed to a Chinese ostrich perched on top of a telephone pole, teed up a golf ball and bashed the bird's brains out with a neat mashie shot?"

"Montague?" asks your butcher, resting his paw on the scale as he tells you that those microscopic lamb chops will be $1.47, thank you. "Montague, did you say? Did you hear about the time he grabbed the four Marx brothers, two in each hand, and stuffed them upside down in the ice box?"

"Montague?" asks your family physician, presenting you with a bill for service rendered that brings on another relapse. "Montague, did you say? Did you hear about the time he beat Bing Crosby by four strokes at Lakeside, using only a cigarette stand, a floor lamp and a buggy whip for clubs and a brass door knob for a ball?"

———

Grantland Rice was startled by what he had wrought. He also was defensive. The story had gone out of control, a layer cake built on top of a simple slice of whole wheat bread. Montague, who had become Rice's friend, never had asked for any of this, never had said he could beat anyone. Rice was the one who had started everything. He was embarrassed.

The story was at least two years old. That was another thing that troubled Rice. Golf games come and golf games go, as all golfers know, the magic wand of today turning into a foreign object tomorrow, sent without an instruction booklet. Montague's golf game now was not what it once was. He hadn't been playing much. He wasn't ready for the tests everyone wanted him now to take.

Rice tried to set matters straight. On April 7, 1937, he wrote another Montague column. He tried to explain, take some air out of the gale-force blather that had developed. He still misspelled Montague's name:

> So many conflicting stories have been written about John Montagu, the so-called mystery golfer, so many wild guesses have been launched in so many directions, that a number of readers have asked us to tell the real story of this California expert.
>
> We happened to write the first stories about Montagu two years ago after playing with him for a number of rounds. At that time he was as fine a golfer as we have ever seen. He was shooting various courses steadily between 65 and 70—hitting the ball a long way and following this up with a brilliant short game.
>
> After that, Montagu gave up golf for the greater part of two years. Apparently he has little interest in golf now except for the game's companionship. As a result, his game has naturally fallen below the standard of some years back, although he still hangs on in the immediate neighborhood of 70. The old groove isn't quite there as it once was.
>
> He has put on added weight since I first met him in 1935 and is now up around 220. But he has lost at least 30 yards from his cannonading drives.
>
> John Montagu began playing golf in California at the age of 7 some 25 years ago. He has never played in any tournament. Many have asked why it was that a golfer of

this caliber never cared to take a shot at some championship. I pushed the query along to Montagu.

"Because," he said, "I never was interested in tournament play. Golf to me has meant only a game that would give me a chance of being with my friends. At one point, when I was playing the best golf of my life, averaging around 67 or 68, I quit the game for four years. I have never given it any serious attention in the last two years. I have never offered a bet in my life or suggested any amount to play for, merely accepting any amount my opponent might name."

Montagu is one of the most powerful men I've ever known. The strength in his hands and wrists is incredible. He has what Ty Cobb calls "quick strength," always the strongest type. He is one of the most friendly, likable fellows you'd care to meet—modest, generous to a fault. He always has had a deep-set aversion to publicity of any sort—especially to photographers and interviewers. Nearly all the pictures printed have been someone else—not Montagu.

One of his main interests is with mining and mining claims in Arizona. He can take care of himself under any conditions, but I have never seen him start any form of trouble. He has as many friends as anyone I know and his popularity is deserved.

How good a golfer was Montagu at his best? I asked George Von Elm, who isn't given to soft criticism. "Two years ago—the best I ever saw," he said. "I played with him once for a month at a stretch and never saw him over 68. I was playing well then and never had a chance to win a match. At that time he could have won any tournament— open or amateur—he might have played in. He had every shot in the bag—a great long game and the best all-around short game I ever saw. He hasn't been playing much lately and his timing is way off. Yet he still is good for a 70 or 71. And without much sleep."

How good is or was John Montagu? I put the same story up to Oliver (Babe) Hardy of the famous Laurel and Hardy combination. "I'll tell you how good he is," the Babe said. "I've played with him for years. I've lived with him. I know his game is off now, but I'll be glad to take Monty against any golfer in the world for a $10,000 bet—if they give him a month to get ready. I played my last game with Monty at Pebble Beach some time ago. He was out in 31. He finished the first nine 2-3-3. He had a 4 on the last 580-yard hole for a 65. After one of the longest drives I ever saw, he planted a brassie on the green. He had two putts for a 65, but two old gentlemen were putting on the green so he told the caddie to pick up the ball. The course record is 67. That's how good Monty is. That $10,000 bet still goes."

How good is Montagu? I asked Bing Crosby—a 74 shooter and a top-notch sportsman. "The best golfer I ever saw," he said. "I was shooting around 74. Montagu started me 5-up and took me in his stride. The story about him playing me with a baseball bat, a shovel and a rake against my regular clubs is all true. He started with a birdie 3 on the 370-yard 10th hole at Lakeside. I called it a day—we settled on the green. Monty isn't playing the golf now he played two or three years ago. He doesn't seem to care about it, one way or another. But I've played with a lot of the leading pros and leading amateurs. I've never seen one that could beat Montagu when he was at his best."

Ask Frank Craven—who certainly knows his golf. Ask Adolphe Menjou. Ask Guy Kibbee. Ask Sid Sutherland, one of the best of the reporters. Ask Leo Diegel, who was out in 33 at Lakeside to find himself two down in a nine-hole match. I've played more than 40 rounds with Montagu in the past two or three years. He isn't playing the game he did two or three years ago—but still he slipped only to 70 or 71.

They have called him a golfer looking only for bets. In the last four rounds we played, Montagu had no bets at all. He's never asked for one—and those who knew him were too canny to suggest anything. I've heard of some of his incredible feats. I can believe most of them, for I have seen him do incredible things on a golf course. He has power and control—and he can play every shot in the bag. What is still more important—he is at his best under pressure.

His private career? Montagu still insists—and correctly—that this belongs to Montagu and no one else.

Rice's attempt didn't work. An itchiness had developed around the tale, a desire to know the result. New to all of this information, these claims of great deeds and talents, bystanders didn't want caveats or explanations. They wanted to see what this Montague could do, wanted to see for themselves. They not only wanted him to play, but play against the best competition. They also wouldn't mind if he came out of the house and knocked a starling or two off a telephone wire.

Various rumors of grand propositions made their way into print. A group of Hollywood backers, including Crosby and Hardy and the rest, supposedly were ready to put up fifty thousand dollars to see Montague play a challenge match against

Bobby Jones, who would come out of retirement. A match with socialite Thomas Suffern Tailer Jr. in Long Island supposedly was going to be played for ten thousand dollars a side. Or maybe Montague was going to play in the next British Open in Carnoustie.

His story certainly had reached England. The headline in the *London Sunday Express* shouted "Man Plays Better-Than-Scratch Golf Using Shovel, Garden Rake, and Baseball Bat." The lead sentence by C. V. R. Thompson, special correspondent, was "This is the true story of the greatest golfer in the world." Montague supposedly was already entered in the tournament. British champion Henry Cotton, among others, said he welcomed the challenge. He also said he didn't believe the wonder stories.

Montague said, alas, none of these confrontations would take place. He liked his life the way it was.

"I have no need for money," he told the United Press. "Although I have won high stakes playing golf I have never made a penny at it. In fact, I have made it a point to spend every cent.

"Secondly, I have no ambition to play in a tournament. Golf with me is recreation, not competition. There is nothing to be gained by tournament play because if I won I wouldn't care, and if I lost there wouldn't be anything settled anyway. I won't play Cotton or anyone else and I won't be lured into the Open."

His words meant nothing. The editors at the American Golfer section of *Sports Illustrated* persisted. The following full-page editorial appeared in the June 1937 edition. The names of the magazine's associate editors—Francis Ouimet, Harry Cooper, Willie Macfarlane, Jesse Sweetser, George Trevor, and Bernard

Darwin, all prominent players or golf writers—appeared across the top of the page.

The headline was "An Appeal to Mr. Montague."

A new golf season is with us, one that bids fair to rival in competitive interest the grand slam year of Robert Tyre Jones. Some of the factors that will contribute to making this year a banner one include the Ryder Cup matches, participation of America's leading professionals in the British Open and the chance that a South African, A. J. Locke, may be a definite factor in the British and United States' Amateur Championships.

From this brilliant competitive scene there is one person missing. He is John Montague, the most talked of golfer in the world today. During the last four months, there has been an enormous amount written about Montague. Some experts say he is the best golfer in the world, others that he is pretty close to it, a few that he is far from it.

With so many diversified statements emanating from different authorities, it is still fairly obvious that the true answer to John Montague's prowess on the links is an unknown quantity. This situation will continue just as long as there is no basis on which to compare his game.

We know that John Montague never wished to heap so much comment upon his own play, but the fact remains that such has been the case and he is the most talked of golfer in the world. Today, the mystery surrounding him has reached such proportions as to become a menace to those whose business is golf.

We ask Mr. Montague to give the golfers of this country, a large percentage of which we represent, a fair opportunity to judge the merits of his game. Such judgment can only be made by his appearance in competition. We know he considers his golf as a recreation and enjoys playing in the company of his intimate friends, but without wishing to make an intrusion on his privacy, we ask him to compete in at least one tournament during his present sojourn in the East.

We are sure that Mr. Montague is the last person to want such a state of uncertainty to exist, especially when, in the long run, it may do infinite harm to the game of golf. We can only hope that he will see his way clear to appearing in competitive play to establish definitely his ability—or inability.

THE EDITORS

Some kind of showdown seemed inevitable. The court of public opinion can be a noisy place when the public doesn't get what it wants. As well-oiled Bob Myers of the AP had demanded as a representative of the people, the newly famous man had to "put up or shut up." Even if the newly famous man hadn't said a thing. The Mysterious Montague had been backed into a well-lit corner.

What next?

New York State Police inspector John Cosart of Troop D in Oneida, New York, had read most of the articles with growing interest. The article in *Time* magazine with the two pictures, even though they didn't show Montague's face, especially caught his eye. Cosart cut it out and sent it with a package of clippings to Inspector Joseph Lynch at the state police barracks in Malone.

Cosart and Lynch had worked together intermittently on the same case of an unsolved robbery in Au Sable Forks, New York, for almost seven years, tracking leads that went nowhere. Cosart had always thought they would find their man somewhere on the sports page. The message the inspector sent to Lynch basically was, "We've got the son of a bitch now."

A request for help was sent to the Los Angeles Police Department on June 11, 1937. Fingerprints were obtained and matched. On July 9, 1937, John Montague was arrested as he left his apartment on North Crescent Heights Boulevard. He was charged with armed robbery as the fourth bandit in the holdup of the Hana restaurant in Jay, New York, on August 5, 1930. He was taken to the Los Angeles County Jail.

"When arrested," the *Los Angeles Times* reported, "he was nattily attired in a brown sports coat, striped white slacks, two-tone sports shoes, brown swagger hat and accessories to blend." Forty-three dollars in currency and change was in his pockets.

John Montague admitted at the jail that his real name was LaVerne Moore and he came from Syracuse, New York.

CHAPTER FOUR

SYRACUSE

July 10, 1937

The headline that ran across eight columns on the front page of the *Syracuse Herald* on the morning of July 10, 1937, was "Mystery Golfer, Syracusan, Held as Bandit." The long-absent face of LaVerne Moore—Verne, sometimes called "Bull" Moore—smiled at local residents, friends, and family in a two-column head shot.

With no need to hide anymore from photographers, he had posed at the Los Angeles County Jail. He was wearing the snappy movie star hat, and a patterned silk necktie hung from his well-starched collar. A matching handkerchief peeked from the breast pocket of his expensive sport coat. He looked untroubled by his troubles, confident, almost cocky. He looked like his old Syracuse self.

News of his arrest was everywhere. The big story of the day was the ongoing, sad search in the Pacific for the lost plane of Amelia Earhart, Toluca Lake resident, which had disappeared on July 2, but the discovery of John Montague's alleged larcenous past was in headlines across the country. From the *New York Times* ("Montague, Golfer, Gets Robbery Bail") to the *Los Angeles Times* ("Montague, Golfer, Held as Bandit"), to the *Yuma Daily Sun and Yuma Arizona Sentinel* ("7-Year-Old Crime Charged to 'Playmate' of Bing Crosby and Other Film Greats"), to the *Lowell (Massachusetts) Sun* (" 'Greatest Golfer in the World' Held for New York Roadhouse Stick-Up"), this sudden solution to the sports-page puzzle was great stuff, true tabloid melodrama.

Bing Crosby, Oliver Hardy, and other Hollywood notables expressed their surprise and offered support to their country club friend. He spent the night in jail, was arraigned in the morning, and was released on $10,000 bail, reduced from the $25,000 requested by Deputy District Attorney Howard Hinshaw. Crosby and Hardy both offered to post the bond, but E. A. Ralston, a Hollywood contractor, and F. S. Calendar, a friend, signed the papers. The freed man signed his name as John Montague, and listed LaVerne Moore as an alias. An extradition hearing was scheduled for July 26, 1937.

"I made a mistake when I was just a kid back East and I've been trying to make good since then," Montague/Moore told waiting reporters at the courthouse. "I was going to go back and straighten the whole thing out."

He answered a few questions, easy and light, but didn't say much. He wouldn't talk about his mining interests, his ability to drink, wouldn't talk about his life with the movie stars. He wouldn't identify the woman who picked him up or describe their relationship. He danced with the questions more than answered them.

"How'd you make so many friends out here?" one reporter asked.

"The way to get along with guys in Hollywood is to keep from trying to steal their girls."

"Since you're so good, why don't you ever play in golf tournaments?" another reporter asked.

"I'm modest, I tell you."

"Did you ever have any lessons?"

"No, I'm just a natural born golfer."

"Have you got plenty of money?"

"Getting personal, huh?"

The members at the Lakeside Golf Club were suitably stunned. They reexamined their experiences with John Montague, replayed their rounds of golf and conversations. There had never been any indication that he was on the run, looking over his shoulder. He was a mystery perhaps, quirky, but he was a good guy, a lot of fun. He was a terrific golfer.

"Yes, we all wondered just what was back of Monty's mask," Hollywood screenwriter Sid Sutherland said, "but he never asked any questions of us and we treated him the same way. We'll do all we can to help him."

Montague had been Sutherland's houseguest in Rancho Santa Fe for three days at the beginning of the week. The implausibility of the news, the tale, was a shock, a weird twist of plot even for a writer who now was working on his eleventh movie, *Adventure's End*, which would star John Wayne. If you didn't know the person sleeping in your guest room, whom did you know? Sutherland was a Lakeside member and had played golf often with . . . LaVerne Moore? The new name and the sudden news were hard to assimilate.

"Why, only the other day he spent hours mixing a huge dish of spaghetti, washing dishes, cleaning house and working in the garden," Sutherland said. "He said he never had enjoyed a trip so much in his life."

There was no great shock in Syracuse, New York.

On the other side of the country, 2,335 miles from Sunset Boulevard, the syncopated industrial city that spewed out steel and typewriters and furniture and china and shoes and caskets, banged and clanged and belched with lunch-pail commerce on the shores of Lake Onondaga, was as far away from the back nine of the Lakeside Golf Club as a man could travel. Syracuse, New York, was a place of deep snow in winter, hard work all year round, a draft-beer, shot-of-whiskey mill town that had grown, population slightly over 200,000, with a touch of dignity added by the university on the hill.

This was an export city, not import, the place where local resident L. Frank Baum imagined his faraway Oz. The dreamers here dreamed about Hollywood. Nobody anywhere dreamed about Syracuse. The Depression had whacked the city's economy, no different from anywhere else, but the production lines had started moving again. Carrier air-conditioning had recently moved into the large plant left vacant when the Franklin automobile company went bankrupt. Workers were working. Money mostly involved sweat and calluses. Nobody dreamed about

sweat and calluses. Good transportation out of Syracuse histor-
ically was its greatest feature.

First the Erie Canal had sent products—salt was a big one
at the beginning—off into the world, and then the railroad
dominated the downtown landscape. For over one hundred
years the tracks of the New York Central ran straight down the
middle of Washington Street, the main business thoroughfare
lined with department stores, banks, and offices. Activity stopped
as often as sixty-eight times a day, nobody able to cross the
street, as the North Shore Limited or the Empire or some other
train bound for wherever creaked though at six miles per hour,
the passengers staring out at the citizens of Syracuse, the citizens staring back, both wondering what it would be like to be
on the other side of the glass windows.

"They'll be missed...," Edward Hungerford wrote in *Pathway of Empire* in 1935 when the plan, now completed, was announced to divert the trains to a new station. "They brought a
curiously alien touch at all hours into the workaday life of the
brisk town, a sort of daily, almost hourly, rubbing of the shoulders by New York and Chicago and St. Louis and Detroit."

LaVerne Moore was born in Syracuse on August 25, 1903.
His father, Matthew, worked at Crucible Steel on West Fayette
Street as a pot puller, an honest and physical dollar earned in the
glow of the blast furnace. His mother, Mary, had come from
Ireland at age eight, part of the exodus from Tipperary County to
Syracuse that was so great that the ethnic Irish neighborhood on
the far west end of the city was called Tipperary Hill. The distin-
guishing landmark in Tipperary Hill was the only upside-down
traffic light in the United States, hanging from the corner of

Milton Avenue and Tompkins Street, created because young immigrant men used slingshots to perpetually extinguish the sight of the British red placed higher than the Irish green. The city finally listened and in 1925 formalized the thought. The green was on top, the red on the bottom; color-blind drivers beware.

LaVerne had a brother, Harold, three years older, and two younger sisters, Madeline and Mary. When he was growing up, the family lived in a rented two-family house at 303 Avery Avenue, the middle of Tipperary Hill. Harold was the good son, grew up to raise his own family, teach music, play the organ, and sing in and lead the choir, all at once, at Sunday Mass at St. Patrick's Church, the cornerstone of Tipperary Hill clean living. Matthew Moore passed the collection basket every Sunday.

LaVerne was the rascal, the rapscallion; some said "bully." He was different from the rest of his family, different from everyone else around him. Electricity, energy, seemed to shoot through his every movement, every thought. He was one of those kids who couldn't sit still and grew into a young man who couldn't sit still. He was always moving, doing, thinking three steps ahead of everyone else. Planning. He saw challenges, angles that no one else saw. Huckleberry Finn comes to mind.

Friends would go to his house when he was young and find him in the attic. He was swinging from the beams, one to the next, doing chin-ups, walking on the beams to work on his balance. He lifted weights, then sometimes, at the end of the workout, tied weights to his wrists and ankles and simply stood in the dark for an hour, letting his developed muscles settle into his body. He was the best athlete on Tipperary Hill, the strongest and also the fastest. Big as he was, he was still timed in ten seconds flat for the one-hundred-yard dash.

Sports always seemed easy, part of his nature. He played them all, played them well. When he was just a kid, pitching for St. Pat's, he struck out eighteen Syracuse University freshmen in a game. When he was older, he hit the longest home run ever seen in Utica, a shot over the left-field fence, which was five hundred feet from home plate and never had been cleared before or since. When he was older, he went to Florida to try out with the Boston Braves, then went back again to try out with the 1928 New York Yankees, the defending world champions, Murderer's Row, the best lineup in recorded history.

He played a little minor-league baseball in Providence, a little more in Buffalo. He once took himself to the Polo Grounds for a week and pestered New York Giants manager John McGraw for a tryout. McGraw surrendered after three days. He grabbed a bat himself and stood at the plate to see what the kid could do. LaVerne threw him every pitch in his repertoire.

"How many things can you pitch?" McGraw finally said, no two pitches alike.

"Speed, hooks, and three kinds of knuckleballs," LaVerne replied.

"That's more than my ball club and this league can handle," the little manager said. "Besides, you're too young. Get a job in the minor leagues first."

LaVerne was good enough in football that Chick Meehan, the coach at Syracuse University, arranged for him to attend Dean Academy, a prep school in Franklin, Massachusetts. This didn't work out, although football should have been his best game. He had the size and speed to play almost any of the twenty-two positions. He played basketball and pool, hunted and fished. He skied. He played golf.

Golf, with its complicated challenges, with its solitary moments, an individual sport, no teammates needed, was perfect for him. He learned the game early. Burnet Park Golf Course, built in 1901, one of the first public courses in the country, was at the edge of Tipperary Hill, walking distance from 303 Avery Avenue. LaVerne always said his career started when he found a golf ball in the street. He was a natural from his first swing.

"I was seven or eight years old," he said. "I took the ball home and found an elbow from a gas pipe. I whittled down one end of a broom handle so it fit the elbow. I took my new club outside and put the ball on a tee. I swung and broke a plate glass window in a cigar store across the street. My dad, after he paid for the window, bought me a set of clubs and told me I should play the rest of my golf on a golf course."

Burnet Park was a nine-hole layout, par 33. It became LaVerne's playground. He first took lessons from his brother, Harold, who was a good golfer. Harold was ambidextrous, could play left- or right-handed, later became a club pro for a while. LaVerne was an easy pupil. He had the coordination to pick up the basics easily, then had the curiosity, the competitiveness, to learn more.

As he grew into his body as a teenager, he developed the big drive, could pound the ball past "the trees on the right," a drive of 350 to 380 yards on the 400-yard par-4 5th hole, longest on the course. He developed tricks. He would bury three balls in a sand trap, one of top of the other like they were green, yellow, and red on the upside-down traffic light. He would ask his audience which ball he should hit, top, bottom, or middle, then whack the proper ball out on a fly, the other two falling lifelessly to the side. He would drive a ball off the tee blindfolded, became pretty good at it. He would set the nine-hole course record, so he said, at 24. The old-timers at the course never believed him. They said he'd only played six holes.

The most interesting hole at Burnet Park was the par-4 4th. Out-of-bounds to the left, over a fence, was the Burnet Park Zoo, a place where bison, deer, and boar roamed. A hooked tee shot therefore really was out of bounds, the ball lost among the animals. A well-placed hook or maybe a straight cannon drive, the golf ball aimed that way, often would whack one of the animals somewhere on its body. The animal would react. LaVerne also became an expert at that.

A boar butted him once when he climbed the fence, trying to retrieve a ball. He broke a hickory-shafted club over the boar's head. The boar simply looked at him, as if it hadn't felt a thing. LaVerne looked back, half a golf club in his hand.

Burnet Park was everyday fun and adventure. The course was redesigned one spring. The 3rd hole became the 1st hole, something like that, a confusing arrangement for a while. LaVerne set up shop at the former 1st hole and collected greens fees from golfers who hadn't heard about the change. Did it for two weeks before anyone discovered what he was doing.

Stories swirled about him from the beginning. He took a mashie one day outside Burnet Park, dropped a ball, pointed at the passing car of a friend, and told another friend, "Watch this." He swung the club easily; the ball went in that big parabola, and, *whack,* bounced neatly off the hood of the car. Life was everyday fun and adventure.

"How'd you do that?" other kids would ask after he did something they could never do.

LaVerne developed a standard answer. He invented a second

name, a performer's name, a circus kind of name. This performer was the one who accomplished great feats.

"I am," LaVerne Moore said, "the Mighty Montague."

It was because of this—and more, much more—that the news out of Hollywood on July 10, 1937, was not surprising in Syracuse. Dozens of people had suspected, even before his arrest, that the Mysterious Montague and the Mighty Montague were the same person. The wild and talented kid from Tipperary Hill seemed to be one of a kind.

"The first time I read about him in somebody's column—it told how he'd beaten Bing Crosby in golf using a shovel, a baseball bat and a rake, how he could throw a 250-pound man over a bar without even breathing hard—do you know what I did?" one local resident told the *Washington Post.* "I called up a friend of mine and told him I'd bet anything the Mysterious Montague guy was LaVerne Moore of Syracuse. It really wasn't much of a call on that, because I knew that there was only one man who could do those tricks."

There was a difference from Hollywood, though, in many of the wonder stories that had been collected in Syracuse. In the Syracuse pile with the blindfolded golf shots, the lifted cars (LaVerne Moore often picked up the power end of a balky car, lighter than they were a decade later, and spun the wheels to get it started instead of asking for a push), the long-distance homers, and consecutive strikeouts, were stories that had a darker spirit running through them. For every story about him boosting a nun's habit at Holy Rosary School, wearing it, and standing in a window, mimicking the gestures of the visiting monsignor on the front steps as he addressed the assembled kids in front of him, everyone in stitches, there was a story about how he liked to lock teachers and kids in rooms at the school every time he found a key in the door.

His devilish streak had some certified devil inside it. The menace was remembered as much as the mirth in Syracuse, often trumped the mirth. He brought a box of eggs to a rally by visiting members of the Ku Klux Klan, winging the eggs off the white sheets and pointed hats of the marchers. Good thing. He winged rotten tomatoes anytime he could at anyone he saw. Not such a good thing.

"Did I ever hear of him?" Syracuse newspaper columnist Joe Ganley, nine years younger, would repeat for years anytime Moore's name was mentioned. "The son of a bitch stole fifteen cents from me when I was a caddie at Burnet park. He snatched the nickels from my hand, laughed in my face, and walked away."

His antics in his old touring car—some people said it was a high-wheeled Cadillac, others said it was a Pierce-Arrow with the big headlights on the fenders—were something out of a Mack Sennett movie. He would drive through the North Side Regional Market, oops, take a sudden turn, and crash through some poor farmer's stand of melons, leaving the melons rolling on the street, the farmer out of business. He would spot a derby hat, blown off a pedestrian's head on a windy day, skittering across the pavement. He would aim for the hat, oops, and if he missed, he would stop the car, shift into reverse, and hit his mark.

Old-timers, codgers waiting for a bus, learned through hair-raising experience never to accept a ride in the touring car, even in the rain or snow. Moore would stop, act as if he were a Boy Scout on a mission, but once the old-timer sat in the passenger seat, the Boy Scout would turn into Barney Oldfield, roaring through downtown, around the State School on South Wilbur Avenue, around and around, the old-timer bounced and jounced, whipped into dizziness before the ride finally, mercifully, would stop. It was crazy stuff. LaVerne once opened the hood of the police chief's car at Burnet Park and tied the chief's golf sweater around the fan belt. The chief started the car, but soon encountered problems. The car stalled. He opened the hood and found a busted fan belt and many small pieces of his own sweater.

"Verne Moore had too much vitality and too much energy for one human being," the police chief, Thomas Carroll, a forgiving soul, said. "But there was never anything vicious or mean-spirited about him."

Maybe.

One story was told and retold in assorted versions. They all began with Moore driving up to a group of construction workers on a sunny morning. He got out, asked the workers how much they were making per hour, offered to double the figure. He brought the men to the home of some prominent official. (Pick one: high school principal, mayor, other.) He assigned the workers a job to do. (Pick one: rip out all of the shrubbery, dig a large hole in the lawn, other.) After promising to deliver pay envelopes at the end of the day, he then left, never to return. The workers toiled all day for nothing. The principal-mayor-other then came home to discover the missing shrubs, the large hole, or whatever other indignity had been done to his property. LaVerne, somewhere far away from the scene, laughed and told the story.

He was a loner more than a joiner, a ringleader of his own

gang of one. There was an unpredictable quality about everything he did. He could put on that curious formality of the true imp in public, deferential to older people, a defender of ladies' honor, pleasant as a ward politician. He could hatch a plot two minutes later. The other kids called him "Bull" or sometimes "the Indian" because of the way he moved, his speed and balance. Nobody called him his real name very often. Some kids thought his real name was part of what made him the way he was.

"All us kids had names like 'Mike' or 'John' or 'Frank' or 'Bill,'" one friend said. "With a name like 'LaVerne' he had something to live down. Funny, though, he always was a polite kid.... Our mothers, who didn't know anything about his deviltry, used to ask us why we couldn't be nice, polite boys like LaVerne Moore. On top of having that name, he used to wear a coat with a real fur collar... while the rest of us were wearing lumberjacks. He had to be strong and tough."

He did get paid back in full every now and then. He showed up one night, early morning, really, about 2:00 A.M., at a restaurant on East Fayette Street in the touring car, which was either the high-wheeled Cadillac or maybe the Pierce-Arrow with the big headlights. He offered a ride to a bunch of fellows—Bozo Corbett and Red Tomamey, Bushel Gooley, Mush Mulane, Rubber Coleman, and Hung O'Hara—took three of them out to Onondaga Hill, where the car mysteriously stopped. LaVerne asked everyone to get out and push. The three friends pushed the car up the hill, he fired up the engine, the car started, then he turned around and waved good-bye, leaving everyone stranded.

Luckily, a cab soon passed and the three friends caught a fast ride back to the restaurant. The high-wheeled Cadillac, maybe the Pierce-Arrow with the big headlights, was parked out front. Bozo Corbett checked the ignition switch, found it was on, and drove the car to a South State Street storage garage. He went for the long-term parking.

"I told the manager I had a job to do out of town," Bozo reported. "I wouldn't need the car for a couple of months."

LaVerne was walking for a couple of months.

The Syracuse wonder stories, like the Hollywood wonder stories, were preserved only in conversation, memory, never transferred to the written word until LaVerne hit the front page in California. The only few mentions of his name in the *Syracuse Standard* before his arrest were two one-paragraph reports of athletic performance, the eighteen-strikeout game and a course record he supposedly set at a nearby layout for shooting a suspicious 66. The good stuff was only local, oral legend that was passed along over coffee and cold beer. Crazy kid, crazy stuff, what's the weather like tomorrow?

There was a point in all of the stories, though, and there must have been thousands of stories, seldom heard, since forgotten, stories every day about the young LaVerne Moore, where the listener wanted to intercede, put himself into the tale, walk up to the subject and start talking to him like some high school guidance counselor, some parish priest. Shake him. What are you doing? Tell him about lost opportunities, the talents he had. Tell him how to harness the electricity.

The best local story of all came from Ten-Yard Steffins, who had received his nickname and a certain amount of fame as a fullback at Colgate University. The story took place in Utica. LaVerne spent a bunch of time in Utica.

"He came down to a cigar stand I used to keep in Utica one

night and we got to talking about how accurate a golf ball could be hit," Ten-Yard said. "He always carried his clubs around with him in his car, so he went across the street and brought back a brassie and a ball. He took a couple of wooden matches off my counter and went back out in the street.

"He put down the matches, about half an inch apart, and set the ball upon them. He said, 'See that electric sign down the street?' It was, I'd say, two and a half city blocks away or about 200 yards and it was hanging from the second floor of a building. Well, he drew back with that short hard swing he's got—right there in the middle of that traffic, with headlights coming at him, and the ball hardly visible—and wham! We couldn't see the ball, but we stood there a second or two and bang! You could hear something hit the sign and a couple of the sign's lights went out."

The image was spectacular: the matches, the mighty swing, the cars and their headlights, the ball lost in the darkness, Ten-Yard and LaVerne watching and waiting. *Bang!* The ball hits the sign. The lights go out.

There.

That was what the curious, untamed kid from Tipperary Hill could do. That was the potential inside him.

His entry into the shadow world of bootlegging, of course, seemed almost preordained. If he couldn't harness his recklessness—if the Braves or the Yankees or John McGraw couldn't see what he could do—there was a place where it would be a definite asset. The alcohol distribution business was made for someone like LaVerne Moore.

The specifics of his involvement were never laid out, but there was little doubt that he was a player in the illegal game being played along the Great Lakes and St. Lawrence River. He always had money, always dressed well, always drove a good-looking car. He never had a meaningful, honest job that anyone ever saw, nothing more than his baseball career or stints as a caddie at area country clubs. His friends, many of them, were people exactly like him. He ran with the runners, the young men of upstate New York who sided with the sinners against an unpopular law.

The glamour of the job was as attractive as the money. In later years, he would mention the name of Al Capone in his few recollections of his bootlegging time. Capone, the Purple Gang, all of the underworld characters from the front page were as magical as characters from the sports page. The bush-league rumrunners were touched by the notoriety of the big-timers the same way the bush-league ballplayers were touched by the fame of Babe Ruth. The foot soldiers shared the glamour of the generals.

LaVerne's one arrest during this time is the one official peek at his role in the operations. He was picked up in 1927 for posing as a police officer. He had presented himself as a policeman to a grocery store owner who sold alcohol. His message was that the owner could stay out of trouble, remain in business, if certain payments were made every month. If the payments weren't made, the owner would go to jail. The business would be closed.

The owner reported the offer to the real police, who waited for LaVerne and arrested him. The charge was extortion.

Nothing serious happened—LaVerne pleaded guilty to a reduced charge, a misdemeanor, paid a fine—but the implications were obvious. He worked as muscle in the liquor business. He worked as protection. An integral part of any smuggling operation was silence from everyone involved, and silence sometimes had to be enforced. LaVerne, with his size and almost unnatural strength, was a perfect choice as an enforcer.

There was speculation that he did other things—he certainly had the driving skills and the bravado to hurtle down the back roads himself, car filled with contraband, roadblocks to be avoided—but those stories were told in private. Friends didn't tell them the way they told the golf stories, the driving stories, the wacky stories. Families never mentioned them in front of their children.

LaVerne Moore was in the game. Enough said. He was part of it.

When the robbery in Jay occurred, it seemed like a logical final step. Once a man crossed the line of illegality, he was doomed to be pulled in deeper and deeper. Wasn't that what happened here? This was a moral tale.

The details had been known in Syracuse for seven years; the men with masks, the revolvers, the members of the Hana family bound and tied and left on the floor, the grandfather beaten and left by the river, the crash of the first bandit car, the death of the bandit in the passenger seat, the apprehension of the two other bandits, the disappearance of LaVerne. He and the robbery had been the subjects of conversations for seven years.

There was little doubt about his guilt when people talked. Why else would he have fled? The other three men named in the robbery—William Carleton, Roger Norton, and the late John Sherry—were his friends. The plan for the whole operation sounded like something out of a dime novel, concocted by Jesse James or another shady character, elaborate and daring, very much like something that LaVerne would do. Elaborate and daring were parts of his daily thinking. He had simply thought too much here.

Foolish.

No, there was no surprise when LaVerne was arrested in far-away California. There was no surprise that he had done all the things he had done in Hollywood, that he had become the golfer he had become, that Oliver Hardy and Bing and everyone else had fallen for his charm. There was no surprise at anything LaVerne Moore did.

He was different.

CHAPTER FIVE

COAST TO COAST

July—August 1937

The Hollywood community moved into action. Friends of John Montague's on the West Coast sensed an injustice here. How could he be prosecuted for a seven-year-old robbery that netted only $750? He was only a kid when that happened. He was a man now, his character well formed. He was polite, solvent; able to reach the 18th at Pebble Beach in two. His past—I mean, he didn't kill anyone—didn't matter.

"We're all back of him 100 per cent," Bing Crosby said at the DelMar Turf Club. "Naturally, we want to know what is back of the whole case, but for the time being you can say that Monty is entitled to the benefit of the doubt. He is a grand fellow, always a gentleman, a great guy on the golf links and the type of chap you just naturally enjoy being with. If, as said, his trouble is the result of some prank or mistake when he was a kid I think he's entitled to some consideration."

"He is one of the finest fellows that ever lived," Oliver Hardy said. "What more can I say?"

The approach that Hollywood had toward scandal was simple: throw money at the problem. If that didn't work, throw more money until it went away. Everything from traffic accidents to murder to awkward situations involving sexual ambiguities was handled that way. Crosby and Hardy and other Lakeside friends went for their wallets and brought in the best help for Montague they could find. They hired fifty-year-old Jerry Giesler to be his lawyer.

Known as "the man who handles the film capital's troubles from peccadillo to perjury," "the magnificent mouthpiece," and "the man who beats the rap," Giesler was the premier defense attorney in Hollywood. Not as flamboyant as his mentor, Earl Rogers, the first famous Hollywood lawyer, who blustered and swooned and always found the purloined letters in a case at the last dramatic moment, he was just as effective and had become just as famous.

In 1933, writer Erle Stanley Gardner had introduced a character based on Rogers to popular fiction. The character, Perry Mason, described himself in *The Case of the Velvet Claws*, the first book of an ongoing series, as "a specialist in getting people out of trouble. They come to me and I get them out." This was also a fine description of Giesler.

He had helped old Alexander Pantages, the famous theater owner, through two trials to an acquittal on rape charges filed by a seventeen-year-old showgirl. He had saved both Otto Schnauber, known as "the Little Fellow in the Attic," and his paramour Walburga Oesterrich from the gas chamber. (Otto lived secretly in her attic for almost twenty years, came downstairs during the day for romance while her husband, Fred, was at work. They were accused of killing Fred.) He had also saved former welterweight boxing champion Kid McCoy from a first-degree murder conviction, the charge reduced to manslaughter. The jury deliberated for ninety-nine hours before delivering the verdict.

In Giesler's most recent celebrated case, he had defended movie executive Busby Berkeley after Berkeley had plowed his car into two other cars late at night on Highway 101 between Santa Monica and Malibu Beach. Three people died in the crash, Berkeley's acknowledged fault. He admitted he was returning home from a Hollywood party, but said he was not drunk. The prosecution claimed otherwise.

After two hung juries, Giesler pulled out an acquittal from a third with an argument that a blown-out tire, not Mr. Berkeley's debatable state of sobriety, was at fault. The lawyer used an elaborate scale model to show the twisting roads Berkeley had navigated before the crash happened. Giesler's point was that Berkeley couldn't have been impaired because if he were, he surely would have crashed much earlier in the complicated drive. The tire must have blown out.

The first thing Giesler did with Montague was to tell him to shut up. That first quote—"I made a mistake when I was just a kid back East and I've been trying to make good since then. I was going to go back and straighten the whole thing out"—was never to be repeated. The second thing Giesler did was to try to make sure that Montague never would go back east and that the mistake would never be straightened out.

The lawyer's plan was to fight extradition to New York. The order for extradition had to be signed by Governor Frank Merriam, and Giesler mounted an all-out appeal to Merriam to simply allow Montague to remain in California. Merriam, a Republican, was always sympathetic toward the movie industry, a group that had aided him greatly in the bitter election campaign against Upton Sinclair. He would seem to be sympathetic here.

Before the formal extradition hearing was held at the governor's office on July 26, 1937, Giesler wanted Merriam to be bombarded with pleas topped by famous letterheads, signed by famous names, requesting that Montague be allowed to stay in California. The bombarding began. The Lafayette Escadrille, the Luftwaffe, or Eddie Rickenbacker himself couldn't have done a better job.

Merriam's office received sixty-six letters on Montague's behalf, so many letters that the governor publicly requested that no more people write. Bing Crosby, Spencer Tracy, Humphrey Bogart, Frank Craven, Oliver Hardy, Johnny Weissmuller, and Howard Hawks were among the contributors. Guy Kibbee's letter was typical of the pleas. After stating that Montague had been a visitor in his home, liked and appreciated by the entire Kibbee family, always a gentleman, he wrote: "If my good friend, John Montague, went astray as a mere youth, it is my opinion he has done everything in his power during the time I have known him to arise above the occasion and has convinced me he has done a great deal to live down the little incident which happened to him in the East as a boy."

Giesler's argument was the same argument used by Kibbee and all of the Hollywood friends of Montague's: the pile of Cal-

ifornia good deeds, obviously witnessed by a number of prominent, respected people, trumped any one alleged misdeed in the
long ago on the other side of the country. Montague had already become a valued member of a famous community. Rehabilitation was not necessary in this case because it had already
occurred. Merriam could simply allow a good man to stay where
he was.

The governor announced he had taken the matter under
advisement. He scheduled a hearing for June 26, 1937. Montague, per orders, dropped out of sight. There were no more
press conferences, no more interviews.

"He is playing no golf these days," Giesler said about his
client. "There is no change in our plans. Montague will fight any
attempt to extradite him to New York."

The only request the lawyer and client granted was from a
newspaper photographer, who asked Montague to re-create the
bat-shovel-rake sequence for a string of pictures. This was publicity that had no pesky questions attached.

The photographer, alas, showed up at Lakeside with equipment that was all wrong. The bat was not a fungo bat, but a regular bat, far heavier. The shovel had a long handle. The rake was
not a traditional garden rake but one of those fan-style bamboo
rakes. Montague grumped at the discrepancies, but went out to
the 3rd hole with the photographer anyway.

He swung the bat...and the ball went straight down the
fairway, maybe 280 yards. The photographer picked up the ball
and placed it in a trap next to the green for the next shot. Montague took a mighty swoosh with the awkward shovel...and the
ball landed on the green, four feet from the pin. The photographer moved the ball back to twenty feet, maybe thirty, to give his

shot of the putt some drama. Montague went to his hands and knees, used the awkward rake as a pool cue...and, yes, that's right, the ball went into the hole. He was ecstatic.

"That was the thrill of my life," he said in the Lakeside shower room. "I thought I could do those shots, but not as well as I did."

———

Demand for this newest celebrity was great, even if his availability was somewhere between limited and nonexistent. Estimates were made about how much money he could earn if he could escape a jail sentence and then stage exhibitions, compete on the pro tour, sign a lucrative movie deal playing strongman characters like Paul Bunyan. The figure of $1 million in a year, a phenomenal amount, was mentioned more than once. Top professionals speculated on what he would do against actual competition on the Tour. Pundits wondered if he was mostly a con man, more than an alleged bandit in hiding.

Small sparks seemed to fly off his name every time it was mentioned. His name—both names, actually—was mentioned often.

Time magazine jumped immediately onto the news it had helped create. The headline this time was "Mysterious Montague (Concl.)," with four times as many words in this story as in the last one, and a head shot of a smiling and dapper LaVerne ("Bull") Moore, smiling this time from page 39 of the July 19, 1937, issue.

"Surest way to attract attention anywhere is to appear to shun it," *Time* philosophized. "In Hollywood, where attention is

the population's bread & butter, this technique is doubly infal-
lible. And what Montague did on a golf course would have
brought him notoriety anywhere, whether he shunned it or not."

Newsweek, Time's plucky competitor, which had started in
1933, came late to the game. It said, "John Montague played
golf too well for his own good," under the July 17 headline,
"Mysterious Montague Caught in Bunker of the Law."

Grantland Rice was mum for the moment, but Westbrook
Pegler couldn't resist. "It would be unwise to speculate on the
mighty Montague's fate at the hands of the court," he wrote,
"but now that the wraps are off the man it is worth hoping that
he will be allowed to enter the tournaments and the ring to
demonstrate whether he's all that legend said of him. That
would almost be called the public's due."

There was little doubt that Montague would make some fast
money if his court problems disappeared. Three different studios had already mentioned the possibility of making movies
about his double life. (Hollywood worked fast. Two movies had
already been proposed for a life of Amelia Earhart, one with
Katharine Hepburn starring as the missing aviatrix.) Darryl
Zanuck said his studio was preparing a story about an athlete
whose amazing feats of strength make him famous, even though
he refuses to be photographed because he fears a past, minor
misdeed will be exposed. Eventually his true identity is discovered and he is tried, found guilty, and sent to jail. In jail he falls
in with a bad element and becomes a hardened criminal.

One report suggested that Bing Crosby was ready to sign his
friend to a million-dollar contract to play golf and star in
movies. Crosby quickly denied it, but said, "I'm sure Monty will

have many opportunities." Endorsements certainly were a possibility if he was found innocent. Sporting goods companies already were in contact. Telegrams were arriving with all kinds of propositions. Exhibitions were probably his fastest way to make a buck. Promoters wanted him. He might revive the exhibition business.

Except, of course, he would have to prove his credibility.

"Montague, alone, might bring back the big dough to golf exhibitions, for he has become a legend, and a lot of people would pay to see if he were true," columnist Bob Considine wrote in the *New York Daily Mirror* about the possible bonanza available if the legend were acquitted. "But there are a couple of little obstacles yet to be cleared. For one thing, he would need a year of steady golf to get himself in physical shape and bring back that deft touch that made him a 65 shooter. And then there's that minor matter of proving that his seemly life in God-fearing Hollywood has cleansed his being of the clouds of a misspent youth."

The quickest way to prove that he was for real, of course, would be to play in some tournaments, play a stretch on the pro Tour. The money wasn't wonderful, but if he won a few titles, the other money would flow even faster. A U.S. Open championship, a British Open championship, would cement all opportunities, be a great exclamation point to his strange story.

Question: Could he do well on the pro Tour?

"That John Montague, that fellow from Hollywood, is all that they say he is," Ralph Guldahl, newly crowned U.S. Open champion of 1937, said in the affirmative. "I don't think he'll knock birds off wires—although I don't doubt that he did once—but he sure does knock those birds off the greens and fairways. He has a marvelous short game and is good coming out of traps. He's really a good golfer."

Guldahl was in the minority. Most of the players on the Tour were skeptical about Montague's chances. They wanted him on the circuit, bringing along that rush of newly intrigued paying customers, but they downplayed his showbiz tricks and his reported low scores and course records. Golf is different when it's played inside a tournament structure, everyone hungry, after the same prize, the results in the newspaper and a gallery keeping count of the strokes. Make a putt in the sunshine with a couple of actors and a sportswriter in your foursome, okay, good for you. Make a putt in a money tournament against great competition, then you're doing something. The pros couldn't understand the big fuss.

"Wasn't it rather ridiculous, this Paul Bunyan business some of the reporters fell for, head over heels?" Horton Smith, winner of the Masters in both 1934 and 1936, asked. "Has Montague proved his ability as a golfer? Not by my idea of a test. Has he beaten the top-notch pros? I've seen Montague play and I've seen better. . . .

"It wasn't those rave reviews of his trick shots—it was those of his golf game that got me. It's one thing to shoot hot rounds when they mean nothing. It's another when you're under pressure. Wait until you see what Montague can do when the chips are down before you go ga-ga over him. Montague, in my opinion, is not the super golfer."

The pros said that as far back as the winter Tour of 1934–35 they had been trying to get a crack at Montague. As word of this fabulous golfer at Lakeside moved through locker rooms that winter, word of a betting proposition moved with it. Babe Hardy and some backers were willing to bet three thousand dollars on Montague against any pro on the Tour. The pros checked out the deal and liked it.

"This pro golf is a hard business and no guy who isn't known can break in on a gang like ours over night and beat a good pro golfer," Tour veteran Wiffy Cox told Shirley Povich of the *Washington Post*. "We saw him play. To us he looked like just another fair country club golfer. He wasn't any pro and we figured he would be a cinch for the guy we selected to play him."

Cox said the pros ran for their wallets. He was one of the runners.

"I put up 500 bucks of the bet myself," he said. "Horton Smith put up $500 and inside of half an hour we pros had that $3,000 covered. We'd pick the man to play Montague and glad to do it.

"And then he started crawling. Said he ought to have a three-stroke handicap. That was all right with us and we said we'd give it to him. Then he pulled out of it altogether. Said he didn't like all of the publicity. It's easy now to see why. With that stick-up job in New York hanging over his head, he didn't want any pictures in the paper. So we had to call the whole thing off."

Money seemed to be involved in all conversations about Montague as his story unfolded. "Where'd he get his money in the first place?" was even more interesting than "How much is he going to make off all of this?" People who had known him at Lakeside, people who had seen him in action were stunned at the report that he had only forty-three dollars in his pocket when he was arrested. He was known for always carrying a wad of hundred-dollar bills. He also carried traveler's checks totaling at least one thousand dollars. He was ready for any kind of proposition.

At the Crosby golf tournament, when he spent time with bridge champion P. Hal Sims at Rancho Santa Fe, there had been a proposition about a combined bridge and golf bet for five hundred dollars. Sims was ready to go for it. Montague peeled off five hundred-dollar bills, tapped his pocket, and said, "And there's more right here if any of you fellows want any of it." Somehow, as often happens with propositions, the match never took place, but there was no doubt that he was ready. Sims did come away with a memory.

"I saw Monty have breakfast," the bridge champion said. "It was a bottle of scotch and eight gin fizzes. Didn't bother him at all."

The memory of that always ready cash, always a mystery, still a mystery, had assorted anonymous Lakeside members now adding up numbers that showed John Montague made a lot of money from golf. Made a lot of money from them. No one ever saw him work, but a lot of people saw him make money at golf.

"I know he made a lot of money from bets," one anonymous member said. "You wouldn't exactly call it gambling because he never seemed to lose. You know that George Von Elm and Grantland Rice called him the greatest golfer in the world. Well, I can name a hundred mediocre golfers in Hollywood who believe he's just a trick-shot artist and not a consistent player.

"The reason for this is that Monty measured his man. When an expert turned in a 73, Monty would finish in 72. But an amateur, playing for $100 a hole and making the course in 93, would only lose four or five holes to Monty, who'd manage an 87. Now $400 for an afternoon's work isn't bad wages."

"A funny thing about Hollywood is that everybody knew Montague was playing 'em for suckers, but they loved it," another anonymous member said. "What's a couple of hundred bucks, or even five hundred, to a guy who's making a lot of dough and who can play with the greatest golfer in the world and talk about it for months afterward? That's how some of the fantastic stories about Montague were born—his victims made 'em up."

The "mining interests" in Nevada or Arizona—the locations changed depending on who was speaking—now were believed to be fictitious. They were mentioned in all of the stories about Montague, but were accompanied by some kind of typographical wink, as if they didn't exist. Montague did nothing to prove their existence, like mention one place or name for a mine, but he also did nothing to stop the references to them.

"I'm sure Monty made his living from golf," one of the anonymous members said. "We've all heard talk and hints about some gold mine somewhere, like the one Death Valley Scotty is supposed to have. But that's a lot of bunk and we knew it."

Death Valley Scotty was a well-known character who had appeared in Hollywood in 1929 and was quickly called "America's Number One Mystery Man" when he unrolled plans to set a world air-speed record, break the bank at Monte Carlo, and buy a string of polo ponies to raise on his ranch in Death Valley. He roared around town in a fast car, red necktie flying in the breeze as he scattered promises and talk about his millions, maybe billions, in mining interests in the desert. Cases were still in the courts as investors sued, trying to recoup losses on those Death Valley mines that didn't exist, none of them.

"I'm no Death Valley Scotty," John Montague proclaimed in one of few definitive answers on the courthouse steps after his arraignment.

The other character from the twenties mentioned often was Alvin Clarence Thomas, better known as Titanic Thompson, once front and center as the country's foremost golf hustler, cardsharp, and heavy bettor on anything, anywhere, at any time. He became a public figure when he was part of a three-day card game from September 8 to 10, 1928, at the Park Central Hotel in Manhattan that included noted gambler Arnold Rothstein, architect of the 1919 World Series fix involving the Chicago White Sox. When Rothstein was murdered three weeks after the card game, presumably for unpaid debts from that night, everyone at the table became famous.

Thompson hated the notoriety. He was a crack shot, an expert at any game of cards, a top-notch pool player, a patient craftsman of the hustle. One of his standard tricks was to eat from a bag of peanuts while he discussed life and times with a freshly minted sucker. On what seemed to be a whim, he would wonder if he could throw one of the peanuts from his bag over a nearby building. The sucker would say that that was impossible. Thompson would propose a bet, reach into the bag, find the lead-filled peanut he had inserted for just this purpose, and throw it over the building. Worked every time.

Thompson's golf career had wandered through several states, but flourished in Los Angeles in the mid-twenties. He didn't play at Lakeside Golf Club, but there was a connection through Howard Hughes and George Von Elm. Able to play left- or right-handed, willing to play badly for days and weeks simply to set up a big-money match, Thompson stalked Hughes, trying to get a piece of the rich young man's money. The rich young man, though, played all the time with Von Elm. They played those days mostly at Rancho Golf Club. Unable to reach Hughes, Thompson settled for Von Elm. He agitated the former U.S. Amateur champion, the "businessman golfer," to such a point that Von Elm made a crazy bet.

"I'm one of the best golfers in the country," Von Elm said. "I keep hearing you're pretty good, but I don't see you entering no tournaments. Hell, yes, I want to play. We'll play eighteen holes and I'll spot you nine. Hundred dollars a hole."

Oh, my. On the 9th hole at Rancho, Thompson had a three-foot putt to virtually close out the match. He had won the first eight holes, now would win the 9th. Von Elm, thirty feet from the pin, picked up his ball and stalked off the course. He paid the nine hundred dollars.

"Montague batted in the same golf league with Titanic Thompson, the Western plunger who played in Arnold Rothstein's ill-fated poker game at the Park Central," Jack Miley wrote in the *New York Daily News*. "Titanic was a trick bettor, too. He used to carry an Ozark hillbilly pro around with him and what they did to those oil millionaires around Tulsa and Oklahoma City was nobody's business.... He and Montague, who played with spades, rakes, and pool cues, would have made a helluva two-ball team."

The comparison didn't really hold up—none of the losers in Thompson's schemes would have talked to him, much less put up bail for him—but that didn't matter. One golf bettor seemed to look like another. Stories of nonexistent gold mines, thousand-dollar Nassaus, and strange propositions all sort of melded together.

One newspaper reported that John Montague had thrown a lead-filled peanut over a building to collect a bet.

Essex County sheriff Percy Egglefield and state troopers Paul McGinnis and Harry Durand arrived from New York in time for the July 26 extradition hearing. They were ready for the appeal to be denied, to take Montague back across the country for justice. Merriam postponed the hearing. The three visitors had to wait some more.

"I am giving consideration to the many communications from Mr. Montague's friends in and near Los Angeles," Merriam announced, but added a warning to the letter writers. "This is a semi-judicial proceeding at least and no question of sentiment is involved."

The case had taken on the definite look of Hollywood over-statement. Cannons had replaced BB guns in a hunt for a squirrel. Montague was like a Hollywood star stopped for speeding or caught slipping a necktie into his pocket in a men's store without paying. Small time was big time simply because of the person involved.

Three law officers coming from the other side of the country to bring back a suspect in a seven-year-old, $750 robbery? Alvin Karpis wouldn't have received that treatment. The famous lawyer, Giesler, to present the defense? Usually a body and blood were involved in the work he did. The governor? Paying attention to all of this? He had hard decisions about labor strikes and unemployment on his desk at the same time.

The cartoon qualities were obvious. The *Des Moines Tribune,* all the way in Iowa, could chuckle in an editorial:

> We notice that LaVerne Moore (John Montague to us) has hired an expert on extradition law to help keep him out of the tolls of New York law for allegedly participating in a robbery 6 or 7 years ago.
>
> This inspires two observations: (1.) that someone with fewer influential friends than Montague, or Moore, would have been extradited to New York with far greater dispatch than is now being shown, but (2.) that if the man were virtually an unknown, the State of New York wouldn't have three men in California to extradite someone they suspected of being involved in a $750 robbery 7 years ago.
>
> We aren't exactly certain of what that proves.

The extradition hearing was finally held on August 2, 1937, in Los Angeles. Governor Merriam, in town for two weeks, presided in his chambers at the state building. Montague, Giesler, and a second attorney, Gregson Bautzer, representing Montague's Hollywood friends, sat at a long table to present his case. Six character witnesses, headed by Guy Kibbee, also sat in the room.

"LaVerne Moore can be considered dead after seven years and a new man with a new soul born in his place," Giesler argued in front of Merriam. "It was exactly seven years ago that this robbery occurred and since that time records will show that this man has led an exemplary life."

Deputy Attorney General James Howie presented the opposing viewpoint. He said the papers from New York were sufficient and should be signed. He added that any evidence of Montague's rehabilitation should be presented to New York governor Herman Lehman, not here.

No witnesses were called. Montague's lawyers presented affidavits from his supporters for Merriam to study. Affidavits also were received from Percy Egglefield and the two New York state troopers. One of the prosecution affidavits, the testimony of Roger Norton, one of the bandits in Jay, New York, was leaked later to the press. Norton accused Montague of being the ringleader, not just part of the robbery gang.

"We originally started out to hijack some liquor," confessed-robber Roger Norton said, "but LaVerne said, 'To hell with the liquor, let's get the money.' "

Another affidavit was from Matt Cobb, the grandfather who was beaten during the robbery. He thought he could recognize his assailant.

"I have seen photographs of this Montague," Cobb said. "I think he is the man."

Merriam closed the proceedings by saying he would take all of this material under advisement and make a decision in the future. This was not a good sign for Giesler and Montague. The words of Assistant Attorney General Howie were ominous. If the attorney general's office ruled that Merriam had to sign the order by law, the governor would have no choice in the matter.

Giesler quickly forwarded copies of the letter and the appeal to New York governor Lehman. This was another long shot. There was little chance Lehman would rule against his own state police.

A week went past with no announcements anywhere....

Ten days...

Eleven...

Twelve...

The fight against extradition was quietly dead. Merriam obviously wanted the matter to disappear. He'd received other messages, too, besides the letters from his Hollywood constituents. The other letters, not from movie stars and hit parade singers, said that the famous should have no more consideration in these matters than ordinary workingmen had. There was little political gain for the governor from going against his own attorney general and rescuing this celebrated golfer. Better to do nothing.

Giesler and Montague went to Plan B, the only plan still available. Giesler made calls, arrangements. Montague started packing. He would go back. He would take his chances.

Simple as that.

On the morning of August 21, 1937, a Saturday, Montague and Giesler walked into Municipal Judge Leroy Dawson's court and dropped all appeals. Everything would now happen in a hurry. He would not only go back to face the charges, he was leaving straight from the courthouse. Percy Egglefield and the two troopers were present, ready to accompany him.

"In the interests of justice, Mr. Montague wishes to return to New York, face trial and be exonerated of the charges," Giesler announced. "He feels the New York courts will afford him justice and he will be exonerated for all time."

The only dispute about anything arose when Montague signed his name to the waiver of extradition. He wrote, "John Montague." The New York representatives wanted him to sign

"LaVerne Moore." Montague refused. Finally, lawyer Giesler took the paper, signing it as "LaVerne Moore, known as John Montague."

Now a prisoner, the Sphinx of the Links, the Phantom of the Fairways, the Garbo of Golf, traveled with Egglefield and the troopers to Union Station. His departure was a picture. Trailed by porters carrying his Hollywood-style wardrobe contained in twenty trunks and bags, he was cheered by more than a hundred bystanders as he walked to board the Union Pacific. He stopped, waved, swung an imaginary golf club, and was off to discover his fate. He was allowed to travel without handcuffs.

The trip took three days. Montague traveled in his own drawing room. The ultimate destination was Elizabethtown, New York, location of the Essex County courthouse, no more than twenty miles of winding roads from the location of the robbery in Jay. Egglefield later said his prisoner was affable and entertaining. They stopped on Monday morning in Chicago, where Montague refused to answer any questions—notably, "Why'd you drop your fight against extradition?"—signed an autograph for a porter, and went into the city with his guards for breakfast. Reporters trailed.

"Do you think you can beat the rap?" one reporter asked at the door to the restaurant.

"Nice breakfast they're having in there," Montague said. End of interview.

The overnight New York Central from Chicago took him to Albany, where he switched to a Delaware and Hudson train headed north. This stopped on Tuesday morning at Saratoga Springs, where a prominent friend was waiting. Bing Crosby, some of his horses running at Saratoga, was standing on the station platform, talking with columnist Damon Runyon of the *New York Daily Mirror.*

"Thanks for coming down, Bing," Montague said, shaking his benefactor's hand.

"Not at all," Crosby replied. "I'm awfully glad to see you again."

They talked on the siding for ten minutes. Crosby wished him well. Montague hopped on the train for the final leg of the trip. Damon Runyon got on with him. Crosby went back to the racetrack.

Shortly before noon the train finally stopped at Port Henry, New York, on the banks of Lake Champlain. John Montague and his three guards jumped into a car and headed for his afternoon court appearance in Elizabethtown, a distance of nineteen miles. His twenty trunks and bags followed in a second car.

If nothing else, he'd come home with more than he took with him when he left.

LaVerne and Harold Moore. Maybe two years after LaVerne's birth on August 25, 1903.

LaVerne and Harold, older. LaVerne was the rascal. Harold was the solid citizen.

The house at 303 Avery Avenue in Syracuse. The family poses on the front porch, LaVerne again next to Harold.

The golf career has begun. The family laundry is a first gallery.

LaVerne circa 1930. His life changed and his name changed when he reached Hollywood.

The garden shovel became a part of Montague's arsenal after his bet with Bing Crosby. The bet became a basic part of his story.

Afraid to be photographed before his arrest, he was not shy later. Here he is posed and ready to attack a small white ball in various and diverse ways.

The Montague smile promised weird propositions. Money usually was involved in those propositions.

Montague and Oliver (Babe) Hardy. The golfer lived in the famous comedian's house for a while.

Montague and Jerry Geisler, attorney to the stars. In this case, the stars hired the attorney for their friend.

The Hana Restaurant. The scene of the crime.

Reunited. Montague returns to Syracuse to see his mother and father before his trial. Mary Moore would take the witness stand. Matthew Moore would not.

Centerfielder Joe DiMaggio, actor George Raft, and Montague share the spotlight at the party celebrating the New York Yankees' 1937 World Series win. Montague is out on bail. Actor William Frawley is in the background.

When his train stops at Saratoga on the way to Elizabethtown, New York, Montague is met by Bing Crosby, Damon Runyon, and attorney James M. Noonan. Runyon and Noonan accompany him the rest of the way. Bing stays in Saratoga to watch his horses run.

Fan mail arrives from everywhere during the trial. The case makes headlines across the country.

Montague takes the stand in his own defense—a surprise. Attorney Noonan lobs soft questions at him.

The jury of farmers and local workingmen will determine Montague's fate. None of them has ever played golf.

The courtroom in Elizabethtown is packed for all proceedings. Women make up a large part of the crowd.

Acquittal. Montague is carried from the court-room by his supporters. Judge Harry E. Owen is not happy about the verdict or the celebration.

Babe Ruth and Montague play a practice round in preparation for their big match at Fresh Meadows Country Club in Flushing, Long Island. The match is Montague's public debut.

Is John Montague the greatest golfer in the world? All eyes—including the Babe's—want to see.

The gallery for the Ruth-Montague match turns fairways into tight and dangerous alleys. The match is stopped after nine holes.

Always the baseball bat, the shovel . . . and the rake. Montague worked the story until the end.

Late in life. He died on May 25, 1972. He was sixty-eight years old.

CHAPTER SIX

ELIZABETHTOWN, NEW YORK

August 24–26, 1937

The arrival of such a celebrated defendant was an occasion in Elizabethtown, a definite summer highlight. With his brown pepper-and-salt sport coat, his gray slacks, green shirt, green tie, and two-tone shoes, John Montague was like a captured exotic bird brought back to be displayed to the townsfolk when he walked without handcuffs down Court Street between his two guards. He could have stepped off a spaceship, he was so different from his surroundings.

Elizabethtown was one of the smaller tourist hamlets in the Adirondacks, full-time population no more than one thousand, summer population double or triple that, depending on the economy. Two rambling Victorian hotels, the Windsor and the Deer's Head Inn, both with more than a hundred rooms, plus assorted smaller bed-and-breakfast operations in the town catered to visitors who came from New York and Boston and Philadelphia to hike the local trails, fish the local streams, breathe the clean local air.

Normal entertainment in Elizabethtown might be a piano player in one of the lounges, a band concert in the center of town, a traveling minstrel show, or a carnival every now and then. Elizabethtown was in a valley. The surrounding mountains, the woods, the daytime vistas were the attraction. A good book or two was essential to an Adirondacks vacation.

This Montague business was as exciting as anything that had happened in a long time. Not only was he from *Hollywood*, rumors were circulated everywhere that his Hollywood friends might appear for his bail hearing. A noontime crowd had gathered near the courthouse, everyone looking to see somebody famous. The crowd was heavily female, wives and daughters of the hunters and fishermen, husbands and fathers who had tramped off to the woods for another day. There was finally an intriguing alternative in Elizabethtown for the women to pursue.

"Is it true that Clark Gable is going to be here?" one woman asked Damon Runyon.

Runyon didn't answer, but scribbled her question in his notebook.

Montague ate lunch with Sheriff Percy Egglefield, then walked with him to the old Essex County courthouse. Built in 1823, the courthouse was set far back from the road, so Montague crossed a large, tree-shaded lawn. This was where the women smiled and he smiled back and every now and then someone shouted his name. He moved like a political candidate whose election was already assured.

Waiting for him was his new attorney, James M. Noonan. Jerry Giesler was not a member of the New York Bar, so Noonan took his place. A forty-five-year-old criminal defense lawyer with offices both in Albany and New York City, Noonan was a large man, taller than Montague, and heavyset. He had already gained some fame for his defense of Arthur Simon Flegenheimer, better known as gangster Dutch Schultz. Twice, the government had taken Schultz to court on income tax charges in similar small Adirondacks towns. Twice, Noonan had brought home Not Guilty verdicts.

"Bing Crosby just called me up," Noonan told his family when he was retained to defend Montague. "He wants me to defend this guy."

"I can assure you that I have not discussed the case with Crosby," the lawyer told reporters. "I have not had time to thoroughly look into the case. I am not prepared at this time to say just what my plans are at this point."

Noonan had met Montague in Albany, ridden with him on the train. All the lawyer knew about the case was what he had been told by Giesler, but that was more than enough for now. He had more than a month, maybe two, before any trial would begin. This bail hearing was simply to determine whether he would be meeting with his client in his office or here in a jail cell.

Montague stopped in an anteroom at the courthouse and talked with an old acquaintance, a Catholic priest, the Reverend Edward McCarthy, for ten minutes. McCarthy came from the meeting and said he vouched for the defendant, liked him very much.

The crowd filed into the courtroom as if it were going to see a prizefight or a Hollywood show. Sprinkled among the summer people were locals, also attracted to the bright lights. More than one report said "the entire town" had shown up. This was an overstatement perhaps, but true in spirit. This was a carnival, a grand legal circus. Anyone who could be here was here.

There was nothing like seeing some dirty laundry flap in the clean, vacation air.

A large painting by artist David Lithgow, six feet by nine feet, dominated the courtroom. The self-explanatory title was *John Brown's Trial at Charlestown, Va.* On December 6, 1859, the Essex County courthouse was a stop for the funeral cortege carrying the body of the famous abolitionist on its way home to the Adirondack town of North Elba, New York, for burial after he had been hanged in Charlestown for his participation in the raid on the federal armory at Harpers Ferry, Virginia (West Virginia did not become a state until 1863), that left seven men dead, ten wounded. Brown's body lay in state in the courtroom that night as neighbors and friends and the curious from the surrounding area paid their final respects.

Though additions had been made to the building since that time, the courtroom itself, cramped and tiny and solemn as a small Methodist church on a Sunday morn, had changed little. The crowd was what gave it life, packed to see the proceedings, color and bustle, excitement, again more women than men, everyone craning for looks at a certified star, at anyone famous.

No Gable, no Bing Crosby had arrived, but Otto Kruger, a respected actor on both Broadway and in Hollywood, a member of the Lakeside Golf Club, a friend who had played golf with Montague and owned a summer home in the Adirondacks, was in attendance. Actress Pauline Lord, also from Broadway, also a summer resident, and magician Nate Leipzig were spotted. And, of course, the defendant was famous. He was a beacon of affability as he smiled and talked with Noonan while they awaited the start of the proceedings.

"Everybody liked John Montague's appearance and sympathized with him, without knowing just why," wrote Damon Runyon for the *New York Daily Mirror.* "He is a short, block-built fellow, weighing 220 pounds, but he does not look that heavy. He has a round, pleasant, moon face, and a nice smile."

The smile was still in place as Supreme Court Justice O. Byron Brewster gaveled the proceedings to order. The rumor was that this hearing was a formality; that Montague was assured of being released on bail. A bondsman from the National Surety Company was in attendance, supposedly with instructions from Crosby, Hardy et al. that virtually any amount would be covered.

Noonan opened with a plea for a reduced bail, pointing out that his client had dropped extradition proceedings and arrived by his own free will to face whatever verdict the court might render. The lawyer said his own idea of bail was that it should in no way be determined as a punishment, that the only purpose of bail was to ensure that the defendant appear at the trial. He said there was no worry here about whether or not the defendant would appear at the trial.

"Am I to understand that Mr. LaVerne Moore is here in person?" Judge Brewster asked.

Montague stood and bowed. He formally recognized his previous name.

"I am, Your Honor," he said.

Essex County district attorney Thomas W. McDonald followed Noonan in front of the bench. Another large and vigorous man, bald, wearing glasses, McDonald was confident about his case. He had already earned convictions on Carleton and Norton with much of the same evidence he had here. After a decade as DA, prosecuting the backwoods domestic-abuse cases, the common thefts, and the occasional Saturday night homicide in the region, this was his chance to work for once in front of a national audience. He was prepared.

A hard line was established at the beginning. He wanted no bail for LaVerne Moore, aka John Montague. McDonald said the crime being considered was "the most vicious I have had to do with in the ten years I have been the district attorney." Any one of four criteria could be used to determine if a charge should be first-degree robbery, and McDonald said this case met all four. He said Moore was armed, masked, that he bound and gagged his victims, and engaged in violence.

The district attorney offered a sample of that violence. He re-created the scene outside Hana's restaurant.

"An old man, then sixty-seven, offered some resistance, and the defendant beat him over the head and face with a pistol," McDonald said. "After throwing the old man to the ground, he called for a blackjack and again beat him on the head and face, left him on the bank of the Au Sable River in a dazed and semi-conscious condition."

McDonald said Moore had escaped and changed his name once. What were the chances he would escape and change his name again? There were none if he were not released on bail.

"Mr. Noonan says his client wants to face the charge," the

district attorney said. "But it has taken him seven years to make up his mind to do it; and then only after this defendant had opposed extradition for months. Then, finally and suddenly, he decides to waive extradition."

The smile had disappeared from John Montague's face.

Every reporter in the courtroom noted that the defendant seemed shocked, stunned by McDonald's presentation. The seriousness of the situation arrived in dispiriting detail. That night at Hana's, seven years ago, dark and sinister and chaotic, was alive again and on full display in the courtroom. McDonald, with his graphic description of the crime, left no doubt about how important he thought the punishment should be for that crime.

The carnival show had stopped, dead still at this point.

Judge Brewster, fifty years old, was more than able to evaluate McDonald's words. He knew his local crime history. A descendant of some of the first Adirondacks settlers, a full-bred Yankee with roots back to the *Mayflower,* he had preceded McDonald as Essex County DA for eleven years before being named to the bench. He lived in Elizabethtown on a thirty-acre estate and had been mentioned prominently as a possible Republican candidate for governor in 1936 before withdrawing his name.

He listened to a brief rebuttal from Noonan, then addressed the interested parties. He talked slowly and thoughtfully, his voice sounding like the voice of justice. He said he had a dilemma.

"On the one side we have the picture presented by the district attorney," the judge said. "It is a picture of a very vicious crime; a crime of the highest grades of moral turpitude. It is a picture of outright viciousness; robbery in the first degree committed in every possible way that crime can be committed. One life was lost, that is, one of the robbers was killed. Two others were captured. They paid the penalty they owed to the law. The fourth escaped and has only recently been taken after seven years, during which time he has changed his name and his activities.

"Then comes the other side. He went far away to a new land and turned over a new leaf. He built himself up, we are told, to be a useful, respected and honored member of society. He was rehabilitated. On the other hand, he could not, by that conduct, pay the debt which by law, in its inexorable demand, requires him to pay. . . ."

Montague waited. The district attorney waited. The summer crowd waited. This, my God, was just like a Hollywood melodrama, like a Perry Mason novel. The judge continued his slow, voice-of-justice appraisal of the matter.

"The protection of society—not necessarily at the hands of this defendant, but for others like-minded, others who are impulsive, young, rash and weak—that is the concern of our laws," he said. "It is upon that the court is called to exercise its discretion as to whether this man should be allowed to go at large until the day of his trial. So severe and so mandatory is the law to self-preservation, the true law of nature, that it might try to impel or force a man to go seek parts unknown to escape the inevitable consequences of the trial.

"I am not prepared at this time to rule. I want to do full justice to the client, Mr. Noonan, but I want to be just to society, too."

Everyone would wait some more.

Judge Brewster adjourned the case until two o'clock Thursday afternoon. That meant John Montague would spend at least the next two nights in jail.

The Essex County jail was not exactly Sing Sing. The residents in the five cells, if there were any residents, ate whatever Percy Egglefield's family ate. That was because the sheriff and his family lived at the jail, an apartment part of the inducement for someone to take the job. Prisoners often sat at the family table, said grace with the family, passed the rolls and then the butter.

"I'm going to let you out for the afternoon to walk around town," Percy Egglefield would tell some of the county's captured desperadoes. "But you have to be back by six. If you're not, I'm locking the doors and I won't let you back in."

The sheriff worked with a small-town ease that better resembled law enforcement in the Old West than any more sophisticated, big-city approach. His personal car, a siren and a light mounted on the roof, was the county patrol car. When he left town, his son would sometimes "borrow" the car and take his friends to the movies in Westport. This was an adventure.

"We'd put on the light and siren and drive to Westport flat out, 45 miles an hour, maybe 50," Percy's nephew, Spencer Egglefield, said. "We'd pull up, park right in front of the theater and just leave the car. Pretty good."

Montague was not happy to be Percy's houseguest, no matter how loose the rules were. This was not what he expected. He undoubtedly was the first visitor to stay in an Essex County cell with twenty pieces of checked luggage somewhere on the premises. He had places to go, people to see, certainly things to do.

The jail was only thirty feet or so from the courthouse, and now, depending on what happened on Thursday, which way Judge Brewster ruled, there was a chance he might be a resident for the next month or two before he went to trial. There was a chance, if the trial did not go well, that he might not be free for a long while.

DA McDonald told reporters he expected the case to go to court on October 11, the opening of county court. He continued to express confidence.

"Even though seven years have passed since this man became a fugitive," the district attorney said, "I still believe I have an airtight case against him."

McDonald was another familiar local figure. He had grown up in Port Henry, gone to Union College, served as an officer in the World War, then returned to open a law practice, first in Keensville, then Port Henry. He was a likable guy, honest, a hunter and fisherman, a left-handed golfer. He was the county commander of the American Legion. His work on the earlier cases against Norton and Carleton, the other two bandits, had been flawless. Norton turned state's evidence and served two years. Carleton served six.

"I think I have a stronger case against Moore than I had against the other two men who went to prison for the crime," McDonald said.

The day in jail, Wednesday, August 25, 1937, was Montague's thirty-fourth birthday. A number of newspapers somehow got the age wrong, said he was thirty-two years old, but he was thirty-four. His present from the state of New York, maybe with an assist from Percy Egglefield, was a leisurely trip down the street to Lawton Metcalf's tiny drugstore for an ice cream soda. Four state troopers accompanied him.

Reporters tried to question him while he walked, but he said nothing they wanted to hear. He was upset with the stories he read in the morning papers from New York. They tended, some of them, toward unflattering portraits of a Hollywood dandy back among the common folk to receive his just deserts. The

New York Daily News called him "the chunky wizard of the links." The Hollywood dandy and chunky wizard of the links was not amused. He let his displeasure be known to certain reporters.

"I am grateful to my friends" was his one statement for publication. He said he had received a number of telegrams in jail wishing him good luck with his problems.

An awkward moment developed at the drugstore. Montague and a trooper sat down at a table not far from a table being used by an older man, a middle-aged woman, and two young women. The older man was Matt Cobb, the middle-aged woman was Elizabeth Hana, and the two young women were her daughters, Naomi and Harriet. These were four of the victims of the August 5, 1930, robbery in Jay.

If Montague recognized the people, he did not acknowledge them. They certainly recognized him—the two daughters had been among the female spectators at the bail hearing—but no words were spoken between the two tables. Montague finished his ice cream soda and returned to the jail. The victims, who had studied him with interest, talked with reporters. They admitted, all of them, that they couldn't be sure he was the fourth robber on that long-ago night.

"We can't positively say that he was one of the men," Elizabeth said. "You must remember that it was dark and that all of them wore masks."

The robbery was seven years and three weeks old now. The family still owned and operated the restaurant, but Naomi Hana was now Naomi Beattie, twenty-four, married, and living in Washington, D.C. Harriet was nineteen, living in New York City, working at the Roosevelt Hotel, and trying to become an actress. Matt Cobb, sixty-seven when he was attacked, was now seventy-four. The changes were reminders that other lives had also been lived while LaVerne Moore became John Montague and picked up Oliver Hardy and placed him on top of a bar. Naomi was seventeen when the robbery occurred. Harriet was twelve.

"I was sleeping on the couch in the dining room because my sister was sick," Harriet said. "Loud voices woke me up and I saw a man with a flashlight and a gun. He was going into my mother's bedroom.

"I said, 'What're you doing with my mother?' I didn't know it was a holdup. He hollered to some fellow, 'Hey, Slim, take care of this kid.' . . . Slim tied my hands behind my back and tore the sheets right off my bed and stuffed them in my mouth."

"Slim" was the nickname for the late John Sherry, the bandit who died in the crash of the roadster that night. He certainly had paid for his crime. Mrs. Beattie said that a different man tied her up. She also remembered his name.

"I remember very distinctly that the man who tied me up was called 'Verne' by the others," she said. "I think that the man who tied me up was the same man who beat Grandfather over the head."

Matt Cobb mostly remembered the beating. He said he had never been beaten the way he was that night.

"The guy must have hit me a dozen times with the butt of his revolver before he called for others to 'bring me that black-jack,' " Cobb said. "How many times he hit me after that I can't recall. He wore out that blackjack."

The identity of "Verne" did not seem to be much of a mys-tery to the members of the family. Though none of them could positively identify him, they had read the stories about LaVerne Moore and talked to DA McDonald. They could add up the circumstantial evidence and tie it to a name.

Harriet Hana, the aspiring actress, had no doubts about what she wanted to have happen to this John Montague, this LaVerne Moore. His appearance in town, his movieland success, the big buzz around him were a personal affront, a repudiation of any thought that crime doesn't pay.

"His twenty trunks of clothes!" she said. "I hope he gets a long term."

The characters reassembled in the redbrick courthouse on Thursday afternoon. The seats again were filled, predominantly with women. The two Hana daughters were back. Otto Kruger and Pauline Lord, the two celebrities, were back. The many reporters filled the jury box. John Brown, frozen forever on that day he was found guilty in Charlestown, stared down at the scene.

Montague again was abrupt with questioners on his way into the room. There was no smile now, no confidence. He was obviously nervous when called to stand and learn his fate from Judge Brewster. He touched the table in front of him, just with his fingertips, and stared directly at the judge.

Again, O. Byron Brewster talked in that slow voice of justice. Again, polysyllabic words rolled into the audience to be parsed and internalized, finally understood, the sound of the law at work.

For the first few minutes, Montague's fate did not sound favorable. Judge Brewster talked about the "high grade" of the charge, first-degree armed robbery, and how in historic interpretations of common law, bail would not be possible. He then, however, said that those interpretations had been relaxed in recent years. He was now able to take into account other considerations:

> Among those considerations thus permitted are the character and means, and standing of the accused in the community where he has lived. Taking these into account, I must in fairness consider your comparative youthfulness at the time when the crime, of which you are accused, was committed.
>
> Also the fact which also appears that since that time and for upward of six or seven years you have made your life over and have been a useful and respected and, I think it may be added, a distinguished citizen in a faraway land: and consider also that it appears from your life and conduct there that you, yourself, have worked a complete reformation within yourself for, it is plain to be seen, from the showing you have made here, that if criminal instincts and propensities still lingered within you there, they would have long since manifested themselves in such a way as to have long ere now brought you within the toils of the law.
>
> It seems impossible that you may now escape paying any penalty which the law may finally extract from you, and I think I may add your history for the past six or seven years seems to indicate to me that you will be willing to meet the charge here in a fair, upright, honest and courageous manner.
>
> Indeed, you seem to present to me in many respects a modern portrait having great likeness to that famous char-

actor painted by Victor Hugo—in sooth you appear to be a modern Jean Valjean....

But different from Jean Valjean you are returned here not to suffer from the vindictiveness of the law. Our criminal law proceeds in its enforcement from no motives of revenge, and you have been returned not for the purpose of persecution but in order that you may be prosecuted in a decent and humane manner for the crime whereof you are charged.

It is because of these considerations, Mr. District Attorney, that I feel that the exercise of a sound discretion must turn in favor of the admission to prisoner to bail, and I accordingly grant his application....

The clouds in Montague's head lifted for the first time in two days. The smile returned to his face. Jean Valjean! Finally someone had it right. The important person had it right. The dignity of the greatest tragic hero in literature, poor Jean Valjean of Hugo's classic *Les Misérables,* imprisoned for stealing a loaf of bread for his family, persecuted by his past, forced to find a new identity—Monsieur Madeline, not much different from Monsieur Montague—was so much more appropriate. John Montague was Jean Valjean, not Death Valley Scotty or Titanic Thompson. He beamed as he stood next to Dutch Schultz's former attorney.

Justice Brewster was not finished.

He, too, had received the many letters from famous people defending Montague's character. He, too, had followed the case in the newspapers. One comment had made him angry. Gene Tunney, the former heavyweight champ, known for quoting

Shakespeare and commenting on any and all subjects, had dismissed the proceedings in Elizabethtown, characterizing them as an attempt by some small-town people trying to make bigtown news. Tunney thought the case was ridiculous.

"I take occasion here, now, publicly, to resent in particular the statement of a former heavyweight champion prizefighter and alleged Shakespearean scholar to the effect that the District Attorney was seeking your return for reasons of publicity and an effort to put a 'hick town' on the map," the voice of justice said. "And, in turn, I send him this question: Does he consider that in this case the District Attorney is more to be honored in the breach than in the observance of his sworn duty as a public officer?"

Bail was set at $25,000. A trial date, probably in October, would be established at a hearing on September 1. The National Surety man wrote out a check. John Montague filled out forms at the jail and collected his luggage. His tone, softened by the judge's decision, was much different with reporters. The Jean Valjean of the golfing greens—a term the *New York Times* would use—was a more humble character.

"I'm going home to see my mother in Syracuse," he said. "She is very ill, about to undergo a major operation. I haven't seen her in seven years.

"I am fortunate enough to have a family I love and love dearly...."

His voice choked with emotion.

He was driven away from the courthouse in a car. His luggage followed in a second car with California license plates. The cars did not have far to travel.

"Number 26," Otto Kruger had said to John Montague shortly after the decision was rendered. "Come right over."

The freed man went to a cocktail party celebration at the actor's house. He would see his mother tomorrow.

Otto Kruger was appearing in theaters across the country at that very moment in a Warner Bros. film called *They Won't Forget,* directed by Mervyn LeRoy. This was a courtroom drama, set in the fictional Southern town of Flodden. Unscrupulous district attorney Andy Griffin, played by Claude Raines, uses circumstantial evidence to convict a Northern stranger, Robert Hale, in a murder case at fictional Buxton Business College. The townspeople, all of them worried that one of their friends might be the guilty party, embellish their stories on the stand to create an aura of guilt around the stranger. Otto Kruger played Michael Gleason, the stranger Hale's frustrated lawyer from New York. Gleason can't help his client. Hale is a goner.

"Now that it's over, Andy," a reporter says to Claude Raines as Andy Griffin at the end, "I wonder if Hale really done it."

"I wonder," Claude Raines says.

In a positive July 15, 1937, review, the *New York Times* compared the plot to the case of Leo Frank, the Jewish stranger from New York who was wrongly convicted, then lynched, after the 1915 rape and murder of thirteen-year-old Mary Phagan at an Atlanta pencil factory. The review also mentioned the ongoing case of the Scottsboro Boys in Scottsboro, Alabama. That was the case of nine black teenage boys wrongly convicted of raping two white girls, another miscarriage of justice inflamed by headlines and false testimony that was still being appealed.

The film, in short, showed the vagaries of the American justice system. Anything can happen.

CHAPTER SEVEN

NEW YORK

August 26—October 13, 1937

The reunion between the man with the new name and his family with the old name took place at 5:30 the next afternoon, the day after he made bail. A dozen reporters and photographers had staked out the house at 2115 South Geddes Street in Syracuse since early in the morning and the family had been assembled for much of the day, but it took a while for John/ LaVerne to make his way down and then across the state from Elizabethtown.

He called from various stops, giving his mother details of his progress. Everyone fidgeted.

"I can't wait to see him," sixty-year-old Mary Moore said. "I talked with him on the phone and he told me how happy he is to come and see me.

"I haven't seen my boy in seven years and now that I will, it's wonderful. I have been quite sick and must undergo an operation. I have been delaying the operation purposely so that I could see LaVerne beforehand.

"He has known of my sickness and has wanted to come back to Syracuse to see me. He told me after the court hearing that he would have come directly to Syracuse, but it was necessary for him to take care of some important business first."

There had been changes at home, too, while LaVerne was stuffing George Bancroft into that locker, upside down, and driving a golf ball three-quarters of a mile in five shots for the boys at Lakeside. The house was a change, for one thing. The family had moved here from Stolp Avenue two years earlier. It was a significant social move, from Tipperary Hill to an area called Skunk City. Skunk City, despite the name, was a more desired location of broad streets and more fashionable homes with lawns and garages.

Another change was that everyone else in the family had gotten married. Harold, LaVerne's brother, finally had tied the knot two years ago at age thirty-five and lived in nearby DeWitt, New York. Madeline, now thirty-one, was Mrs. Madeline McGrath, lived in Chicago, and had two girls. Mary, twenty-seven, was now Mary Allen. She and her husband, Richard, lived in the second floor of the new house. LaVerne's father, Matthew, now sixty-one, worked at Sanderson Steel. The color of his hair had changed dramatically. Black when LaVerne had left, Matthew's hair was now a perfect white. The parishioners called him "Whitey" when he passed the basket at St. Patrick's and wondered if his son's indiscretions had been a cause in the change of color.

When LaVerne finally reached Syracuse, he called the house again and his brother-in-law Richard Allen drove to pick him up. They arrived together at the house, greeted by reporters and a boyhood friend, Eugene Grobsmith.

"Hey, Moorey," Grobsmith shouted. "You look like a million bucks."

"So do you," LaVerne said.

He shook Grobsmith's hand, nodded to the reporters, and bounded up the steps, two at a time. He shook hands with his uncle, William Whalen—"Hello, my boy, how are you?" his uncle said—and went into the parlor to see his mother. This was almost a scene out of bad fiction.

"Hello, Mother darling, how are you?" he boomed, pulling the gray-haired woman close.

"You look well, son," she said when she was able to back away and appraise him. "You do."

"You look well, yourself, Mother," he said. "How are you feeling?"

The reunion went from there as he hugged his father and brother and sister, met his new in-laws and new nieces. These were private moments, unrecorded, but he soon went onto the front porch with his parents to talk with reporters and pose for pictures. There was a wedding-reception formality to the shots, everyone dressed in good clothes, even on a Friday, smiling in that awkward, overstated way that people do in front of a camera.

"Kiss your mother," a photographer asked.

"That's a very easy thing to do," LaVerne said.

"Put your hand on your dad's shoulder."

"You bet I will."

Left unsaid in public were a lot of facts about this reunion. Had his mother talked to him during his seven years in Hollywood? Had anyone in the family talked to him? If they had, did they try to convince him to come home and give himself up? If they hadn't talked to him, did they have any idea where he was? Had they, too, been suspicious when those John Montague stories started to appear? Did they think that John Montague was LaVerne Moore? Or did they always know? None of this was mentioned during the hugs and kisses, the poses for the newspapers.

"Will you be with your family tonight?" a reporter asked.

"I don't know anybody that could get me away," LaVerne said.

He stood on the porch and looked out at the view. A field was directly across the street, and then the eye could see the rolling fairways of the Bellevue Country Club. The view was terrific.

"It sure looks like home," LaVerne Moore said.

Newspapers pointed out the next day that he never before had been to this house.

———

The next public sighting of John Montague/LaVerne Moore—except for a brief gossip item that he was spotted at the Rainbow Room in New York City—did not come until ten days later in Elizabethtown, where he had to enter a plea on September 7, 1937. One of the people waiting for him was Henry McLemore.

Thirty years old, McLemore was already the lead sports columnist for the United Press, a deft and often cynical writer, his words from New York pumped around the country under column heads that read "Today's Sport Parade" or "Henry

McLemore's Parade of Sports" or "Henry McLemore Says." He was originally from Macon, Georgia, an Emory University graduate, one of the new generation walking in the footsteps of Grantland Rice.

Though he had become friends with Rice—since everybody became friends with Rice—he had a zany quality that Rice never had. He often told how his first job in the newspaper business was writing editorials for the Ku Klux Klan, not exactly his favorite organization, during the 1928 election. His best Klan editorial detailed how the pope was already planning to build a tunnel underneath the Atlantic Ocean from the Vatican to the White House if Democrat Al Smith, the Catholic, became president. Not true, perhaps, but an inspired thought.

He had a tendency to put himself into the middle of the action, usually after a couple of cocktails for literary inspiration. At the 1932 Winter Olympics at Lake Placid, for example, he wound up at the bobsled run at Mount Von Hoevenberg at midnight with a trained black bear and one of the Stevens brothers, a member of the U.S. two-man bobsled team. The Stevens brother had claimed, after some cocktails, that he and the bear could beat the world two-man record. Why not see? McLemore, the Stevens brother, and the bear had broken into the course in the dark.

McLemore stood at the finish line with a stopwatch. The Stevens brother shouted from the top and he and the bear took off. On the first turn, the Stevens brother driving, the bear fell off the back. The Stevens brother kept zipping down the course in the bobsled, now without a brakeman. The bear kept zipping along the course in quick pursuit, not in the bobsled and howling all the way. McLemore at the finish clocked Stevens at two-tenths of a second under the world record. The bear, missing a big patch of fur on his backside, tied the world record.

At the 1936 Summer Games in Berlin, after more cocktails, more inspiration, McLemore was apprehended late at night by the Gestapo as he climbed the wall of Adolf Hitler's residence, singing, "Is It True What They Say About Hitler?"—a parody of the popular song "Is It True What They Say About Dixie?" He told his captors that he was simply having fun, that he didn't even know which building he was climbing, that it was all a mis-understanding. He was released in time to write a scathing col-umn about the German leader in the press box the next day, detailing Hitler's crazy eyes, weak mouth, Charlie Chaplin mus-tache, ridiculous strut, and totally classless demeanor.

"Is that how you feel about the German leaders?" a small and quiet man asked, looking over McLemore's shoulder.

"In spades," McLemore replied. "Have you ever seen a sillier-looking bunch of men?"

Joseph Goebbels walked away.

In the past year, McLemore had moved away from sports a bit, covering the flood of the Mississippi River in New Orleans in the spring and the natural gas explosion at a school in New London, Texas, that killed 294 people, but now was back at a story that combined both sports and the real world. His mission in Elizabethtown, as he perceived it, was to take some of the mystery out of this Mysterious Montague character. He was skeptical of the wonder stories. He was curious about the court case, about what would happen next. He wanted to see what he could see.

Checking into the Deer's Head Inn, across the street from

the courthouse, he decided first to gauge local feelings about his subject. The place to do this kind of research was obvious.

"So I went to the tavern with its substantial mahogany bar, ugly barmaids, electric phonograph and straight-back booths, and hung around," McLemore later wrote. "Hung around a long time, just listening—listening to college kids, semi-pro baseball players, still in dusty suits and wearing spikes, farmers, dressed-up members of the summer colony, laborers and those indistinguishable men and women you find in bars everywhere."

Fermented lubricants did their work. There was indeed a lot of conversation about the man from Hollywood, about the trial. The surprise was that no one ever used the name "LaVerne Moore." Why was that? Montague was always "Montague" or "Monty" or "Johnny." The stage name had stuck. The old name was no more. Young women talked about "Monty's good looks." Young men talked about his strength. Could he really pick up cars?

McLemore asked no questions. He spread out a menu and simply wrote down the comments he heard:

"I'll lay three to one he doesn't beat the rap. That Norton fellow the district attorney brought in from Cleveland is a clincher in the case."

"He's a cinch to get out of it. It all happened seven years ago and who around here cares? Besides, he knows a lot of important people and that helps in a little town."

"He made a monkey out of himself when, after they let him out on bail, he went to a cocktail party with those actors instead of going to see his mother like he said he was."

"The other guys in the job paid, so why shouldn't he? Knowing those fancy people don't mean anything."

"He never should have come back."

"It'll be a sin if he is sent to jail. He's thrown off all that crime and made a man of himself."

"I hope they let him loose. He was just a boy then."

Reactions, McLemore decided, were definitely mixed.

The next day, the sportswriter went to the arraignment. This would be his first sight of the subject in person. He settled into the jury box with the other reporters, the courtroom only half filled now that the last post–Labor Day remnants of the summer crowd were headed home. A perfect small-town hitch developed—nobody could find a gavel for Judge Harry E. Owen, entailing a delay and a mad search before Sheriff Egglefield saved the day—but then the parties settled down to business.

Attorney James M. Noonan had consistently refused to say anything about what his client's possible plea might be. Now, in response to Harry Owen's question, "How do you plead?" he gave the answer.

"At this time, on behalf of the defendant, I hearby enter a plea of Not Guilty," Noonan said. "Reserving the right to demur to the indictment or to make any motions with reference thereto."

The hearing took no more than five minutes. The trial date was set as October 11, 1937. Montague, dapper and seeming almost disinterested as he sat next to his lawyer, said nothing. The Not Guilty plea obviously meant he was going to fight the charge, but what were his weapons? How was he not guilty? Hadn't he tacitly admitted guilt in California, when he fought extradition? What? None of those questions was answered.

McLemore trudged with the rest of the reporters across Court Street to Montague's room at the Deer's Head Inn. The lawyer and the defendant had promised that they would talk. The lawyer, though he explained little, kept his promise. Montague did not. His few answers were clipped, brusque.

One of the reporters asked what his thoughts were about Norton, the witness for the prosecution. Was Norton his friend?

"I never heard of him," Montague said.

A woman reporter tried to get him to talk about what he had done from the time he left Syracuse until he became the star at Lakeside Golf Club. There seemed to be a couple of years missing in his personal history.

"You've said enough," Montague said.

The situation became uneasy. The reporters became nervous that their subject would snap at them. The subject appeared ready to snap at anything. He was as uneasy with the reporters' questions as the reporters were with his answers. McLemore noted his unease.

"He sat heavily, staring fixedly out the window, looking something like Buddha with his heavy-lidded eyes," the sportswriter wrote the next day, "and each time one of us asked a question, he'd jerk his thumb toward his lawyer without uttering a word. Finally, he jumped up and without so much as a bow to us, said to his lawyer, 'You've said enough. Hell, let's get going, Jim.' "

The verdict, for McLemore, had arrived.

The man, Montague, was definitely not a charmer. He was rude and surly, his personality "as vibrant as a broken ukelele string." He seemed like a chunky country boy, not too smart, in a situation that was very much over his head. How had he made all of those Hollywood glamour people fall for him? What had they seen?

The other reporters hurried off to file their little stories with meager quotes about the Not Guilty plea at the arraignment. McLemore stuck around. For what, he didn't know. He needed more information for a column titled "Henry McLemore Says." He needed more to say.

With everyone else gone, he was able to introduce himself and start a conversation with the man of the moment. The words tumbled out. McLemore said he wasn't like those other reporters, of course, he was a sportswriter. They were news gatherers and scandalmongers. He was interested in sports, just like his friend Grantland Rice. You know Grantland Rice, don't you?

The man of the moment relaxed.

He chatted with McLemore, back and forth, normal, on an assortment of subjects. McLemore eventually told him how he was skeptical about some of the stories he had heard, wondered about how good this John Montague really was on a golf course. Crazy thought, he had golf clubs in his car. Would Montague want to accompany him to the local course and play a round?

Montague said that wasn't possible, he didn't have his clubs. McLemore said they could both play out of his bag. Montague said too many people would follow, that it would be a mob scene. McLemore said they could drive awhile, to a course where no one knew him. Montague said he didn't have time for eighteen holes. McLemore said they could play as many holes as Montague wanted.

They found a course. They played six holes.

McLemore fell in love.

There was a truth about intimacy here: an average man's golf clubs in a talented man's hands will make the average man gape at the results. It was as if Brahms or Mozart had sat down at the family piano. Notes that didn't exist in a balky piece of furniture suddenly were let loose. Montague made wonderful music.

He birdied two of the six holes, parred the other four. His drives went farther than McLemore thought possible, especially with his clubs. The rest of Montague's performance on an ill-maintained, overused vacation course at the end of a season was even better. McLemore rubbed his eyes at Montague's work.

"His approach shots were so perfect that he did not have one long putt," the sportswriter said. "And it was his short game that was most amazing. I never saw chip shots played as he played them. There was no follow-through. Just a flick of the wrist. And the result was deadly. Both his birdies were on chips that, despite the poor fairway lie and spotty greens, stopped 'gimmie' distance from the pin."

The sportswriter and the golfer returned to the hotel after the golf. They went back to Montague's room, where they talked some more. McLemore, somewhere in the conversation, asked Montague if he was as strong as everyone said he was.

"Punch me," Montague said. "Hit me anywhere you want."

Punch me?

Anywhere?

McLemore, as part of good journalistic inquiry, punched Montague in the chest, then the stomach. McLemore punched him over the heart. McLemore punched him in the chin. Montague never moved, never reacted. McLemore's knuckles ached.

"Is it true you once picked up the back end of a car and held it over your head?" McLemore asked.

"Sure," Montague said. "Just like this."

"And with the quickness of a cat," McLemore wrote later, "he reached for the heavy bureau, picked it up easily, swung it over his head and deposited it lightly on the other side of the room. Then, to make it more convincing, he grabbed me by the nape of the neck with one hand and held me dangling and kicking, much as one might hold a cat between thumb and forefinger."

Never before had there been a pad-and-pencil witness to anything outrageous Montague did. Grantland Rice had caught him on the golf course, marveled at the way he played the game, but had never detailed any feats of strength performed in front of him. Never had Grantland Rice been lifted in the air like a house cat or Oliver Hardy. The wonder stories by everyone else had been repeated tales, many of them validated by eyewitnesses, perhaps, but none of them chronicled as they happened. McLemore had stumbled onto journalistic gold.

He hurried to his own room and wrote two stories, not one. The first was his column, where he described the feeling of being lifted into the air, of punching the country's most famous alleged armed robber in the stomach. The second was an extra story, an appreciation of Montague's six holes of golf:

ELIZABETHTOWN (NY)—LaVerne Moore, the man who masqueraded for years as John Montague, won friends in high circles, made his name into a legend, and now is charged with having been an ordinary thug, is, in the opin-

ion of this correspondent who has a professional knowledge
of the subject, a champion golfer. The man of the flesh is no
less than the man of the legend. . . .

The superlatives went on from there.

Montague apparently liked this column. Three weeks later
he was in New York City and invited McLemore, who lived in
Manhattan, to his hotel room for a visit. The sportswriter gladly
accepted. He hurried to the hotel. A third party was also in the
room when he got there: Montague's fat golf bag had arrived
with his oversize golf clubs. Montague was clearly delighted.

"Gee, these babies feel great," he said, swinging his oversize
niblick.

McLemore wondered at the size of the clubs. They were bigger than any clubs he had ever seen. They looked like the mon-
strous bats that Babe Ruth was reported to have swung. Only
a man with Babe Ruth's size could swing bats like that. Only a
man with Montague's size could control golf clubs like this.

The big man, on impulse, placed a glass on the table in a
corner of the room. He dropped three balls onto the carpet.

"What odds will you give me that I can't knock one of these
balls into that glass?" he asked.

"Anything," McLemore said. "It's a 100-to-one, 200-to-one,
300-to-one proposition."

"Don't be a sucker," Montague said.

He swung the niblick easily at one of the balls. The ball went
in a nice arc, close to the ceiling, and dropped into the center of
the glass with such force it shattered the glass. McLemore was
astonished. He said the shot had to be luck. Montague agreed,
luck was involved, but he had McLemore place another glass on

the table. He then missed three times, but put the ball into the glass on his fourth try. This time it did not break.

Montague decided to put on a little indoor clinic for the sportswriter. He did tricks with a golf ball, each more eye-catching than the last one:

A window in the room was open about six inches, maybe eight. A vacant lot was on the other side. Montague tossed a ball on the carpet, took his oversize driver from his bag. He said the ball would either break the window or fly free through the gap. He took a full swing—a full swing—and the ball took off like a rocket, straight through the opening. McLemore estimated that he himself, tossing the ball underhanded, would have trouble from anything more than two feet away.

Next, Montague buried a ball in a seat cushion. He took out a sand wedge and told McLemore to sit on the sofa on the other side of the room. He promised to put the ball in McLemore's lap. *Swoosh*. The ball landed next to McLemore on the sofa.

Finally, Montague opened three drawers in the desk, top, middle, and bottom. He chipped three balls, one-two-three, into the top, middle, and bottom drawers.

"He did it so quickly," Henry McLemore said, "that it sounded like Bill Robinson doing his famed tap dance on steps."

The sportswriter was still in love.

Montague played one round of golf in the next five weeks while he awaited trial. Grantland Rice convinced him to come to the North Hempstead Country Club in Port Washington, Long Island, on Wednesday, September 29, 1937. Montague wasn't hot on the idea, said he had only played three times since February, but finally agreed. He asked that there be no publicity, just a round of golf among friends.

The host for the foursome was Clarence Buddington Kelland, a member at North Hempstead. Kelland, an author of wildly popular fiction, eventually wrote more than two hundred short stories and sixty novels. His work was pummeled by the critics but beloved by readers of the *Saturday Evening Post* and *Collier's*, who waited for each installment of his character-driven serials featuring Scattergood Baines, the homespun philosopher, and Mark Tidd, the fast-thinking fat boy. Many of the tales had been made into movies.

The fourth member of the group at North Hempstead was Alex J. Morrison, regarded as the foremost teacher of golf in the United States. He had written the best-selling instructional book ever printed, *A New Way to Better Golf,* wrote a syndicated instructional column twice a week called Golf Facts, Not Theories, had his own radio show, and owned a driving range underneath the Fifty-ninth Street Bridge in Manhattan. He headlined golf clinics for as many as a thousand people at a time. His claim was that he had given golf lessons to more than a million people in his life.

He also sometimes traveled the vaudeville circuit, preaching the virtues of an easy swing, good balance, and the proper groove and arc to the audience in between the jugglers and comedians who preceded and followed him on the bill. His private clients included Babe Ruth, Jack Dempsey, Annette Kellerman, Charlie Chaplin, Paul Whiteman, and Rube Goldberg.

Fascinated by the first reports of Montague's abilities while in California to shoot some instructional film shorts, Morrison had shown up at the Lakeside Golf Club in the late summer of

1936. He tried to convince Montague to play a round with him. Montague declined, but after a lot of coaxing agreed to hit some shots for the teacher. Morrison was duly impressed by the big man's game.

"From the tenth tee, a short distance from the clubhouse, he drove probably ten balls," Morrison later wrote. "Every one of them carried in the face of a stiff breeze and through an atmosphere heavy with evening mist, over 300 yards. Prodigious clouts, which proved to me that in addition to his great strength he had agility, flexibility and above all a fine touch which enabled him to swing the club with enormous power, yet smoothly. In short, he produced almost perfect co-ordination, perhaps as fine as I ever had seen in a golf swing."

Morrison looked forward to watching Montague for eighteen holes. The teams were Rice and Morrison versus Kelland and Montague. Dr. Leander Newman, another North Hempstead member, joined the group. A women's tournament had been held at the club in the morning, newspaper reporters on the job, so Montague's request for privacy was the first casualty of the day. A gallery of maybe one hundred people that included a couple of reporters, a bunch of the women, and anyone else who heard the news that famous men were playing golf gathered at the 1st tee and would follow the group for the entire round.

Montague shrugged and accepted. He then played one of the best rounds of golf in his life.

He shot a 65, one off the North Hempstead course record set by professional Harry DeMeo almost ten years earlier. He had five birdies—birdied two of the first three holes—and no bogeys on the par-70 layout. He dazzled Alex Morrison, who shot a 71, dazzled the two writers, both fiction and nonfiction, who were on the wrong side of 80. He dazzled the gallery.

It was one of those near-perfect rounds of golf. None of the putts he made was more than ten feet. If he'd sunk a couple of longer putts, and he rimmed out on a few, he easily could have shot a 61, a 62, easily could have broken the record. This was a round without luck, a round of pure skill. He didn't even beat the course into submission with long drives, mostly hitting the ball 250 yards down the middle, shorter than Morrison on most holes. He carved the course into submission.

"To illustrate Montague's confidence and his ability, let me describe the play at a short hole, the [par-3] second," Morrison gushed. "The hole is 125 yards long. The carry is over a pond and on this day the pin was placed in a small corner of the green, centered on a surface approximately 20 feet square. Only a perfect shot would give the player the certainty of a two.

"I played my shot safely to the big section of the green and advised Montague to do likewise. He grinned at me and took a stance to play straight for the pin. He then made one of the most daring shots I ever have seen. Taking an exceptionally long wooden peg, he teed the ball to a height of almost two inches from the turf. He struck a powerful, downward blow with an 8-iron and the ball took a flight that was never more than 20 feet high. It struck the green, bit in and stopped less than three feet short of the flag. He got his two there where I had to take three."

Morrison wrote a long story about the day and about Montague, which was shipped to newspapers around the country by King Features as part of a full-page spread that included pictures of Montague in action, drawings of Montague in action, even an equipment shot that pointed out the size of the head of his driver compared to the head on a normal driver. There was little doubt that the foremost golf teacher in the country was in accord with the foremost sportswriter in the county on the subject of John Montague.

"There never seems to be any doubt in his mind as to the successful outcome of anything he undertakes to do," Morrison wrote. "The spectator, too, senses that same assurance when Montague approaches the ball, more so, I think, than even Bobby Jones conveyed when he was at his best."

Grantland Rice wrote a brief, syndicated story for the next day and said that Montague had "proved his case." He pointed out that even though this was the end of September, leaves and debris on the course, Montague refused to play "winter rules," which would allow him to improve his lie. The *New York Times,* which had stumbled upon the action, ran the headline "Mystery Golfer Breaks Par by 5." One of the smaller headlines on the one-column story was "Takes No More Than 2 Putts on Any Hole to Give Conclusive Proof of His Skill."

All of this was for a round of golf among friends.

Whatever dust and question marks had gathered on the legend of John Montague had been removed. Just like that.

He had talked about going back to California during the five-week wait for the trial, but never did. He spent some time in Syracuse, more time in New York. His lawyer, James Noonan, still refused to discuss whatever strategy he had for the case. Montague also kept quiet about it.

He quietly hired a business manager in case things went

well. His choice was fifty-nine year-old Marty Forkins of New York, a veteran of the vaudeville circuit, known primarily as the longtime manager of dancer Bill (Bojangles) Robinson. Forkins had experience in handling man-of-the-moment celebrity. He had managed track star Jesse Owens only a year earlier, when Owens had returned from Berlin with the four Olympic gold medals that had embarrassed Hitler.

Montague's most public appearances were at Yankee Stadium, where he watched the home team batter the New York Giants in five games to win the World Series. The golfer even joined the baseball players in their victory celebration at the Waldorf=Astoria. The next morning, Monday, October 11, 1937, his picture was on the front page around the country as he sat at a table with actor George Raft and Yankees star center fielder Joe DiMaggio. Left to right: the accused felon, the cinema felon, the idol of American youth. It was quite a picture.

The trial was supposed to start that morning, but had been postponed for two days because Tuesday was Columbus Day. On Wednesday, October 13, 1937, John Montague was back in Elizabethtown to learn the fate of LaVerne Moore.

CHAPTER EIGHT

ELIZABETHTOWN, NEW YORK

October 19–25, 1937

One report called this "the first sports page trial since the Black Sox affair." Another said that not since Bruno Hauptmann was found guilty of kidnapping the baby of Charles Lindbergh had a trial "dredged up so many people of renown." Heady stuff. The participants gathered for the start of the proceedings on October 19, 1937, under a well-seeded cloud of anticipation.

Telephone workers had been in Elizabethtown for a week installing extra lines for the many reporters who would be on the job. The summer people were long gone, the local population now listed as 636, the weather cool to cold, the trees in late color, deer hunters in the woods, but the hotels had retained staffs and ordered extra food. John Montague himself had rented seventeen rooms, an entire floor, in the annex of the Deer's Head Inn to accommodate his lawyers and friends and friends of friends.

This was going to be a show.

"All the adjacent sport writers, sob sisters, newsreel, radio men, columnists and a few newspaper men are on hand to see that justice is done in a few million well chosen words," *New York Mirror* columnist Bob Considine reported. "The little town is like a college station on the eve of the big game, with lights in the dormitories and songs in the pubs.

"Hear ye, Hear ye—make way then for the only man who was ever brought to trial for being too good a golfer."

The entire drama would take place in a square of real estate no more than five hundred yards by five hundred yards, the red-brick courthouse with its white columns on one side of Court Street, the Deer's Head on the other, the players going back and forth for meals and strategy sessions, testimony and judgments, cocktails and conversation. The now familiar oil-painted stare of the late John Brown would follow all movement.

Jurors, prosecutors, defendant, reporters, attorneys, bellmen, waitresses, spectators, and a short-order cook or two would be thrown together in an around-the-clock stew, everyone eating, sleeping, arguing, and, ultimately, listening to the same decision together. This would be intimate, personal debate. No one would be a stranger to anyone else by the end.

The first tactic of Montague's lawyer, James M. Noonan, was familiar. In his defense of notorious gangster Arthur (Dutch Schultz) Flegenheimer in a similar situation two years earlier in two trials for tax evasion in the small Adirondacks town of Malone, Noonan had won the hearts of the local residents before they had a chance to use their minds. He had hired two popular Malone attorneys as assistants. He had brought his client into town early, showed him around, had him meet local people, patronize their stores, give to their charities. It was this humanized, likable Dutch Schultz, this friend of the town, who was acquitted twice to cheers in the courtroom and frowns from the bench.

"I have to say that your verdict is such that it shakes the confidence of law-abiding people and truth," federal judge Frederick H. Bryant bellowed from the bench at the end of the first trial. "It will be apparent to all who have followed the evidence in this trial that you have reached a verdict that is not based on evidence but on some other reason. . . ."

The judge's words were of little significance. The Dutchman was free, albeit to find a different fate, which happened to be a .45-caliber bullet slightly below the heart at the Palace Chop House in Newark, New Jersey, on October 23, 1935.

Noonan had followed the Dutch Schultz approach in Elizabethtown already. He had hired two local attorneys, Robert Dudley and Albert Forthmiller, and made sure that his client was an affable and accommodating guest in earlier visits to the town. Seventeen rooms at the Deer's Head made John Montague a substantial boost to the local economy without saying a word.

The rest of Noonan's strategy was still as mysterious as his client ever was. The lawyer still said nothing, gave indications of nothing. The most popular guess was that he would take a similar approach to the one Giesler had taken in the extradition hearings, paint John Montague as a good kid, maybe pulled into some affair reluctantly once in his life, an obviously solid citizen ever since. The name of Jean Valjean would possibly be repeated.

District Attorney Thomas McDonald's case was still obvious. Roger Norton, the truck driver now living in Cleveland who was one of the bandits, then served almost two years in jail for the crime, had been a guest of Percy Egglefield, since the bail hearing, held as a material witness. He would place Montague at the scene. The physical evidence, Montague's golf clubs and clothes and personal effects, would back up his story. Any other testimony would only add to the pile.

The judge, Harry E. Owen, was a familiar local figure, seventy-two years old, with a face distinguished by a large gray mustache. He had already been involved in a prominent case that fall in Elizabethtown, acting as a surrogate to decide conflicting claims about the will of multimillionaire Edward H. R. Green. The late Mr. Green, who lived part of the time in nearby Lake Placid, was the son and heir of Hetty Green, the famed and eccentric "Witch of Wall Street," the first woman to make a fortune in the stock market in the early part of the century. She had left much of her money to Edward, and now Edward had left all of his money to his sister, Mrs. Matthew Astor Wilks. His wife of nineteen years, Mabel Harlow Green, contested this decision despite the prenuptial agreement she had signed long ago.

Judge Harry Owen was still considering which way to rule. Five different states waited on the side, ready to fight one another for the substantial taxes from the estate. It was a rich man's leftover mess.

The Montague trial also had its subplots, its fault lines and imponderables. The case was so old, cut from the yellowed headlines of long-gone Prohibition with talk about speakeasies and bootleggers, that it seemed like quaint ancient history. Did anybody except the DA care what happened back then? Did any of it still matter?

The celebrity of Montague was an issue. Did it help? Or did it hurt? Homespun jurors could be dazzled, simply by being in the presence of the friend of all of those famous people far, far away. Or they could be repulsed by his clothes, his money, his big-time waltz. Who does he think he is?

A subtle factor was race. Every day another story appeared about the Japanese army's relentless assault on Shanghai, its imperial march through China. The Japanese were seen as the upstarts, the provocateurs in this business. Anti-Japanese senti-ment was on the rise across the country. Would Kin Hana's broken-English testimony be heard with favor? His daughter Harriet, quoted often in stories about the bail proceedings, was described as an "almond-eyed beauty, a mixture of the Orient and Occident." The victims here were the only Japanese people for miles around.

The New York papers, captivated by all of this, had sent some of their best people—Considine of the *Mirror,* Meyer Berger of the *Times,* Jimmy Kilgallen of the *Journal-American,* Dick Lee of the *Daily News*—and the wire services were all rep-resented, ready to ship the news across the land. The few mil-lion well-chosen words promised to be inventive ones.

"The foreign papers like to call our jury trials 'Roman cir-cuses,' and there is a pretty good chance that they are right," Considine wrote. "The trial of John Montague, which has its first inning here tomorrow morning, probably will earn the cir-cus sobriquet, but it seems to be a little more like a combination between a big football game, a serio-comic aspect of the Haupt-mann trial and the 19th hole."

The stakes were pretty good. If the defendant won, he could walk across the street, shake hands with his business manager, sign a few contracts, take out his sand wedge, and start flailing away at that million-dollar buried treasure that supposedly awaited him. If he lost, he would go to jail for the next ten years. He wouldn't see a golf course for a long, long time.

At 9:30 on the Tuesday morning of October 19, 1937, as the bell rang from the top of the courthouse, John Montague put out his cigarette and went inside to watch his future unfold in the hands of other people. He wore a conservative double-breasted gray business suit, no Hollywood clothes now, and a solemn expression. He sat down next to his attorney.

The courtroom was less than full, the spectators mostly women, free again while their husbands marched through the soggy woods in search of deer and pheasant. Dramatics prom-ised to be kept to a minimum as the mechanical process of jury selection took place.

Strangely, sex was one of the first issues. For the first time in the history of Essex County, women were included in the jury pool. Four women were in the panel of thirty-six names. The de-fense was hoping to see at least one of them on the jury, thinking that women might have a sympathetic ear for a good-looking friend of Bing Crosby. The prosecution was against the idea for the same reason, though District Attorney McDonald said he objected because "we don't have facilities for women in the courthouse. Nothing comfortable enough."

At any rate, the women were ruled out quickly. One reporter wrote that McDonald objected to the "plump" Mrs. Ethel Betters of Lake Placid, the "plumper" Mrs. Helen Mitchell of Westport, and the "plumpest" Mrs. Katherine Lamoy of Lake Placid. The fourth woman, Mrs. Hazel Chambers of Lake Placid, was dismissed by the defense after she said she was acquainted with District Attorney McDonald.

McDonald's basic question for prospective male jurors was, "If the testimony in this case convinces you that Moore is guilty, would you be inclined to temper your decision because he apparently led an exemplary life since the date of the crime?" If the answer was yes, or if the prospective juror thought twice about an answer, he was released. Attorney Noonan's basic question was, "If, at the conclusion of all testimony, there is even a faint doubt in your mind that Moore is guilty, will you give him the benefit of the doubt which every man deserves?" Noonan also was quick to send a candidate home.

Montague sat quietly between his lawyers for the first hour, watching the process, but as he heard more, caught the rhythm of the questions and responses, he began to make suggestions to Noonan. The lawyer seemed to react to some of them.

The reporters, when not looking at the cream-colored walls, the high ceilings, or their fingernails, studied the defendant's slightest reactions. Each story mentioned his two dimples, his long eyelashes, his kinetic-energy bulk, his suit coat stretched across his wide back as he sat through the words. His lunch across the street, stop the presses, included a shot of eighteen-year-old bourbon.

"His hands look like an Irish washer-woman's—pasty, short-fingered and thick," Considine wrote. "But that section between the heel of his hand and the first knuckle of the little finger makes you start. A great gable of muscle sticks out, making his paws as wide as they are long. When you shake hands with him you remember it for an hour after, even though you might not know him from Joe Doakes."

The net result of the first day's work was six jurors, half of the panel. Two farmers, a carpenter, a plumber, a gas station owner, and a laborer were selected. The laborer was from Jay, lived less than three miles from the scene of the crime. None of the men played golf. The day passed with only the few bits of levity found by invention on a dull job.

"Do you believe everything you read in the newspapers?" Judge Owen asked prospective juror Oliver Euro of Elizabethtown.

Euro nodded affirmatively.

Dismissed.

The second day of the trial was pretty much a repeat of the first except for the fact that the defendant's conservative suit was switched from gray to blue and the lawyers on both sides asked longer questions and wrangled more in finding the final six jurors to fill out the panel. Noonan used nineteen of his twenty challenges in the process, McDonald ten. Court had been in session for over an hour before Juror No. 7 was chosen and ran late, until six o'clock, before the final selection was made.

A truck driver, a carpenter, a painter, a farmer, a lumberman, and a laborer completed a group completely comprised of workingmen. The twelve-man jury of John Montague's peers probably couldn't fill his twenty traveling bags of clothes between them.

The humor again came from the tedium.

"You would, if chosen as juror, vote for conviction or acquittal based on the evidence?" DA McDonald asked Frank Harper, a salesman from Crown Point.

"I would acquit him," Harper answered.

Dismissed.

The tabloid *New York Daily News,* "the Picture Paper," used the day to unveil its newest technological advance, the portable Wirephoto machine. The first on-the-scene photo ever transmitted to the paper with the machine, announced with appropriate fanfare, showed the defendant in his blue suit signing an autograph for four drop-jawed teenage girls who stared at him as if he were a famous singer who had stepped straight out of the family Victrola.

One of the girls was the daughter of O. Byron Brewster, the judge who had called Montague "Jean Valjean." Another was the daughter of Percy Egglefield, who had escorted him across the country and lodged him at the family jail. Part of the Dutch Schultz strategy seemed to be working very well. The defendant signed his name, "John Montague, 1937."

The picture that emerged from the courtroom the next day was quite different from the *Daily News* shot. The affable, almost debonair John Montague 1937 of today was deconstructed into a venal, mean, dangerous LaVerne Moore of seven years ago. He tied up crying children and stuffed their mouths with gags so he wouldn't hear their noise. He repeatedly hit an old man on the head and left him by a river, bleeding and unconscious. He was the mastermind of dark doings on a dark August night in the middle of nowhere.

The prosecution went to work.

District Attorney McDonald laid out two revolvers and a taped-up garden-hose blackjack on a table to set the scene, the blackjack somehow more lethal in appearance than either of the guns, and in his opening statement proceeded to draw the outlines of a LaVerne Moore who was no more than a common thug, a vicious thug at that. After James M. Noonan for the defense waived the right to make an opening statement, McDonald brought his witnesses to the stand, one after another, to add dramatic swatches of color.

The star of the production was Roger Norton, fresh from his voluntary stay in the Elizabethtown jail. A slender, blond character, dressed in the wrong-sized jacket and tie of a workingman, an ill-at-ease outfit worn only for weddings and funerals and court appearances, the thirty-five-year-old Norton detailed the plan and execution of the robbery of Hana's restaurant.

The dialogue sometimes sounded as if it came from *Gangbusters,* the popular radio show that featured the dramatization of actual FBI cases. Only the opening sound effects of sirens, squealing tires, and rat-a-tat tommy guns were missing.

"Moore passed me the revolver," Roger Norton said at one point, describing the chase when Moore was driving the getaway car and the state police were on their tail. "He said, 'Give it to them.' "

"Did you 'give it to them'?" DA McDonald asked.

"No, I threw the gun out the window," the witness replied in a soft voice.

Norton said the night began in Mechanicville, New York, when he and Moore met up with William Carleton and John Sherry. They supposedly were going to Hana's, almost one hundred miles from Mechanicville, to discuss a deal to buy thirty cases of whiskey to resell to bootleggers in the southern half of the state. Norton, through his uncle, Matt Cobb, was the contact with Hana. The four men made the trip in two cars.

"Thirty miles before we got to Hana's place," Norton testified, "Moore, who was driving the car, told me that they were going to stick up the place. I couldn't do anything about it. He had a gun and a blackjack in his lap."

Norton said Moore told him he was in some trouble in Syracuse and needed money for a getaway. The robbery would finance his immediate disappearance. That was the reason for going to Hana's.

"When we got there, we parked two hundred yards away from the tavern and Carleton went down to scout," Norton said. "He came back and said we'd have to wait until the last customers left before we could begin. Finally, they left, so the four of us drove up close. They all got out, but I stayed in the car with the lights out.

"After a while I heard the girls crying and Uncle Matt hollering and suddenly Uncle Matt came running out. I guess he had broken free. He ran to a little storehouse behind the tavern yelling for Kin, and then Moore came out in the yard.

"He knocked the old man down and while they were rolling around, the old man hollering, Moore yelled to the others to bring him a blackjack. Finally Sherry brought it to him and Moore hit the old man over the head a few times with a thudding sound and they rolled down the bank toward the river.

"I got out of the car and hollered, 'Leave the old man alone; let's get out of here.' "

Norton said the two other robbers left first in the Ford roadster, and he and Moore followed in the green Pontiac sedan, Moore at the wheel. He said they were chased and stopped near Schroon Lake. The state troopers mostly questioned him, but also talked to Moore, who gave his name as Lawrence Ryan. Free to go, they resumed their trip.

"I left Moore at the station in Schenectady," he said. "He said he was going to Syracuse to change his clothes and see if Carleton had showed up."

That, Norton said, was the last time he had seen LaVerne Moore. Until today.

"Is the man you refer to as LaVerne Moore here in court?"

"Yes," Norton replied, pointing at Moore, who stared back at him.

"Is he the LaVerne Moore that was in Kin Hana's restaurant at that occasion?"

"Yes," Norton said.

James M. Noonan now took over the questioning. He approached his subject with an air of lawyerly disgust and disbelief. He clearly considered Norton's account preposterous. His questions and Norton's replies consumed the next two and a half hours.

Noonan not only questioned everything Norton had said, but questioned Norton's character. He made the witness admit that he had been involved in another run-in with the law, stealing a car battery, since he had been released after his two-year sentence for the Hana robbery. He brought out signed statements by Norton after the Hana arrest, statements that Norton now had to admit were false. He pointed out that Norton and his wife had dined at the restaurant only two weeks prior to the robbery and that Norton knew where the safe was located. Wasn't that true? Norton admitted that it was.

Noonan constructed another reason for the robbery, that it was an act of vengeance because Carleton thought that Hana had given the state police a tip about a shipment of liquor that was ultimately confiscated. Norton denied this. He said again that he didn't even know there was going to be a robbery until Moore told him, thirty miles before they reached the restaurant.

"You weren't forced to participate, were you?" Noonan asked.

"No," the witness replied, "but Moore had a blackjack and a revolver in his lap."

The rest of the day was spent in descriptions of the robbery from the victims' point of view. Members of the Hana family, plus employee Paul Poland, came to the stand, one after the other, to describe their feelings as they were manhandled and tied. They, too, gave their impressions of being on the wrong side of those revolvers on the table. The revolvers and the masks, they said, made identification of the robbers hard.

"You couldn't recognize any of them?" DA McDonald asked Poland, who told how he had been trussed and forced to lie facedown on the floor.

"One of them had something in my back," Poland explained.

Poland did say he recognized Montague from a chance encounter at a gas station in Jay two days prior to the robbery. He said he saw Norton, who he knew by sight, in the car, and Montague was sitting beside him.

Kin Hana was hard to understand on the stand. Between his accent and a tendency to talk fast, his words were often lost on his audience. The court stenographer kept asking him to repeat what he had just said. Harry Owen asked him to speak more slowly.

Hana gave his version of the robbery, how he came in from the storeroom outside and found the crime taking place, how he was thrown to the ground and bound. He identified his own flashlight, which had been found outside with the blackjack. He said his biggest worries during the dark night came when the robbers were tying up his daughters and they were crying.

"I said, 'Don't hurt my girls,'" he said. "'Take what you want, but don't hurt my girls.'"

Hana admitted, under cross-examination by Noonan, that he had been arrested twice for violations of the Prohibition law. He said fear of a third arrest had driven him from the illegal liquor business. He claimed he had never been a big distributor of alcohol, that he "only sold to friends."

His wife, Elizabeth, and daughters Naomi, Harriet, and Doris also gave details from the robbery. None of them could make a positive identification of the defendant, though Mrs. Hana and Harriet both testified that they heard one of the robbers call another one "Verne."

"The robber said, 'Verne, we better get out of here,'" Mrs. Hana said. She also said she heard one of the robbers referred to as "Carleton."

All four of the women talked about the screams they heard from Mrs. Hana's father, Matt Cobb, from outside. Doris Hana testified that one of the robbers said to her mother, "Hurry up, or we will blow this place up." All four women talked about how frightened they were by the pistols.

"Did you make any noise before you were tied up?" Attorney Noonan asked Naomi Hana.

"Well," she replied, "I spoke a lot!"

Noonan asked that the testimony of the girls be stricken from the record because of their ages when the robbery occurred. The motion was denied.

Matt Cobb finished the victims' version of the robbery the next day. The seventy-four-year-old father of Elizabeth Hana, described in one account as a look-alike for "Popeye's father," was not the greatest witness. The loss of hearing sustained in the beating seven years earlier was evident. District Attorney McDonald had to stand within a foot of him and shout questions into his right ear. Cobb often seemed confused, sometimes giving answers that did not seem to match the questions.

"I was in bed," he said in his basic re-creation of the event. "It was about one o'clock in the morning. A tall man with a mask over his face came into my room, shoved a gun in my face and said, 'Stick 'em up.' I pulled the mask from his face and we struggled. He shouted, 'Van,' I mean, 'Verne.' Then another man came in. He hit me across the head with the butt of his gun. Then they tied me up and threw me on the bed.

"I got loose and I got out of the room through a window."

Cobb said he was dazed and wandering, perhaps twenty feet

from the restaurant, when his problems grew worse. He was attacked again.

"I saw a man coming on the run," he said. "He had seen me. He hollered to someone to give him a blackjack. Then he took the blackjack and hit me across the face and head. He knocked my teeth out. I fell onto the ground."

District Attorney McDonald asked, shouted, if Cobb could identify the man who attacked him in the bedroom.

"I think I could identify the man outside," the witness said.

Defense Attorney Noonan objected to the phrase "I think I could identify the man outside." The witness should either be able to identify the culprit or not, not "think" he could. Judge Owen denied the objection.

"How about the man who hit you in the bedroom?" McDonald shouted.

Cobb said nothing.

"Well, could you identify the man who hit you outside?"

Cobb spaced his hands wide and said the man was broadly built. McDonald asked, shouted, if Cobb could see the man in the courtroom.

"Yes," the witness said.

He pointed at Montague.

McDonald asked the question again.

"I think that's the man there," Cobb said. "He looks the same across the eyes."

Then he wavered.

"He looks too fat for him across the face."

Paul Poland, when asked to identify Montague as the man he had seen in a car with Roger Norton, had walked across the courtroom and placed a hand on Montague's shoulder. This identification was less convincing. What was the old man saying? Yes? Or no? Montague simply stared, no reaction, at the witness. He hadn't reacted to any of the testimony since the state's case had begun. The fact was duly reported that his suit today was green, the fourth different suit he had worn in four days.

When the cross-examination of Cobb began, Defense Attorney Noonan also had to shout. The longer the question-and-answer process went, the less Cobb seemed to understand. Noonan made important note of the fact that the witness sometimes said "Van" instead of "Verne" in his account of the attack. Noonan also tried to pick at Roger Norton's story through Cobb. In the detail of what happened outside the restaurant, when Cobb ran into Norton, the lawyer found openings.

"Did Norton say, 'Hello, Uncle Matt'?" the lawyer asked.

"No," Cobb replied.

"Did he have a gun in his hand?"

"Yes."

Norton's answers had been a direct opposite. Yes, Norton said he said, "Hello, Uncle Matt." No, he said he did not have a gun. Cobb also was unable to identify either the revolvers or the blackjack as the implements used in the crime. Noonan made him admit that there was no light in the bedroom when he was attacked the first time, and no lights outside the second time. Everything had happened in the dark.

A better set of witnesses for the prosecution were the golf clubs and the Gladstone bag that belonged to Moore. There was little doubt, as his driver's license and his baseball clippings and clothes and the pictures of assorted girls were displayed, that all of this physical evidence was attached to him. The golf clubs consisted of thirteen hickory-shafted irons, and a driver, brassie, and spoon. They were all average-size, not the built-up monsters that Montague had used in California. The balls in the bag were the older, smaller version used in 1930. A pair of spiked shoes was also in the bag.

Sgt. Paul McGinnis of the New York State Police and former trooper Donald Wood testified that they had found all of these items in the rumble seat of the wrecked Ford coupe on the night of the robbery. They detailed how they had chased the car, come upon the crash, then found John Sherry dead and Carleton wandering in the vicinity. Former trooper Wood testified that during the chase he had spotted a green Pontiac being driven fast in the opposite direction. He tried to catch the license plate, but saw only that the first letter was "D."

This led to the next witness, Trooper Harry Durand. He testified that he was on the lookout for a green Pontiac with a "D" plate due to Wood's report. At six in the morning near Schroon Lake, he spotted a car that fit the description and stopped it. The occupants, he said, were Roger Norton and LaVerne Moore, who gave his name as Lawrence Ryan.

Durand described what Moore was wearing that night—"a blue suit, no stripes"—and pointed at him in a positive identification. This was a corroboration of Norton's story, a second set of eyes to put Norton and Moore together on the night of the robbery. This was the heart of the prosecution's case.

Defense Attorney Noonan quickly tried to find holes in that corroboration.

"You have testified, Mr. Durand, that you stopped this car at six A.M.," Noonan said. "If Norton said it was 3:30 A.M., he was mistaken?"

"If he said that, he was," Durand said.

Noonan said he estimated that Durand probably had stopped more than five thousand cars during his career with the state police, and wondered how he could remember one man from one Pontiac in the dark over seven years ago. Durand said he had taken notes that night, but subsequently had lost them. He also said that Moore had stood in front of the headlights for at least part of the time. He knew what he knew. Period.

The state rested its case at the end of Durand's testimony. Noonan made a motion for dismissal, heard in Judge Owen's chambers, on the grounds that the state's case had not been proven. The motion was denied. With only an hour left in the day, Noonan opened his defense with three witnesses from Mechanicville: a city court judge, a deputy sheriff, and a policeman. They were all on the stand to give their impressions of Roger Norton, the state's lead witness.

"Have you heard his reputation for truth and veracity discussed by citizens of Mechanicville?" Noonan asked the policeman, Gustave Boucher, a representative question for all three witnesses.

"I have."

"Is it good or bad?"

"It is bad," Boucher replied with a representative answer.

Court was adjourned for the weekend.

The jurors were sequestered on the top floor of the main building of the Deer's Head Inn, another sign that this was not a normal seven-year-old case of a normal $750 armed robbery being tried in a normal way, so the weekend stretched out for them, long and boring. The highlight was "a motor tour of the Adirondacks" on Saturday. State troopers supervised as the men who had grown up in these mountains, these woods, were taken on their field trip through these same mountains and woods. In the rain.

John Montague left town on Friday night, destination undisclosed, but was back by Saturday at the Deer's Head, front and center on Sunday morning for nine o'clock Mass at St. Elizabeth's Roman Catholic Church. Three of the jurors were also spotted in the congregation.

The defendant had developed personal routines during the first week of the trial. He was an early riser every day, took a walk through the center of town in his buttoned-up camel's hair overcoat. Sometimes he walked alone; sometimes a state trooper walked with him, the two of them in friendly conversation.

He ate breakfast at the Deer's Head, sometimes alone, usually with Noonan and Robert Dudley, the local attorney. He ate well, tipped well. So said the cross-eyed waitress. He drank his one shot of bourbon at lunch, switched to a double scotch and water at the end of the day. He mostly ate his meals alone, although various friends from the Syracuse area visited.

The friends told reporters many of the old stories of their man's strength and abilities, added a couple of new ones. He bowled 190 the first time he ever tried the sport; then was thrown out in the middle of the next string for throwing the ball overhanded. He ran the pool table the first time he played nine ball. The reporters themselves added a new one in Elizabethtown when Montague joined Jimmy Kilgallen of the *Journal-American* in an arcade game of SkeeBall, first time, and rolled a 290, a very good score.

The biggest addition to the legend during the week came in the men's room of the courthouse during an afternoon break. Faced with one of those balky dispensers of paper towels that wouldn't dispense, Montague banged it a couple of times with no results, then put his fingers into the little metal slot and pulled it wider, bent it, sort of like opening an alligator's clenched teeth. He put forefinger and thumb through the opening, now large, and removed a towel and dried his hands.

The one embarrassing moment came in the tavern at the Deer's Head. A reporter, drinking, called Montague to come over. The defendant came, not noticing that District Attorney McDonald was next to the reporter.

"Mr. Montague, hey," the reporter said, "I want you to meet the district attorney."

"I think I know Mr. Moore," McDonald said with emphasis on the name.

Montague just walked away.

On Sunday afternoon, for the first time during the trial, he sat down with reporters in a reception room at the Deer's Head. Some of those Syracuse friends, in the middle of their tales, had said that their man had boasted that he could outdrive Jimmy Thomson and Sammy Snead, now the two longest hitters on the PGA Tour, by fifty yards. The words had reached print and Montague wanted to set the record straight: he had never said that.

"I never said a thing like that in my life," he said. "Thomson and Snead are a couple of mighty hitters. I've only met Snead once, but I've known Thomson for some time and he's a wonderful golfer and a wonderful fellow. He knows, and so does everybody else in the PGA, that I'd never go around bragging.

I'd never say a word to hurt those fellows. If I said anything at all about them, I'd boost them, not knock them. A golf pro works hard. He deserves a break."

The denial—attached quickly with the caveat, "I'll take a backseat to no one in my driving, though"—opened the floor for more talk about golf. Soon Montague was verifying that he did knock a bird off a wire once ("But maybe I couldn't do it again") and did put out the lights on the street sign in Utica ("It was just one of those things") and that all of those great scores in Palm Springs and at Lakeside were real. He mentioned numbers, shot in practice, than would never be reached in tournament competition.

"The best round of golf I ever had was a 54," he said. "I shot it at Palm Springs a couple of years ago. It's kind of an easy course if you hit a long ball and pancake your approaches."

He said he did have an average of 68 over two years at Lakeside. He said he did shoot 61-61-61-58 over a four-day stretch at Palm Springs with George Von Elm as they practiced for a match against local hotshots, which never materialized. He said he did a lot of things playing golf.

"But," he said, "golf is not my life."

He refused to say much about the trial, as did Noonan. They both said that Montague's mother and sisters were coming to town for Monday's session, but didn't know if the women would be put on the stand.

The big news on Sunday night came from the jurors. They sent out for three fiddles, then held an all-male square dance on the top floor of the Deer's Head. The sound of "Turkey in the Straw" could still be heard at ten o'clock, rolling over the few and empty streets of Elizabethtown.

The white-haired mother of John Montague did indeed take the stand. Attorney Noonan called the name of Mary Moore late in the morning of October 25, 1937, and the small, frail woman, dressed in black, moved to the front of the room. The remnants of an Irish brogue were in her voice as she repeated the oath. If the lawyer had requested "a sympathetic mother type" from the casting rolls of his client's friends in Hollywood, he couldn't have found a better choice. She was a humble penitent in the great hall of justice.

Four witnesses from Syracuse had preceded her to start the day. Daniel M. Shea, the retired fire chief; Julia Ryan, a member of the board of supervisors; Thomas F. Kendrick, postal worker; and undertaker Michael Callahan all testified that the reputation of Mrs. Moore's son was "good" or "very good," and that he was "honest."

"What is this," District Attorney McDonald asked in the midst of all the kind words, "a neighborhood rally?"

Mrs. Moore presumably would be another contributor to this group. She would talk quietly about a good boy from a good family. The jury would look at her and think about apple pie and pot roast dinners and Sunday afternoons and lemonade. Her testimony would be predictable and positive and, thank you very much, she would be done.

This was not exactly what happened.

"Do you recall the night of August 4, 1930, and, if so, did your son come home that night?" Noonan asked in an early, important stretch of dialogue.

"Yes," Mrs. Moore said. "He came home around midnight."

"And did he spend the night there?"

"Yes, in bed."

"And was he there on the next day, August 5, 1930?"

"Yes."

Mary Moore gave her son an alibi.

Her words were stunning. The defense's strategy, in doubt until now, was laid on the table: the defendant didn't commit the robbery; wasn't even there. He didn't do it!

Never had Montague, or Noonan, indicated once that this was the case they would try to prove. Never had they even indicated that it was an option. Noonan's challenges to the state's witnesses about their identifications of his client had seemed to be pro forma attempts to create doubt, to challenge credibility, but never had he implied that his client was not part of the four-man group of bandits. Montague didn't do it? Never once had Noonan or his client made that case publicly inside or outside the courtroom. Never once, until now, had anyone said that. Jerry Giesler hadn't even said it back in California.

Mrs. Moore said that her son was at home on the night of August 4, 1930, and again on the night of the fifth, and on the morning of the sixth he kissed her good-bye and said he was off to play either professional baseball or golf. She didn't see him or talk to him for over seven years after that kiss.

"On the Sunday after he left, I went down at midnight to answer the bell," Mrs. Moore said. "Troopers and a detective stood at the door. The detective asked if LaVerne was home and I said, 'No,' he wasn't.

"I turned to the troopers and said: 'You can come in and see if you want to,' but the detective said, 'Mrs. Moore, we'll take your word for it.'

"I said he'd left on Wednesday morning. I said, 'He kissed me good-bye and said, "Good-bye, Mother dear, I'll see you later. I'm going to play either golf or baseball." ' "

"Did you hear from LaVerne from the time he left until the time he came back in August this year?" Noonan asked.

"Through my son, Harold," Mrs. Moore said. "Yes."

Her testimony took less than ten minutes—District Attorney McDonald waived cross-examination, seeing no gain with the jury for badgering a kindly old mother—but she had flipped the entire proceedings. There was a new road to travel, and Noonan was more than prepared for the trip. Like a gin rummy player laying out what he thinks is a very good hand, the lawyer now brought one witness after another to reinforce Mary Moore's words.

First were the defendant's sisters, Madeline McGrath and Mary Allen. Both had been single seven years ago. Both had been living at home on Stolp Avenue. Both said LaVerne was there on the night of August 4, 1930. He didn't do it! He was home! Mrs. Allen said LaVerne drove her to work on the morning of August 5. Mrs. McGrath said she was awake when he came home on the night of August 4. Syracuse was almost two hundred miles from Jay, New York. He couldn't have been in Jay at any time during the night. He didn't do it!

District Attorney McDonald did not waive cross-examination privileges with the sisters. He hammered at both of the women, obviously skeptical of their stories. Neither sister buckled.

"Did you know where your brother was between 1930 and 1937?" McDonald asked Mary Allen.

"No," she replied.

"Did you know that he was using the name 'John Montague'?"

"No."

"But weren't you ever curious? Didn't you ever ask where your brother was or what he was doing?"

"I was the baby of the family. The family just didn't discuss these things with me."

Mrs. McGrath said that she knew her mother received messages through her brother Harold once a month, but didn't know much more. She also said she didn't know LaVerne used a different name.

"Did Harold tell you where LaVerne was?"

"No."

"Was LaVerne's absence discussed by the family?"

"No."

"And no one inquired as to where he was?"

"They might have."

McDonald shook his head.

Judge Owen recessed the court for lunch after Mrs. McGrath's testimony. The reporters pounded out fast stories about this new development—"Old Mother Aids Monty" was the headline the next day in the *Daily Mirror*—and wondered what would come next. A new energy was in the trial now.

———

Noonan's first witness in the afternoon was Francis McLaughlin, an employee in the circulation department of the *Washington (D.C.) Star* newspaper. McLaughlin had been the subject of speculation since his name appeared on the defense's list of possible witnesses at the start of the trial. The prosecution had always wondered where exactly he fit. Roger Norton included McLaughlin in a group with LaVerne, William Carleton, and himself that went to Hana's restaurant a week before the robbery to plan a liquor deal, but that was the only mention of McLaughlin.

Now he turned out to be a second piece of the defendant's alibi. That was where he fit.

McLaughlin testified that he picked up LaVerne Moore at a golf driving range on the night of August 4, then drove him home around midnight. He said they had been friends since boyhood in Syracuse and admitted they had been involved in the illegal liquor business together in 1930. They had not, he said, been involved in this robbery.

District Attorney McDonald was able to draw out information that McLaughlin had been arrested for possessing policy slips, for breach of the peace, and for public intoxication, but again was unable to shake his story. McLaughlin repeated that he had taken the golfer home after the golfer hit golf balls. The golfer didn't do it! Couldn't do it! He was hitting golf balls.

The next important witness was William Carleton, the second convicted robber. Carleton had served five years in prison in Clinton, New York, for the crime. Missing a couple of front teeth, defiant and tough, now using the alias "William Martin," he was a picture off the post office wall of the 1930s career criminal.

"The hard-eyed Martin then took the stand," Meyer Berger wrote the next day in the *New York Times*. "His back tight against the witness chair, his shifty eyes going from questioner to defendant, he gave swift and sharp answers. Only when hard pressed on cross-examination did he lose poise. Then he came close to snarling."

Carleton/Martin was the third piece of John Montague's alibi. Carleton/Martin said Moore/Montague was not part of the gang of robbers. He didn't do it! He wasn't there!

"The other man in the crew was named 'Burns,' " Carleton testified.

The name was a convenient alternative to the "Verne" that Matt Cobb and the Hana children had heard shouted in the middle of the robbery. Maybe they heard "Burns" instead. Carleton said he didn't know much about "Burns," didn't know where he lived, where he worked, what he was doing now. Didn't know his first name. "Burns" was a one-night recruit for the job. He apparently did most of the dirtiest work, too.

District Attorney McDonald asked if Carleton had known from the beginning the reason for the trip to Hana's restaurant. Carleton admitted that he did.

"Sure, we went there to rob the joint," he said. "Norton knew the spot. He told me how Kin Hana was afraid of banks and kept plenty of money right in the place."

"Did you tie up the children?"

"The Burns guy was supposed to tie 'em up. I suppose he did."

"Did you see anyone beat Matt Cobb?"

"No. I heard a commotion, but I didn't know the old man was around."

"Do you remember that after you were arrested you were asked if LaVerne Moore was with you and you denied it?"

"I remember that you asked me a lot of questions and you may remember that I didn't tell you nothing."

Carleton explained the presence of Moore/Montague's golf clubs and Gladstone bag in the car. He said he and Moore had taken a trip to Rochester and planned another trip to Saratoga. Carleton said he was going to look for a job in Saratoga; Moore was going to play golf. No, they had not taken a trip to Jay together. The clubs and the Gladstone bag did, but not the man. Carleton admitted that LaVerne Moore was his friend. He also admitted that Moore was with Norton, McLaughlin, and himself when they went to the restaurant in the week preceding the crime.

He said Moore had introduced him to Norton. He said Norton was the reason for the robbery.

"Norton told me that Hana was responsible for a load of my liquor that had been knocked off a few months previous," Carleton said. "Norton told me that Hana had tipped off the load and that's why it was knocked off.

"I decided then and there that I'd rob the place and get even. Norton gave me some dope on how Hana kept his money. I told him not to mention anything to Moore and McLaughlin about our plans. They were supposed to share in our bootlegging deal, if we disposed of some of the liquor Hana was supposed to get, but they weren't in on the robbery.

"On the night of the robbery I came to Mechanicville with John Sherry. Norton was there with a man named Burns. Yeah, Burns. About my size; short, stocky. We went to Hana's and robbed the place."

"Did Moore ever ride with you when you were carrying liquor?" the district attorney asked.

"No."

"What was the purpose of Moore, Norton, and McLaughlin going to the Kin Hana place with you?"

"If I done business, they would get part of the profits."

"About the man Burns? Did he look like LaVerne Moore?"

"I can't say what he looked like."

McDonald treated Carleton with the same distaste Noonan had shown for Norton, acting as if just talking to the man was a sin against nature. At one point the district attorney picked up one of the revolvers from the table and asked Carleton if he had held it over Elizabeth Hana while she knelt down and opened the safe. The robber admitted that he had. The district attorney also had Carleton admit that he had been involved in other burglaries, had been arrested for gun possession as far back as 1923, and had worked as "a payoff man" at a gambling house in Saratoga.

Carleton's testimony concluded the session. Noonan told the judge he had only a few more witnesses and the defense would probably rest its case by noon the next day. Closing arguments could be held in the afternoon. The jury would have the case by dinnertime.

The quote from the witness chair everyone remembered most at the Deer's Head that night had come from Mary Moore. It wasn't a response to any of the questions, was more like an aside, spoken simply to fill air, a thought that seemed to escape from the old woman's head, a sentence without a filter.

"He was always a good boy to me," John Montague's mother had said.

CHAPTER NINE

ELIZABETHTOWN, NEW YORK

October 26, 1937

ight o'clock at night. Maybe eight-thirty. The defendant stood on the porch of the Deer's Head Inn with his cigarette. The collar of his camel's hair overcoat was turned up against the cold as he stared across the street at a small building next to the courthouse. The lights were lit, welcoming and ominous and maddening, all at once. Jesus, God, the suspense was awful.

The arguments were done. The trial was in its last stage.

The farmers and laborers and carpenters, the twelve men good and true, were deciding John Montague's fate. He replayed the presentations and arguments during the past week in front of Judge Harry E. Owen, remembered who had paid attention, who had not, who had laughed, who had sat there like the Sphinx; facial tics and flannel shirts and haircuts, good and bad, everything examined, looking for a clue.

What were they doing?

"There is one place, gentlemen, where mercy and sympathy cannot enter and that is the jury room," Judge Owen had said in his instructions at six o'clock. "Power to show mercy is given to the governor and to the court.

"If you find the defendant committed robbery in the first degree in one or more of the four ways it can be committed, then you must return a verdict of guilty. If, after careful consideration of the evidence, you find you have a reasonable doubt that the defendant is guilty, it is your duty to acquit."

The piano could be heard, noises, from the tavern at the Deer's Head, everybody in the place excited, thinking about going home, leaving this provincial outpost, another sticker on the luggage, a little check mark on the itinerary of life experience, another stop on the road. Not so for the man at the center of the production.

This was the ball game. This was everything. His future was a single question mark, and other people, these now-familiar strangers, were the only ones who had the answer. He had no control. A man of control, who always worked the odds his way, who could bend his fate with concentration and skill, head down, wrists cocked, power rising through his legs, packaged in the full torque of his body, released with grace and determination and a good follow-through, a man who could send his own good news hurtling through the air to land on a green carpet, *plop*, four feet from the given hole, could do nothing now.

Done.

He smoked his cigarette and the reporters left him alone. Everybody left him alone. He spoke, just for a sentence or two with his business manager, Marty Forkins.

"I just want to tell you, Marty, that I wasn't there that night. I wouldn't kid you."

Alone again. Another cigarette.

There had never been a day in the life of John Montague like this one under any name he used. There would never be another.

What were they doing?

The day had begun with a secret. He knew the secret and James M. Noonan knew the secret and maybe the other lawyers on the team knew, but nobody else in the courtroom knew. The idea was to act normal, give no clues, then to lay out the secret with a grand flourish, a rabbit from a hat, a coin plunked from some spellbound child's ear.

John Montague sat in the same chair that he had occupied at the same table for a week. Noonan resumed the work of trying to prove his client was innocent, presenting his case for the second day.

The initial piece of business was to read into the record the letters from the famous friends of John Montague. Noonan did the job. He moved into the witness box, sat down, acted as the voice for all of the Hollywood voices—their representative more than the voice for the defense.

The theatrical attorney, who could have done fine work in

any community production of Shakespeare, a perfect Falstaff, a serviceable Richard III, maybe not Hamlet, sat and read with vigor and feeling the testaments from Bing Crosby, Oliver Hardy, Andy Devine, Guy Kibbee, Richard Arlen, and Los Angeles sportswriter Mark Kelly that his client was "charming and honest."

"I have never known him to behave other than as a gentleman," Noonan read as Crosby. "The circle that I moved in accepted him as an upright man."

"I have gone on fishing trips, hunting trips and golfing trips with him," Noonan read as Oliver Hardy. "He is absolutely above reproach. He has handled sums of money for me where it would have been possible for him to take some if he wanted to. He has been in my home on many occasions where expensive jewelry was kept and he never evidenced any indication to be dishonest. In fact, I would trust him with anything at any time."

The reading took a while. There were fourteen depositions in all: from a Catholic priest in Los Angeles, from businessmen, from film directors as well as the stars. The repetitive quality of the content about the defendant's "peacefulness and quiet," his "honesty and truthfulness" eventually triumphed over Noonan's vigor. It was a relief when he was done.

The lawyer stood up and left the witness box, returned to the defense table as counsel, seemed lost in thought....

Now!

He turned to the judge....

Now!

"Swear the defendant," Noonan said.

John Montague took the stand. The secret was out.

No reporters had predicted that he would testify. Most predicted that he wouldn't. Noonan had led them toward that prediction, never firm one way or the other, but always with that look, that sound in his voice indicating that it would be foolish to put his client on the stand.

The positive side of promising to tell "the truth, the whole truth, nothing but the truth" was that Montague could be the final and possibly best character witness for LaVerne Moore, that frenetic young man who had run free, run wild, and was accused of doing this bad deed seven years ago. Look at who LaVerne Moore was now. Look at what he had become.

The negative side was that he was now open to all questions from District Attorney McDonald. The DA could pick at the details of his story, pound at all questions of character, pick and pound and attempt to leave no more than a pile of dust at the end. A bunch of the mystery in John Montague's mysterious life would be exposed to direct sunlight for the first time and under oath.

Testifying was a flat-out bet on himself, the ultimate five-dollar Nassau, the biggest gamble the gambler had ever made. No one was falling asleep now as he made his way to the witness box and repeated the oath. The courtroom, packed in thin hopes of witnessing this exact moment, was silent.

"What is your name?" Noonan asked.

"LaVerne Moore," the defendant replied.

"Your home?"

"Syracuse, New York."

"Where were you on the night of August 4, 1930?"

"I was home in bed that night and until the morning of August fifth."

If Montague was nervous, it did not show. His voice was even, his eyes on his attorney. He folded his thick hands in his lap. Noonan asked if he had been in a car with Roger Norton on the night of August 4, 1930, if he had been with the members of the gang in the "stickup" of Hana's restaurant.

"I was not," Montague replied.

"Were you in Kin Hana's restaurant the night the crime was committed?"

"I was not."

Noonan acted as if this were a perfunctory exercise, his client filling out a necessary form for the jury. He knew what the answers would be and his client knew what the answers would be and the jury knew what the answers would be. The goal was to get the job, the task, done, get it out of the way.

"Were you ever convicted of a crime?" Noonan asked.

"I was."

"When was that?"

"In 1927 in Syracuse. It was a misdemeanor."

"Are you sure there was no other crime?"

Montague seemed to think about his answer. He took his time.

"Weren't you fined five dollars once for stealing cherries?" the lawyer asked, to help with his client's recall.

The defendant chuckled.

"Yes."

"That was many years ago."

"I don't remember how many years."

"When you were around thirteen, let's say, or fourteen."

"Yes."

That was the end.

"Your witness," Noonan abruptly said.

The exercise had taken no more than four minutes.

The intent of putting Montague on the stand, obvious now, was to have him tangle with District Attorney McDonald. This encounter would resemble the one in the hotel room across the street two months earlier when sportswriter Henry McLemore was invited to swing away, to hit the defendant anywhere he wanted. The hope was that in the end McDonald would walk off, as McLemore had, rubbing his knuckles. Montague would be without dents.

The district attorney, as requested, came out swinging.

"What is a misdemeanor?" he asked for his first question.

"Perhaps I can't define the law as regards a misdemeanor," Montague replied.

"Weren't you arrested for extortion?"

"Yes."

"That's a felony."

"I was permitted to plead petty larceny."

And so it began.

The interrogation would take the next two hours. McDonald would ask every question with an air of disbelief, as if Montague's previous answers had been hollow and wrong to his ears. Montague would answer calmly sometimes, but sometimes contempt would surface, contempt and anger, and he would shout back. The dialogue would sometimes become tavern argument as much as courtroom testimony.

McDonald had Montague explain the facts of the extortion/petty larceny charge, the sixty dollars made from the beer-selling owner of a grocery store. Montague did not like the tone of these questions, answered sharply for the first time, and was admonished for the first time by Judge Owen.

McDonald then turned to the Gladstone bag and the golf clubs, which had been brought back to the courtroom. He asked Montague to step down from the witness chair and identify the items in the bag, affirm or deny if they belonged to him. Montague did as requested. He and McDonald and Noonan gathered around the bag and went over each item. Everything, it was agreed, belonged to the defendant, even the fourteen pairs of socks.

McDonald then asked how the clothes, the clubs, the driver's license, all of the other items—the clippings, the socks—happened to be in Carleton's car. Montague said he planned to take a short trip to Saratoga with Carleton and already had taken a short trip to Rochester with him.

"Why did you take so many clothes for just a short visit?" the district attorney asked.

"I always carried that much," Montague said.

"There are two suits here. How many suits do you wear a day?"

"I change them often. I like to be clean."

McDonald moved to Montague's exodus west. Montague said he left on the morning of August 6, 1930, and drove first to Rochester, where he sold his car. The car was a 1925 Model A Ford and he received $250. He then went from Rochester by train to Chicago.

"From there I went to Los Angeles. I stayed in a hotel for two days, then I found an apartment," the defendant said.

"When did you change your name to John Montague?"

"After that, shortly after I got to Los Angeles. In 1930."

"Why did you change your name?"

"Because it was different than LaVerne Moore."

"Were you ashamed of the name Moore?"

"I was not and am not."

"Then why did you change?"

"Because I was ashamed."

"Ashamed of what?"

"Because my bag and belongings were found in Carleton's car."

"Then you ran away because of that?"

"I did."

"Why did you take the name of Montague?"

"Because it sounded good."

The thoroughness of the change of names and places seemed to amaze McDonald. Wasn't this the man who now was so concerned about the health of his mother? Where was the concern for her during all of the time he was in California? Montague now would be in his eighth year away from his family.

"And during these past eight years, you never wrote to your mother, never sent her a card on Mother's Day?" the district attorney asked.

"I didn't, but I wrote to my brother twice quarterly and told him to tell my mother I was safe and doing well," the defendant replied.

"And did your brother write back?"

"Yes, he did."

Montague explained that he had rented the post office box

belonging to a man named Monroe Eckels from a man named Sweeny. That way he was able to keep up correspondence.

McDonald began a deeper examination of Montague's life in Los Angeles. How did a man survive the way he did, not only survive, but flourish? When did he start playing golf in Los Angeles? How did he find a job when jobs were scarce? Montague said he bought a set of secondhand clubs at a shop and played first at a public course. He said he met a man named Eddie Schaefer at the Rancho Golf Club, a public golf course. Schaefer introduced him to a Colonel Rogers, who owned an automotive engineering firm that sold superchargers among other products for cars. Montague said Rogers hired him as a contact man and salesman, a job he held until 1935.

"What was your salary?"

"I had a drawing account of one hundred dollars a month."

"But what was your salary?"

"I worked on commission."

"What were your average earnings?"

"A hundred dollars a month. Things weren't too good then."

"And you lived on that?"

"I did."

"Were you a member of a golf club?"

"In 1933, I was a member of the Lakeside Golf Club."

"And do you know the fee there?"

"Sixty-six dollars for three months."

The economics didn't fit for the district attorney. A membership at Lakeside, greens fees, food, lodging, transportation, and clothes added up to more than a hundred dollars per month. How did Montague survive with a fast-spending crowd of rich and famous people? Montague said he traveled with "an extravagant crowd, but didn't attempt to keep up my end as expensively as they.

"I traveled with them as a guest most of the time," he said.

"Was your company so charming that they paid your expenses?" McDonald asked.

"I don't know how charming I was, but I was accepted."

"How much rent did you pay for your apartment?"

"Thirty-five dollars a month."

"Out of the rest you bought your clothes, food, paid greens fees and did other things?"

"Yes, I was able to as some things were paid for me."

"How many suits do you have here in Elizabethtown?"

"Four, I believe."

The district attorney looked at the workingmen jurors.

"That may not be a lot in Hollywood," he said, "but around here that's a heap of dressing."

More questions about his economic situation in Hollywood made Montague angry. They made him sound like a moocher, a sycophant on the dole.

"You met a number of people prominent in the public eye, didn't you?" the district attorney said.

"Yes."

"You were entertained by them and you entertained them."

"I didn't entertain them."

"You didn't keep up your end?"

"I kept up my end," Montague snapped. "At least to some extent."

McDonald hammered for a moment at the request to Governor Merriam in California not to sign the extradition papers to New York. In the seven-week process, before Montague dropped his plea, he never denied participation in the crime. He never really had denied his participation until one day ago. Indeed, in that widely circulated quote after his arrest he talked about "a mistake" he had made as a wild youth and that he had been meaning to go back East and "clear that up."

Montague said he had acted solely on the advice of his lawyers in California. The quote? He said that had been exaggerated.

"Was there any time in California you played a lot of golf?" McDonald asked.

"There was."

"And did you object to photographers taking pictures of you?"

"I did."

"And did you once smash a photographer's camera?"

"I did not. I took out the slide. I gave him fifty dollars."

"You were afraid that you might be identified if your picture was taken?"

"Possibly so."

"Did you know that you, Carleton, and Norton had been indicted for this crime?"

"I did."

"I suggest that might be the reason why you didn't want your picture taken."

"Perhaps."

McDonald returned his questions to New York and the past. He asked about the trip Montague took with William Carleton, Francis McLaughlin, and Roger Norton to the Hana restaurant near the end of July to see if it was a good place "for a liquor drop." Montague admitted he was part of that trip. He said the problem was that they never had a chance to talk to Kin Hana that day. He said the possibilities of using Hana's place as a drop were discussed again on August 1 in a restaurant in Utica, but that Carleton didn't think the idea would work. Montague denied being with Norton in a car that was spotted by Paul Poland.

"Isn't it a fact that when you ran away you went to Florida and then to Mexico and then to California?" McDonald suddenly asked.

"No, sir."

"Didn't you play golf for high stakes when you were in California?"

"I wouldn't say so. I have played five dollars, five dollars, five dollars."

Judge Harry Owen interrupted with a question. The judge, who must have paid attention to golf, asked if Montague had played against professional Olin Dutra for a side bet of $2,500.

"No," Montague said with a smile.

"Weren't your earnings in California largely from golf?" District Attorney McDonald now asked.

"I don't think so," Montague said. He added that he sometimes prospected for gold for three years in California. He went sometimes when weather conditions were appropriate.

McDonald now read an affidavit Montague had signed in California in August. In the affidavit, Montague denied that he had ever previously said that he had struck Matt Cobb with a blackjack. McDonald used the words to begin a closing barrage of questions.

The pace would quicken during the barrage. Montague's voice would grow louder with each reply. If this were a heavyweight championship fight or a Broadway musical finale, the customers would have been standing for the last ten seconds. The two men virtually shouted at each other.

"Do you deny that you beat the old man in his room that night?" McDonald asked.

"I deny it," Montague said.

"Did you not later, outside the house, call to Norton for a blackjack and beat Cobb again?"

"I deny it."

"Do you deny that you helped tie Hana and Mrs. Hana and members of the Hana family?"

"I deny it."

"Did you ever wear a mask the night of the Hana holdup?"

"I deny it."

"Didn't Sherry, who was in Cobb's room, call 'Verne,' and didn't you go in and hit the old man with a pistol?"

"I deny it."

"Did you carry a gun into the Hana place that night?"

"I deny it."

"Didn't Roger Norton tell you to let the old man up?"

"I deny it."

"Did you drive away in Norton's car?"

"I deny it."

"Were you pursued by troopers and did you interfere with their efforts to get past you?"

"I deny it."

"Do you deny you were stopped late by State Trooper Durand?"

"I deny it."

"Then State Trooper Durand was telling a falsehood on the stand?"

"He was."

"In fact, you deny being at the holdup?"

"I do."

"That's all."

After a break for lunch, the jury and the participants from both sides and Judge Owen and everybody else returned at two o'clock for the summations by Noonan and McDonald. This again was intense verbal combat. Noonan, selected to replace Jerry Giesler, had been paid premium rates just for this moment. He was a master of the hellfire and damnation school of oratory, part of the American tradition of preacher-lawyers.

He did not disappoint.

His words thundered through the tiny courtroom. He shook the walls with his manufactured passion. For over two hours— a midafternoon recess slowing him down not at all—he stated his client's case. He was an Adirondack version of Clarence Darrow, incensed and bemused and, yes, saddened by the accusations that had been made against a good and honest man.

"John Montague is not on trial!" he bellowed. "The defendant is LaVerne Moore of Syracuse, a boy the state contends was in four different places at the Hana restaurant at one and the same time on the night of the robbery. I'm not trying to pin any wings on LaVerne Moore. I think he used bad judgment when he picked some of the friends he had back in 1930. But he was a healthy American boy full of vitality. He wasn't any sissy.

"You saw Mrs. Moore sit on that stand and tell you where LaVerne Moore was on the night of the robbery. I've been around some time, gentlemen, but I've never seen a sweeter, kinder, more delightful old lady than that. She never would breed a boy who would put a mask on his face, go into a place with a gun and say, 'Gimme your money.' "

LaVerne Moore with a gun? Noonan picked one of the revolvers off the exhibits table and waved it in the air. That was how ridiculous it would look, LaVerne Moore with a gun. He might have been a boy who invaded cherry orchards, "even as you and I did," but he was not one to be found with a gun!

Much of Noonan's time was spent dismembering Roger Norton, the state's prime witness, referring to him often as "that vulture." Norton was "the squeamish, crafty, Norton, a beautiful example of purity" (hah), a "maneuvering master of perjury." Norton surely had lied to save himself from more trouble. Hadn't three people, defense witnesses, come to the stand simply to call him a liar? He was a liar.

Noonan discounted the testimony of the Hana family and Paul Poland and especially poor, disoriented Matt Cobb. None of them could identify his client. The physical evidence, the golf clubs and Gladstone bag, was in the trunk of the car for the exact reason both Montague and the driver of the car, William Carleton, said it was: they were going on a trip to Saratoga. They were telling the truth.

Noonan made special note of the fact that he and his client both were from a different part of the state and the district attorney was not. He pleaded that the jurors give the DA no extra credit or consideration because he was a neighbor and they would continue to see him during their daily travels once the trial ended. The trial should be decided on the evidence, by what the twelve men saw in front of them.

And they saw Roger Norton. Didn't they?

"This case," Noonan said in his finish, "simmers down to this: will you believe Roger Norton, a squealing, squirming, framing mugg, or will you believe that dear, delightful old lady, her daughters, and the men and women of Syracuse and Hollywood who have testified that this is an honest man?

"If you fail to believe Roger Norton—and, gentlemen, how could you do anything else?—you must acquit."

Noonan's presentation was so powerful that even District Attorney McDonald, who followed him in front of the bench for the state's closing argument, was moved to comment. He apologized, in a plainspoken, appreciative way, that he couldn't hope to match Noonan for rhetoric. McDonald then laid out his version of the case in half the time the lawyer for the defense took, an hour, and at half the decibels. His image, his personality, was much more understated. He was the local guy, the public servant, the good guy doing his job.

That didn't mean he was without passion. If he didn't have the drama of Noonan, he had just as much conviction.

"I want to say that I have seldom tried a case where the indication of guilt was so strong," Thomas McDonald said, "where the defense was so weak."

The prosecutor said a parade of perjurers, liars, had taken the stand to help their friend or family member. It was sad to see. Francis McLaughlin, William Carleton—and did you get a look at him?—Mary Moore, Madeline McGrath, and Mary

Allen all had provided a thin alibi for an obviously guilty man. LaVerne Moore himself had lied again and again.

The lies had been concocted after the fight against extradition had failed. Why had the defendant not professed his innocence from the start? The bag of getaway clothes and personal effects, including his golf clothes, showed what he was doing. Roger Norton said it. Moore was going to take off. "Verne," not any "Burns," was at that restaurant that night. Trooper Harry Durand saw him. Why would Trooper Durand lie? The truth was obvious.

McDonald finished by calling the defendant "cowardly and selfish." What kind of man would allow his mother to come into court and "tell falsehoods on his behalf"? This was a man who "hid behind the skirts of his mother and sisters." This was a guilty man.

McDonald asked the jury to convict LaVerne Moore of first degree armed robbery. Moore was no different from the two other robbers who had been convicted, no different from the one who died. Thank you very much, gentlemen. The man was guilty.

Judge Harry Owen charged the jury. The time was five o'clock. The jury walked across the street, had dinner at the Deer's Head Inn, then came back to the small building next to the courthouse and went to work at six. Everybody else began the nervous wait.

The verdict was very much in doubt. This was not a trial shaped by nuance. Somebody was lying. A couple of somebodies were lying, at least. Either Roger Norton was a vulture and Trooper

Harry Durand was mistaken, or John Montague and the women in his family and his cronies had created a fable to keep him out of jail. There was no middle ground to the case, a fact detailed in Judge Owen's instructions. The jurors had to pick a side, either to send Montague to prison for first-degree armed robbery or to set him free. There was no alternative for a reduced charge.

The reporters at the Deer's Head now had to hustle out stories about the day's tumultuous proceedings, then stay close for a possible verdict and a new lead paragraph to be written under a new banner headline. There was no sense of how long the deliberations might take.

Bob Considine of the *Daily Mirror* filled his On the Line column space with an off-the-subject treatise on hunting in the Adirondacks that would withstand any or no verdict. Even here, though, he couldn't keep his thoughts completely off the trial.

"Deer are the star performers in this annual bombardment up in the nearby hills, but they don't complete the larder," he wrote. "This is open season, too, on any bears you might find prowling around Wall Street or anywhere else. And mink, if you do not take them 'by chemicals, gas or poison.' After November 10, you can kill a skunk, if you don't preface the act by digging it out of its hole. The frog season closes next week. It's against the law to shoot a turtle, in case that's been worrying you. It's against the law, too, for a hotel to put venison on its menu, and nothing that's been dragged out of the hills can be sold. District Attorney Thomas McDonald says it's open season on John Montague, too, but this could not be checked at an early hour today."

The rumors started somewhere during the night—one man told Montague that the first ballot had gone 10–2, in favor of "guilty," and Montague grunted—but no one really knew. The small building next to the courthouse was the most important spot in the universe. The lights had not gone out. The decision was still being considered.

Montague smoked another cigarette.

What were they doing?

He stared at the leaf-filled street, the leaves wet and plastered to the ground. The weather had been lousy for the entire trial. There had even been a touch of snow.

Sometime between 10:00 and 10:30 on the night of October 26, 1937, the bells from the courthouse began to ring. People came from everywhere, fast as they could. There hadn't been this much activity this late at night this late in the year in Elizabethtown for as long as anyone could remember.

John Montague joined the crowd that crossed the street. Everyone gave him room.

———

"Gentlemen of the jury, have you reached a verdict?"

"We have, Your Honor."

The foreman of the jury was Alvin Woods. He was a laborer.

"What find you?"

"We find the defendant not guilty of first-degree robbery."

A whoop, a holler, a roar reverberated through the little courtroom. The spectators stood and cheered as if they each had won the Irish sweepstakes. A quick head count showed little dissent, maybe none. The popularity of the decision, the noise from the outburst, was startling, so startling that Judge Owen rapped his gavel, rapped again, and ordered the room cleared. He was flustered, but more than that he was mad.

When the spectators were gone, he turned toward the jury. He still was fuming.

"I am sorry to say that your verdict *is not in accord* with the one that I think you *should* have rendered," he said. "But that's up to you and not to me."

The judge thought the verdict stunk.

This was the Dutch Schultz case all over again. The famous man and the big-money lawyer from Albany had beaten the system in the small-town setting. Or at least that was what Harry Owen believed. He was disgusted by the work of his neighbors.

And, once again, it didn't matter.

Maybe Montague's string of witnesses, his mother and sisters, had created enough reasonable doubt to confuse the jury. Maybe Noonan's eloquence confused them. Maybe Montague's celebrity wowed them, the affidavits from all of the famous people. Maybe the case was just too old, a leftover from a time and a law that just seemed silly now. Everybody was still alive, doing well, what's the problem? Maybe, maybe, maybe.

James M. Noonan moved for release of bail for his client. Judge Owen agreed. Noonan addressed the jury.

"I want to thank you gentlemen on my behalf and the behalf of my client," the lawyer said. "Who will thank you himself."

"Gentlemen of the jury..." John Montague began, standing, a smile across his face.

Owen rapped his gavel.

"This is no show," the judge said, still angry.

Noonan pulled his client back down to the defense table by his sleeve.

"I'm sorry, Your Honor," Montague said.

The judge gaveled the court closed, left the bench, and the doors were opened and, okay, now it was a show. The crowd engulfed Montague, shaking his hand, congratulating him. William Carleton was in the front of the pack. Montague threw his arms around Noonan and kissed him and everyone cheered. It was one of those moments reserved for the ends of close elections and athletic events. Women wanted to touch John Montague, meet him, hug him. The men lifted him on their shoulders—Carleton part of the group—and carried him out the door toward a free-flowing celebration that had already begun at the Deer's Head Inn.

The jury had taken five ballots. The first vote was 7–5 in favor of acquittal, each succeeding ballot closer to the final unanimous decision, plumber Ed Blanchard of Ticonderoga the last holdout for conviction. A good part of the jury had walked across the street to the Deer's Head. Noonan was there. McDonald was there. The reporters were there. The beer was there. Montague was in his room, mostly on the telephone. He called his mother in Syracuse with the good news. He started receiving calls, congratulations, offers. Freedom had seldom held out such lucrative possibilities.

"I'm going to make a million dollars," he told someone, anyone who listened. "I'm the happiest man in the world today. I'll never leave anything behind me again—even my hat."

"He's all set now," business manager Marty Forkins agreed. "He can make a million dollars. We're getting all kinds of offers. He is the greatest attraction there is in the country today. Not just in sports, in anything.

"Movie contracts, radio appearances, endorsements of vari-

ous kinds and golf exhibitions—all these things are before him.
He can't miss. Of course, his golf playing will be the big thing."

Montague left little doubt that he also considered this a victory over the reporters who had covered the trial. He never liked
the ways they characterized him, talking about his "chubby
fingers" and "chunky frame" and all of that. (One reporter, after
Montague said he received a telegram saying "Keep your chin
up," asked in print which chin the sender of the telegram
meant.) Most stories, Montague felt, pointed toward a guilty
verdict. The headlines were worse.

When he finally decided to talk with the press, most dead-
lines for morning papers long gone, he first took everyone down
the hall to another room. A small girl, Mary Louise Bastian,
daughter of the owner of the Deer's Head Inn, was sleeping. Her
mother stood next to her.

"This girl prayed for me," Montague said. "She prayed with
a crucifix in her hand before the verdict came in."

The obvious message was that somebody was on his side. A
little girl was more powerful than all the typewriters and all the
newsprint put together. The naysayers, that's right, you and you
and you, could kiss his ample derriere.

Back in his room, he answered questions the same way he
had answered on the stand. Replies again were brief. The situation again was confrontational, awkward.

"Are you planning any movie work?"

"That all depends."

"Going on the radio?"

"That all depends."

"There is a report that you're going on the radio with Grantland Rice."

"Ask Rice."

"Will you write a golf instructional book?"

"I think it should be written."

"Will you enter the U.S. and British Open?"

"Such plans are remote at this time."

"Have you received a lot of congratulations?"

"Words cannot express my feelings regarding the support my friends have given me."

"Any talk with any producers about movies or movie shorts?"

"I think they [the producers] have all the plans."

"Will you be going back to Hollywood?"

"At a later date."

"Are you going to give any golf exhibitions?"

"There are plenty of golf professionals. Why should I do professional golf?"

"Are you going to get married?"

"Nothing to say."

There was one thing he did want to add. He said he had already received at least fifteen telegrams from other attorneys congratulating Jim Noonan on the job he did. Jim Noonan was a great lawyer.

"He's one of the finest men I ever met," the free and clear John Montague said.

———————

A wire service report the next day declared that Montague had already signed a personal services contract with Everett Crosby, one of Bing Crosby's older brothers, that would guarantee him a million dollars over the next seven years. The contract would cover all of Montague's endeavors including golf, movies, radio, and writing. If Montague made more than a million dollars during that time, he would receive the extra money, minus managerial fees to Crosby.

Montague, no comment, left town early in the morning, headed for Albany and James M. Noonan's office, then to Syracuse to see his mother. He was indefinite about his plans after that. Business propositions had to be considered. Judgments had to be made. Plans would follow.

This was the first time he had been able to make decisions on his own, without the threat of arrest clouding his mind, since leaving in his Model A from his mother's house on August 6, 1930. This was the first time he could take full advantage of his considerable skills. This was the first time he could truly be himself, no strings attached. A different and grand life was possible. Anything was possible.

The difference between when he arrived in Elizabethtown and when he left was amazing. The difference in less than twenty-four hours was amazing.

He was out there in the music now. No doubt about that. He would walk in the direction it sounded the loudest. Maybe even run.

CHAPTER TEN

FLUSHING, LONG ISLAND

November 14, 1937

The public debut of John Montague, free man, tabloid celebrity, and would-be golfer extraordinaire, was quickly scheduled for November 14, 1937, at the Fresh Meadow Country Club in Flushing, Long Island. Nineteen days after his acquittal in Elizabethtown for armed robbery, he would play in an 18-hole exhibition with Babe Ruth, Babe Didrikson, and Helen Hicks to benefit a program to send poor children from New York City to summer camp.

This would be the start, the beginning, to whatever grand moments would come next. This was his first audition for greatness.

"How good is Montague?" Lester Rice, golf writer for the sponsoring *New York Journal-American,* asked in the announcement of the event. "Well, here he is, folks, to look upon and criticize.

"Whether he is phenomenal as so many have said or merely good, bad or indifferent, you can decide for yourselves merely by buying one-buck tickets of admittance to the Fresh Meadow Country Club...."

The prospect was enticing. No undefeated boxer, coming to Madison Square Garden after a string of knockouts across the cramped arenas of the Midwest, matched now against the seasoned big boys, ever brought a bigger buzz of speculation with him. He was the new marvel, the prodigy, the next best thing. Joe DiMaggio himself hadn't arrived from the ball fields of the West Coast with a bigger ballyhoo than John Montague.

"To the public at large he is still something of a mystery," Joe Williams wrote in the *New York Telegram and Sun.* "Everybody has heard of him. Few have seen him. That's what gives his first public appearance as a golfer a touch of piquancy. Interest in him is two-edged. First as a golfer, second as a curiosity. Or maybe the other way around. You know how people are. They were lured by the Cardiff Giant, by the Loch Ness Monster, and, in dad's day, by the seductive Evelyn Thaw as a dramatic actress."

The event was created solely for Montague. The work of business manager Marty Forkins was obvious in the detail. The day promised glamour, but without a lot of risk. The donation of all proceeds to charity, New York mayor Fiorello La Guardia to accept the money, was an inspired decision. John Montague, ladies and gentlemen, was a good guy. That fact was established before he even swung a club.

The course offered a solid test. Fresh Meadow had been the site of the 1932 U.S. Open, a moment in golf history when Gene Sarazen shot a 70 in the morning of the final day, then fired a 66 in the afternoon to break the course record by two strokes and capture the title three weeks after he had won the British Open in Sandwich, England. Any magic number recorded at Fresh Meadow would be legitimate. Sarazen's 66 was still the record.

The competition in the foursome was attractive, but not threatening. Absent were any male professional golfers from the PGA Tour, louder every day about their wishes to play this John Montague any time and in any place for any moment of money, but the three other players matched with Montague all had made sports headlines, golf headlines, in the past. They added stature, class....

The forty-two-year-old Babe, George Herman Ruth, probably still the most famous athlete in the country, even after a second season removed from the baseball wars and his 714 home runs, was an ardent and quite public golfer. He loved the game, loved the clothes, loved the cocktails at the turn.

Born poor, raised in the St. Mary's Industrial School for Boys in Baltimore, he didn't play golf until his first major-league season as a pitcher with the Boston Red Sox in 1914. The attraction was immediate. Throughout his baseball career, golf was his major off-season and in-season conditioning tool. He threw himself into the game, 36 and 54 holes a day during the early weeks of spring training at Hot Springs, Arkansas, or St. Petersburg, Florida. Not necessarily good golf, but golf.

"The orthodox construction of the modern golf course was a disastrous handicap to the Babe's style of play today," Marshall Hunt wrote in the *New York Daily News,* describing Ruth's first round of the spring in 1926 at the Jungle Club in St. Petersburg. "Had the rough been directly in front of the tees and the fairway on both sides of the rough, Mr. Ruth assuredly would have had a much more satisfactory score. Yet, under a ripe Florida sun, Ruth enjoyed a good workout, contracted a handsome case of sunburn and announced that his gross leakage through the hide was entirely gratifying."

His game had improved greatly with retirement. He played virtually every day, usually at St. Albans Golf Club, in Queens, when he was in New York, and had dropped his handicap as low as four. He hit the ball long, if sometimes erratically, and played in the championship flights at some local club events.

"Thank God for golf," he said, still grumpy about leaving baseball. "I played 365 rounds last year."

Babe Didrikson was a golf star in the making. (She called herself "Little Babe" when in the presence of the larger Babe.) At age twenty-six, she already was the country's greatest female athlete—a track star, softball star, basketball and tennis standout—but had decided that golf was her future.

The first time she ever played the game was at the Brentwood Country Club in Los Angeles, the day after she finished winning two gold medals and a silver in the 1932 Olympics. She was invited by Grantland Rice, that man again, to play in a group with Westbrook Pegler, Braven Dyer of the *Los Angeles*

Times, and Paul Gallico, the writer and sports editor of the *New York Daily News.*

Nervous, she took a quick lesson in the morning from Olin Dutra, who was the Brentwood pro and would win the PGA Championship that year. He showed her the grip, stance, and swing and advised her to "look at the ball real hard. That's the important thing."

She and Rice were paired together, the neophyte and the best golfer in the group, against the other three writers. Still nervous, she was the first to tee off. She put the ball on the ground and was ready to hit when Rice stopped her and told her she had to tee up the ball first.

"And he teed up the first ball for me," Didrikson wrote later in her memoir, *This Life I've Lived,* under her married name of Babe Zaharias, "which I've always thought was quite an honor."

Her first golf shot off that first tee went for 240 yards, straight down the fairway. She outdrove all of the men. Her score for the day was reported as 86, but she thought it was higher.

The key moment in the match came on the 16th hole, a par-3 that featured both an elevated tee and an elevated green, a large dip in the middle. Paul Gallico had the best tee shot of the group, was on the green, and seemed destined to win the hole. Rice used a little gamesmanship.

"Babe," he said, "why don't you challenge Paul to race you up and down that hill?"

Didrikson challenged. Gallico, the man who once sparred with Dempsey (and was knocked out in two minutes), once caught a Dizzy Dean fastball, once challenged Bobby Jones to a round of golf, the competitive rower and fencer, had to accept. Didrikson won the footrace easily. Gallico, winded, gassed, four-putted. Didrikson and Rice won the hole and the match.

She had played some different sports in the five years since the 1932 Olympics—toured with her own all-star female basketball team, pitched for the bearded male House of David baseball team, tried tennis—but now she was back at golf, convinced it was the best chance to make a dollar from sports.

"It's not enough to just swing at the ball," she said as her golf philosophy. "You've got to loosen your girdle and really let the ball have it."

Helen Hicks, the final member of the foursome, was the most established female golf professional in the country, if for no other reason than she was just about the only female golf professional in the country. A Long Island girl, winner of the 1931 Women's Amateur over three-time champion Glenna Collett Vare, a member of the first Curtis Cup team in its victory over Britain in 1932, she had turned pro in 1934.

A few other women had turned professional before her, but they mainly worked in pro shops and gave lessons to country club members. Hicks signed with Wilson sporting goods as a spokesperson. The company produced a Helen Hicks line of clubs for the growing women's market. Hicks gave clinics, visited stores, did anything to boost sales. There was no women's professional tour, only three events she could play in that were "open" to both pros and amateurs, so her actual golf career had suffered by her decision to turn pro.

The exhibition promised benefits for everyone involved.

Helen Hicks could play a competitive round, sell her product Babe Didrikson could display her developing talents on a New York stage for the first time in her career. George Herman Ruth could hear the crowd noise again, something that had been missing. Montague? The marketing of the legend could begin.

"Monty has several big-money offers waiting for him on the Coast," business manager Marty Forkins said as the foursome for the match was announced. "They have urged him to hurry. But he won't pass up this match for any of them. He gave his word on this and I don't believe you could shake him for all the dough in Hollywood. I never saw a guy so set on charity. It's a mystery to me!"

The marketing of the legend, check that, had already begun. All the legend had to do was produce.

If John Montague had any doubts about what came next, Grantland Rice laid out in print the problems and possibilities that lay ahead for the character he had brought onto the scene, for better or worse, three years earlier. The famous sportswriter had been quiet during the trial, typical for him, uninvolved with the grittier sideshows of sport, but now that action had returned to the golf course, he also returned. He knew his golf.

In a column on October 28, 1937, two days after the end of the work in Elizabethtown, Rice delivered a combination pep talk and warning to his onetime discovery, which he allowed the rest of the interested nation to overhear:

What place will John Montague, the mystery golfer, take, now that he is in a position to prove his place in the game?

The seven-year shadow has been removed by a jury. He can afford to step back into the spotlight and prove his place among the Picards, Coopers, Guldahls, Runyans, Sarazens, Hagens, Smiths and others. It will be an interesting experiment.

John Montague's chief claim to fame has been golf. It was his golf ability that brought him from Hollywood to Elizabethtown. It will be by his golf ability largely in the future that he rises or falls, in any financial way after the opening guarantee.

I would say that the answer is up to John Montague— up to his willingness to get back in top physical condition and rebuild the game I knew two or three years ago. If golf becomes only a sideline with him, if too many other interests take over his time and attention, he will undoubtedly lose much of the mystery glamour he has known. If he becomes just another golfer, he will lose much of his present prestige as a 60something shooter and one of the game's phenomena.

My first introduction to John Montague was on a rainy day at Riviera, one of the best courses in golf. Tommy Armour nominates this course as No. 1 in the United States. That day I played with Montague; Dick Hanley, then coaching Northwestern; Frank Craven and Babe Hardy, the far from anemic comedian.

I had heard about Montague before. Believed about 20 percent of what I heard. But that day he shot a 66—33 out and 33 in. He played the first hole, 460 yards, with a drive and a six iron. He played the second hole, 450 yards, uphill, with a drive and a niblick. I soon found his bunker play, his chip shots, and his putting were his soundest points. I knew at least I had seen a great golfer.

In the course of the last three years, I have played with Montague 100 times. Up until last winter. I had rarely seen him over 70. Last winter he played only casual golf and his long game suffered—but never his niblick, his chipping and his putting—quite unusual in a 225-pound athlete who is as strong as anyone I have ever known.

But his long game had lost 30 or 40 yards—his long iron play had fallen off through lack of timing, practice and play. Just how his amazing short game held up is still a mystery, for, at that time, he was far from being in top physical form, being 20 pounds overweight.

Here are some authorative opinions concerning Montague's golfing ability:

Gene Sarazen—"A fine shot-maker with an unorthodox style. A fine competitor. I'd like to see what he could do in an Open. I wouldn't know. Maybe yes—and maybe no."

George Von Elm—"The greatest golfer I ever saw. I've played with him four years. I played a month with him over different courses and never beat him a game. As I recall it, his highest score was 69 and he was down around 65 or 66 more than once. At his best he could win any championship."

Walter Hagen—"I never saw him play—but he can make it any amount for 36 or 72 holes and it will be all right with me. I've been taking a chance for 25 years. I'll still take one. Can you fix it up? I'll even be on time."

Paul Runyan—"I would be very glad to meet Montague and let him name his own terms—anywhere or any time."

Charley Lacey—"I've played a lot of golf with Montague. I'd say at his best he could beat any pro or amateur I ever saw six times out of 10 starts. Whether he can get back to his best depends on Montague. He can't loaf and do it. Not against this bunch."

Leo Diegel—"I don't know what Montague would do in an Open. I was the first pro to play with him about four or five years ago. I've played with him since. The last time I played, I shot a 68 and broke even. I still class Hagen, Armour, and Montague as the best money players I ever saw. In an Open—I don't know. I doubt that he would win one. Mac Smith hasn't in 27 years—and that's as great a golfer as I ever saw."

Only a few weeks ago, a number of well-known golf writers wanted to see Montague in action. At that time, he was under indictment. He had played only three rounds of golf since last winter. A new set of clubs had just arrived, which he never had played with.

I told him he was on the spot. The round was at North Hempstead with Clarence Buddington Kelland, the novelist—with Alex Morrison, one of the star experts of golf—with Dr. Leander Newman.

That day, under this pressure, Montague shot a 65. As Alex Morrison said later—"It was a 65 that so easily could have been a 61 or 62—a matter of four or five putts that lipped the cup and refused to drop from six or seven feet. In my opinion, Montague has the soundest and most compact golf swing with every club that I have ever seen. By this I mean that his physical and mental reaction bend more consistently when it comes to a matter of getting results. He has unlimited power and amazing control of the short game. It all depends upon his willingness to work upon his game. Winning golf is not a sideline for anyone."

This happens to be the answer for John Montague. Condition, play and practice can bring him back to as fine a golfer as anyone has seen. But he can't reach that point by the sideline route where other things become more important. And, again, it is by his golf that he will go forward—or be forgotten. In the public mind, he will be only as important as his golf game is.

The exhibition at Fresh Meadow seemed to be the perfect start to all of this. The gallery, the attention, would give Montague a look at what his new life could be like. He could meet and make fans. He would be linked immediately with Ruth and Didrikson, great athletes and eminently popular public figures. He could breathe his possible future.

The *Journal-American,* as newspapers tend to do with their own promotions, publicized the match daily with long stories, cartoons, and pictures. The plan was to sell six thousand tickets, first come, first served, no more, a representative gallery for a big-time event.

Babe Ruth added a flamboyant touch to the promotion with his return to New York from a three-week hunting trip to Nova Scotia on Thursday, November 11, three days before the match. Arriving at 8 A.M. at Pier 19 on the SS *New York,* unshaven and tanned from his time in the woods, he rolled down the gangplank in his Sutz Bearcat touring car with a dead deer tied to his front bumper, two more dead deer strapped across the front fenders, and a large (and dead) black bear stuffed into the rumble seat.

"The deer and the bear weren't all we got," the Sultan of Swat proclaimed. "We also got some ducks and woodcock.... That's over, though. I'm not thinking about big game in Nova Scotia, just a golf game at Fresh Meadow. I hope I can drive and putt as well as I can shoot a gun."

On Friday, Ruth played a nine-hole warm-up with Montague. They were not strangers. Montague had pitched to Ruth and met him during his short foray to the Yankees' spring training camp in 1928. Montague remembered, "He turned my cap around when I tried to sneak a fastball by him. The ball was still rolling when I looked up." The men had been friendly. Montague had an uncle on his mother's side, Ben Egan, who had been a catcher for Ruth, long, long ago with the minor-league Baltimore Orioles.

In the warm-up, Montague shot a 35 for his nine holes, Ruth a 37. Montague had two birdies, one on a 35-foot putt, another set up with a 230-yard blast out of a trap with a four-wood on a par-5. Those were his best shots of the day. Ruth was rusty from all of that shooting at the various fauna of Nova Scotia and New Brunswick. Montague was rusty from his own problems.

"I'm a little bit soft right now—after all I've been through," Montague said. "I can't be sure what kind of golf I'll play Sunday. Guess it doesn't matter if I get off some good shots."

The debut of the mysterious man had finally arrived.

Nobody could have expected what came next.

The weather was spectacular in Flushing, Long Island, on November 14, 1937, spectacular in the entire New York metropolitan area. The temperature was sixty-two degrees. The skies were clear, the sun warm. This was a last blink of summer two weeks before Thanksgiving, the colors on the trees lit up across the countryside. This was a day to pull a city-dweller outside one last time before the cold arrived.

The Fresh Meadow Country Club was outside.

The people started arriving early and did not stop. The parking areas were full by 10 A.M. for the 1 P.M. exhibition, and soon the streets were packed with cars that were parked and double-parked and could not move. The one-dollar ticket price and the weather and John Montague apparently had formed an irresistible combination. The six-thousand-ticket cutoff was breeched and forgotten, as ten thousand people, twelve thousand people, nobody was sure how many thousand people, came to the course. There were guesses that this was one of the largest crowds ever to appear for a golf event in the United States. Certainly it could have been the largest ever to watch a single foursome go to work.

The *New York Times,* on page one the next day, would say the crowd was "reminiscent of the last time Bobby Jones played in a championship at Merion in 1930, the year he completed his 'grand slam,' except at Merion there was semblance of order, whereas here there was none." The *New York Daily Mirror* would say that "there hasn't been a crowd like that since the funeral of Rudy Valentino." The *New York Daily News* would call the crowd "a riotous mob."

Not only did all of these people soon surround the 1st hole, ready to go, but—in the words of Lester Rice from the *New*

York Journal-American—"it was estimated by those who know their hooks and slices intimately that 60 per cent of those present didn't know a bunker from a bung-hole." These were subway-riding New Yorkers who didn't know much about golf, but had doctorates in creating personal space in crowds. Thin bamboo stakes and the few marshals on the job were shoved out of the way. People climbed any available tree. People filled the fairway as close as thirty feet in front of the tee. People engulfed the tee, leaving maybe a ten-foot, fifteen-foot-wide tunnel through which to hit a very-well-aimed golf shot. People were already standing on the 1st green.

Into this mayhem stepped the contestants.

One change had been made in the lineup. Helen Hicks had dropped out due to illness and was replaced by Mrs. Sylvia Annenberg, a noted Long Island amateur who played out of Fresh Meadow. Mrs. Annenberg was teamed with Montague against the all-Babe pairing of Ruth and Didrikson.

The long-awaited first public shot by Montague, his backswing restricted by the crowd around him, was a pushed drive into the rough along the right side of the 1st fairway. Easy to spot in his gray slacks, light blue shirt, dark blue sleeveless sweater, he fought his way through the crowd to reach his ball. His caddie stood over it, waving a small paper American flag, hoping to be seen. Two hundred yards from the green; Montague pulled out an oversize four-iron for his second shot and waited. And waited. And waited.

He waited for fifteen minutes for someone to push back the people in front, for a bunch of someones to have some common sense and get out of the way. Finally, nothing changed, he hit his shot, which flew over the crowd, bounced on the green, and rolled off the other side. He eventually chipped close, sinking the putt for a par 4.

The conditions for the day had been established. Golf would take second place to survival. This was his debut.

"This is worse than any World Series," Babe Ruth grumped. "At least at the ballpark the crowd has to stay in the stands. How can you expect anyone to play under these conditions?"

"Where'd you get that putter?" a fan shouted.

"Shut up!" the Babe shouted back. "It's a good putter."

All four of the competitors were bothered, but clearly the crowd had come first to see Montague. He drew more than twice the attention of anyone else, even Mr. Ruth. The only way he could travel to his ball was between two policemen and surrounded by four or five marshals, a movable eye in a stationary storm.

The final thought for each of the players for every shot was "The heck with it," or some suitable variation. People simply would not move. Half the shots were hit into milling groups of spectators, bouncing off backsides and legs and arms, hopefully not heads. When the balls hit the ground, they were taken much of the time for souvenirs, sometimes replaced with mangy range balls, sometimes simply taken.

"I never was so scared in all my life," Ruth would report later. "I never tried to control a golf ball the way I did today. Did you ever see anything like it? Every time we got on a tee we saw nothing but a fairway of people. You just had to blaze away and hope you didn't crown anybody."

An hour had elapsed before the foursome completed the first three holes. Future holes promised to move even slower. Already a crowd was sitting on the 6th green, waiting for the players to arrive. Idle conversation, shouts, noise continued through every shot. There was no hush to any gallery. There was no gallery, simply all of these people. Babe Didrikson, sick of waiting for the police to clear a pathway to her ball on one fairway, simply stepped backward for momentum, then rushed forward like a football blocker, knocking the paying customers out of her way.

Sylvia Annenberg, the late selection, hit the shot of the day on the 183-yard 4th hole, a par-3. Ignoring the crowd directly in front of her, she unloaded a brassie that went over everyone, bounced on the green, and rolled to within an inch of the hole. The excitement was so great in the crowd, which surged forward, closer to the green, that Babe Ruth was knocked to the ground. He was pulled back up with a twisted thumb and had a few four-letter words of wisdom for the spectators.

"Give us a break," he said repeatedly.

Montague seemed especially bothered by the congestion and commotion. By the 5th hole, he had decided to abandon all drives to the proper fairway. He aimed now for adjacent fairways or the rough, areas less populated, but still danger zones. On the 6th hole, as Montague hit a long iron from the rough, still surrounded by folk, a male spectator moved into the flight of the ball just as the ball left the ground. The bewildered soul stuck his head out of the crowd, as if looking to see if the train was coming. Montague's ball hit the edge of his hat, knocked off the hat, kept on flying. The spectator missed serious injury by no more than an inch. The crowd was so large around Montague's third shot, he simply picked up, didn't finish the hole.

On the 7th, still shaken from the long iron shot on the 6th, he again hit toward the rough. His shot flew through the branches of a tree, just missed someone sitting on one of the limbs, then found some anonymous body in the other fairway. The anonymous body shouted, "Ow!"

"I can't go on," Montague said to Scotty Chisholm, the West Coast golf writer who had come east for the match to wear his kilt for the day and act as a theatrical referee. "I'm afraid of injuring someone seriously."

The match was cut in half, a decision made to quit after 9 of the 18 scheduled holes. This was common sense. All of the competitors felt the same way Montague did. The foursome fought its way through the 8th, then finished at the par-3 9th when all four contestants hit shots that reached the green. The wisdom of the decision was evident as the crowd immediately gobbled up all four balls. That was the end. No putts. The match was finished.

The crowd, festive in its rowdiness, surrounded all the players, grabbing and jostling and offering congratulations. Someone somehow stole Scotty Chisholm's kilt. Reaching the clubhouse was the all-time relief, a celebration of rescue more than accomplishment, sort of like being plucked from a churning Long Island Sound by the Coast Guard. Bill Corum, the columnist who ran the production for the *Journal-American,* said this was "the first, and only, sports show in history that had to be called because of sunshine."

"I'd love to play for you again next year," Didrikson told Corum, "but you've got to get a bigger golf course. I don't mind sugar daddies in their proper place, but I hope I don't ever have to play chip shots again while sitting on their knees."

"Let's make this an annual affair," Montague suggested to the promoter. "Only we'll play it in private."

The man of the moment was still shaken. In their athletic histories, part of their success, Ruth and Didrikson at least had some experience with big and noisy crowds, backslappers and buffoons, but Montague had none. An ad hoc accounting system figured that he and Mrs. Annenberg had lost, two-up, to the Babes, and he personally had shot a 37 against the Babe's 35 for the nine holes. None of this really should have mattered, the day controlled by the madness, but the scores would still be printed in the newspapers. Montague wanted to explain.

"I just couldn't swing freely," he said, still sweating from his experiences on the course. "I deliberately played to adjacent fairways to avoid the crowd. There were other times when the fans crowded around so closely it was impossible to swing with concentration.

"I never did know whether I was playing my ball or not, for at least four times somebody exchanged mine for an old scurvy one. I'm glad it ended as it did without anyone getting hurt."

The good part of the exhibition was that it showed he certainly could attract a crowd. Or at least he could on this day. Marty Forkins could use that Rudolph Valentino crowd quote and a host of headlines—"Mob Stops Ruth, Montague Golf" the *Daily Mirror* shouted from its front page—to show that there was public interest in his client. People surely knew his name.

The bad part of the exhibition was that beside Montague's ability to attract a crowd, it showed little else about him. People were looking for magic, for golf balls to explode in the air, for boundaries to be obliterated, for lightning to shoot out of his ears or some other orifice. True, this exhibition was an unfair, chaotic test, but also true was the fact that John Montague was a heavyset, nervous guy playing golf. No lightning appeared.

"The entire demonstration brings out a curious fact, an odd but vicious circle," Bob Considine wrote in the *Mirror*. "Montague will attract big crowds wherever he plays, noisy mobs made up in great part by people who have only a passing interest in his golf game. He, nor anyone else, can produce first-class golf under those circumstances. It naturally follows that the crowds, who make the exhibitions financially possible, will in turn make them artistically impossible. Montague will be shooting in those Rotarian 80's—and so would Bobby Jones if he had to do his playing before crowds like Sunday's congregation.

"The drab part of shooting in the 80's is that Montague couldn't exist as a drawing card, under those terms—for his reputation is unfortunately such that every time he fails to break par a layer of his glamour and his mystery peels off."

The peeling, alas, had begun.

CHAPTER ELEVEN

HOLLYWOOD, MANILA, MEDINAH, ETC.

1937—40

John Montague finally returned to Hollywood on November 22, 1937, eight days after the fiasco at Fresh Meadow and less than a month after his acquittal in Elizabethtown. He traveled with Scotty Chisholm, the referee who never did find that missing kilt, and stepped off an American Airlines plane and into a movie star's kind of reception at Grand Central Air Terminal in L.A. Flashbulbs popped as he was greeted by comedian Guy Kibbee, actor William Frawley, Sid Sutherland, George Von Elm, and assorted other friends.

He beamed for the cameras, said he was happy to be back at his adopted home. He sounded ready for business.

"My chief aim now is a lot of golf," Montague declared. "I've got to practice for four or five hours a day and then I'm going for the British and American Open titles."

The joy of the moment—he had left town four months earlier, after all, accompanied by Percy Egglefield and two New York state troopers, headed toward possible jail time—was tempered by the marketplace realities that awaited. Hard work was a necessity if he wanted to take advantage of his situation. He had to produce, had to post some verifiable, wondrous results to back up the wonder stories, had to do it in a hurry.

His predicted big bonanza was shrinking already. Hollywood always had been a place of fast talk and big plans, easy words shouted out to capture a piece of the day's headlines, then forgotten when the headlines disappeared. How long would people wait to see something great from John Montague? Perception ruled. Nothing killed the Hollywood deal faster than the first signs of apathy and disinterest.

Time was a ticking factor.

The Garbo of Golf, the Sphinx of the Links, the Phantom of the Fairways had to get going, get busy, put up, yes, or shut up. The legend had to be fortified by facts to stay alive.

"Monty's reputation was built around one thing—his ability as a golfer," Henry McLemore wrote for the United Press, laying out the problem the same way Grantland Rice did. "The only way he can give it foundation, guarantee it withstands the attack of time, is to go out on the fairways and greens and prove it was an honest reputation. Unless he wants to be forgotten, he must, within the next few years, win himself a major title, be it the American Open, the British Open, or the Amateur.

"I know Monty well. I have eaten with him, drank with him, played golf with him. I like him very much. But he must dig deeper than the Hollywood surface to keep from letting a lot of people down."

McLemore, like Grantland Rice, was worried that his man wouldn't rather than couldn't live up to the legend. The Hollywood surface would be too tempting. The task would be too hard. The writers knew John Montague's disposition as well as his talents. The sound of a cocktail lounge piano was a bigger hazard than any number of pot bunkers or patches of uncut rough on a trip through a 450-yard dogleg right to an elevated green. He had to execute a complete change in his life to even have a chance at success. Did he have that kind of dedication, that kind of hunger?

The odds were not good. He was thirty-four years old, overweight, and out of shape. The excesses in food and drink, easily absorbed in youth, now left their mark, sat on him, stayed. He hadn't played serious golf in at least three years. Maybe he had never played serious golf, come to think of it, not the golf he was supposed to play now, competitive, against a full field of talent, judged by flat-out strangers.

He had to step into this different environment and win championships. And not just any championships; he had to win the biggest ones. He had to drive the ball farther, score lower, putt better than any golfer who had ever played the game. It wouldn't hurt if he knocked a bird or two off a telephone wire, either. Good would not be good enough. Great would be a disappointment. He had to be phenomenal.

Whew.

This was the challenge that sat on the horizon as he told reporters that for the moment he probably would be a guest at Guy Kibbee's house, but had a beach house that he was going to open in the next week. The golf would start in the morning. He was ready to go. He denied that he had signed any contracts with anybody to do anything, said that his future still had to be mapped out.

"I never as much discussed contracts in the East," he said. "There are a lot of things in the fire, of course, that must be hashed out.... I have several things in New York and out here that I'm going to look into, but my eyes are on the British and American Open golf championships."

Time was a ticking factor.

If there was any doubt about that fact, all he had to do was read the newspapers. His image took another hit almost before he attacked his first bucket of practice balls.

Three days after the Fresh Meadow adventure, before he left for California, he had tangled again with Babe Ruth. They played a more sedate round at the Quaker Ridge Country Club in Scarsdale, New York. Invited by club pro Jimmy Farrell to the exclusive course, designed by A. W. Tillinghast, home to members like department store magnates Louis Gimbel and Samuel Bloomingdale, publisher Alfred Knopf, and composer George Gershwin, Ruth and Montague played in a sixsome, an informal affair, supposed to be simply a day of golf and fun.

Notoriety, of course, didn't allow this. Word of the match soon spread around the club and a gallery of seventy, perhaps eighty people trailed the action. The seventy, perhaps eighty people, of course, had eyes and mouths and reported the results after the match to their friends and acquaintances: Babe Ruth had thumped the supposed greatest golfer in the world. Some reports added the possibility that the Babe might have taken a sizable amount of Montague's money.

Reporters heard this tale and soon questioned Ruth about it. The baseball star hemmed, hawed, then finally admitted that he had beaten Montague, 6 and 5, in the match and that the medal scores "were nothing to brag about." (Jimmy Farrell, the pro, said Ruth shot a 76. He couldn't remember what Montague shot.) Ruth seemed almost embarrassed to talk about the subject. He denied that there were any wagers.

"Monty's a better golfer than I am," the Babe said. "I can tell you that from watching his swing. He knows all the strokes and he knows all the answers in the book. I think he was experimenting on a lot of his approach shots, and that's why I was able to beat him. He's a great driver—no question about that—and the only reason I was able to keep up with him off the tee that day was that he was a little wild in getting that first smack away.

"Another thing. He hadn't had enough practice, while I have been pretty regular at St. Albans all fall. Anyway, as I said, it looked to me as though he was trying some new shots with his irons and they didn't pan out. That was how I beat him. I don't want to take any credit for it. He is out on the Coast now where he can get the practice and I think he will be a star."

Ruth's remarks, widely reported in the East, were clipped out of the New York papers and brought to California by the intrepid Henry McLemore. He spread them out on a table at the

Brown Derby for Montague next to a breakfast of wheat cakes and sausages. Montague was surprised.

He said the only score he remembered against Babe Ruth was when they played those nine practice holes at Fresh Meadow and he shot 35 and the Babe shot 37. He said there was never a bet and there was never a real match at Quaker Ridge, he and the Babe were both playing for fun. He didn't know what the scores were.

"But don't get me wrong," Montague said. "I'm not sore at Babe. Maybe he thinks he did beat me. Maybe he honestly believes that we bet and he won. That's all right by me. After all, he's a good golfer and it wouldn't be a disgrace to be beaten by him. He's a magnificent putter, isn't he?"

Business manager Marty Forkins, thinking about headlines, took a more aggressive approach. He belittled Ruth's "claim" of a victory and suggested a match be set up in the next few weeks, this time with crowd control and very big stakes. He said his man would take care of Mr. Babe Ruth at any place and at any time.

"To be honest about it, I haven't even obtained Montague's okay on this," the business manager said, "but I know he'll go through with it and I'll back him if Ruth is willing. All I want is for Ruth or his friends to name their price. This will be a shooting match and I'll let as much ride on Montague that anybody will cover—$50,000, any amount offered."

A small item soon appeared out of Bradenton, Florida. St. Louis Cardinals pitcher Dizzy Dean challenged Montague to a match as part of the annual Dizzy Dean tournament on December 11, 1937, at the Bradenton Country Club. Montague quickly declined.

"I told him to stick to baseball," he said. "Forget about the pitching and putting."

Baseball players were lining up at the door. This was not a good sign for someone who was supposed to be the greatest golfer in the world.

The opportunity for the fast million dollars had already disappeared. Sportswriters had been quick to point out that million-dollar payouts had been speculated for other athletes after their big moment—Jim Thorpe after the 1912 Olympics, Red Grange in pro football, Babe Didrikson after the '32 Olympics, for example—and none materialized. Jim Thorpe wound up digging ditches. Montague would break a precedent if he made a million.

His chances at the magic figure largely were tied to his Hollywood connections. From his first blink in the spotlight he had been cast as a natural for movies, a big and powerful man, maybe starring in the role of Paul Bunyan himself in a first feature film. Movie stars made millions much faster than professional golfers did. (Professional golfers didn't make millions.) The speculation about Montague's movie possibilities by gossip columnists had made a movie career seem almost inevitable.

There was no speculation now.

That million-dollar contract with Bing Crosby's brother Everitt, "leaked" at the conclusion of the trial in Elizabethtown, died almost as soon as the morning papers were delivered to the Deer's Head Inn. That same day, Bing Crosby announced that not only had there never been a deal, there never would be a deal. He said the company was going in another direction, blah, blah.

"I don't know exactly what Monty's plans are," Crosby said with the careful words of a diplomat, "but he ought to make a lot of money. I suppose he'll go into pictures. He ought to do very well, because he has a lot of personal charm. I imagine he'll play roles such as George Bancroft plays."

Any possible deal with Crosby had fallen apart during a meeting between the singer, Paramount Pictures producer Emmanuel Cohen, and representatives of the Hays Office. The Hays Office, headed by former postmaster general Will Hays, functioned as the movie industry's self-censoring agency, charged to keep objectionable material from the screen. Montague had apparently been deemed objectionable material.

Crosby wanted to cast him in *The Badge of Policeman O'Roon,* a new movie based on a short story by O. Henry about four retired relay racers and their annual reunion in Central Park. Crosby, Andy Devine, and Sterling Holloway had been signed as the first three retired runners. Montague was supposed to be the fourth. The Hays representatives, according to a Paramount press release, "prevailed upon Crosby and Cohen not to put Montague in the picture."

"There are roles and there are roles," Crosby said, downplaying the decision. "We didn't plan anything important for him anyway."

The implications ran far deeper. The Hays Office, created by the industry after scandals involving comedian Roscoe (Fatty) Arbuckle and other prominent actors in the early twenties brought the threat of government censorship, had become stronger and stronger in the thirties, and now was so powerful that it ruled on virtually every word and every scene that came out of Hollywood. The Hays Office had cut out swearing and nudity, controlled all bodily functions in bedrooms and bath-rooms, and determined the proper amounts of blood that could flow from dead cowboys, Indians, and Chicago gangsters. The Hays Office and its "production code" controlled cinematic life far better than any religion or Ten Commandments controlled real life.

A Johnny Weissmuller movie, *Tarzan and His Mate,* was in-volved in a celebrated decision when nude scenes involving a body double for Maureen O'Sullivan were deleted in 1934. Laurel and Hardy were forever in front of the censors, fighting to keep some borderline, but very funny scenes in their movies. The Hays Office kept Mae West in her clothes, Groucho Marx on his best behavior, livestock in diapers.

No reason was given why Montague was unacceptable, but two of the production code's three basic tenets mentioned that "the sympathy of the audience should never be thrown to the side of evil, wrongdoing or sin" and "Law, natural or human, shall not be ridiculed, nor sympathy created for its violation." The Hays Office seemed to sit on the side of Judge Harry Owen in Elizabethtown, unhappy with the jury's verdict. To the Hays Office, Montague was guilty, no matter what those men in flan-nel shirts said. Unlike Harry Owen, the Hays Office could do something about it.

"The employment of actors is a matter for the producer alone to decide," a spokesman from the Hays Office said, but everyone in Hollywood knew that this was not the case. Nods and nudges from the Hays Office had great implications. A nod and a nudge surely had worked here.

Whether Montague would be banned permanently from movies was not known, but this was not a positive first step for his film career. The armored car would not be arriving in a hurry with that first million from the Crosby empire. Nor would it be arriving from the offices of any movie producer.

"How's Montague going to make that million dollars?" an Associated Press reporter asked Larry Crosby, another of Bing's brothers in the family entertainment business.

"Million dollars!" Larry Crosby said. "He's going to make a couple of shorts showing how he plays golf, but they won't bring in more than $20,000. There's a deal for some magazine stuff, I guess, pictures and life stories. I guess he'll go on Bing's radio program. He'll probably get a thousand or so for that."

The radio appearance would never happen. The magazine stuff would never happen. The movies would never happen. The million dollars would never happen.

The great golf? The wins in the U.S. and British Open? That still had to be settled.

A scouting report from Johnny Dawson detailed the basic difficulty Montague faced. Called "the best amateur golfer in the United States" by Bobby Jones, Dawson worked for Spalding sporting goods. Montague asked to meet with him soon after returning to Hollywood. The meeting took place at the house in Beverly Hills where Montague was living.

The first thing Dawson noticed was 150, maybe 200 telegrams and letters spread across the floor. Montague said these were business deals, most of them offering a fee of one thousand dollars for him to play an exhibition with George Von Elm.

"Well, what do you want me for?" Dawson asked.

"I want to have Spalding sponsor us," Montague said.

Dawson said he would have to check with his boss. The boss asked if Montague was as good as he was supposed to be. Dawson answered that he really didn't know, he had never played with Montague. The boss told Dawson to "check him out, play with him for a week." Dawson played ten rounds with Montague, sometimes with George Von Elm in the group, sometimes with Babe Didrikson. He reported back.

"I was at the top of my game," Dawson said. "I was 66 or 67 every round. And Montague was right there, tying me."

This sounded very impressive.

"What do you think we should do?" the boss asked. "Should we hire him?"

"No!" Dawson replied. "We can't afford him. He orders doubles every time he stops for a drink. He'd run us out of business with his drinking and carrying on."

The temptations were too great. The man was too old to change his life in a moment, especially when the good times had become even better. The wide-eyed new arrival that pounded golf balls down Wilshire Boulevard at two in the morning, golf all the time, was long gone. The worries of Grantland Rice and Henry McLemore were distressingly accurate. Montague couldn't attack his situation the way it should be attacked, despite his occasional bursts of good intentions.

As the days, weeks, then months passed, he coasted, riding the dissipating fumes of his celebrity. He never made the change to become an athlete, never felt the urgency, seldom practiced, only played in comfortable surroundings. No plans were made to enter the U.S. Open for 1938. ("Too soon," he explained.) No plans were made to travel to England, where the tabloids had created a demand with exaggerated, often fabricated, stories that made him sound like a true mythical character.

(One London tabloid reported that Montague drove a big and expensive car periodically into the desert from Hollywood, towing a trailer that was furnished in silk and silver and contained a gold piano. Under the desert moonlight, he sat at the piano and composed many of the popular songs that all of America now sang and whistled.)

Marty Forkins had suggested that perhaps Montague would become a race car driver, backed by Peter DePaolo, and that he might drive in the Indy 500. Never happened. Forkins had suggested boxing as a possibility, with Montague's great strength. Never happened. Montague turned down all vaudeville requests and by the time he finally got around to signing up for exhibitions in May 1938, seven months after his acquittal, Forkins was gone.

While the serious golfers tried to qualify at various sites for the upcoming U.S. Open at Cherry Hills Country Club in Denver, the golfer in Hollywood announced that he would edge into the competitive scene with a series of matches with George Von Elm. Details had to be worked out, but now Robert Harlow, former tournament director for the Professional Golfers' Association, would be the man in charge. Harlow also ran an ongoing series of exhibitions between tennis players Ellsworth Vines and Fred Perry.

Montague showed up at the Open in Cherry Hills in Denver two weeks later only to watch the action and publicize his tour. He was candid in his reasons for not being part of the field.

"I'm not where I want to be with my golf because I'm still

out of shape," he said after a practice round the day before the tournament began. "My putting isn't as good as it should be, but that will be fixed."

He watched Ralph Guldahl win a second consecutive Open title. He socialized with friends. He found the men's bar.

His debut—his return, whatever it was—didn't take place until June 26, 1938, at the Washoe Golf Club in Reno, Nevada. Montague and Von Elm were matched against Washoe club professional Charley Foley and Hutt Martin, a local club pro who had once won the Southern California Open. The event was on a Sunday, well publicized in the local papers, and a gallery of perhaps four hundred people gathered. Montague was presented with a pick, shovel, and sledgehammer as possible clubs for the course in the mining area.

He couldn't have done worse if he used them. Blasting his drives to strange locations, troubled again with his putter, he shot a 77, the highest score in the group. On top of that, he missed a two-foot putt on the 18th hole that would have won the match, the finish now a tie with the local pros.

Reaction came in a hurry.

"One thing was certain, Montague can please the crowd," the sponsoring *Reno Gazette* reported in a tempered review of his work. "He showed them some great golf shots with some booming drives, approaches dead to the pin and some fine putting. But he was inconsistent and it was generally agreed that Monty must work on his game for some time before he can become a top ranking golfer."

Other news outlets were not so kind. In Salt Lake City, the headline called him "a bum." In San Francisco, he was "a dud." He responded with the claim that score did not matter in these exhibitions; that he was simply trying to hit some thrilling shots for the crowd rather than going for score. He also canceled scheduled upcoming shows in Salt Lake City and San Francisco.

"The promoters of this tour have made a fatal mistake," Bill Tobbitt wrote in the *Oakland Tribune*. "Monty should have been given top billing, yes...but he shouldn't have been allowed to play. Despite Monty's frantic efforts to acquire a golfing skill equal to his press notices by secretly taking lessons for weeks on end, he has turned out to be nothing more than a high-class duffer."

A picture of the golfer was in the middle of the column. The caption read "Montague Bubble Bursts."

Two days later at the municipal course in Sacramento, he did much better, shooting a three-under 69 as he and Von Elm played against local amateur Frank Toronto and pro Tommy LoPresti. Toronto, however, shot a 67, and he and LoPresti won the match, 3 and 2. The next day Montague shot another 69, one-under, on a nine-hole course in Woodbridge, California. He shot a 71, one under, the day after that at the Fort Washington Golf Course in Fresno, to break par for three straight days. He then tied the course record at Hillview Golf Club in San Jose with a 66 a week later.

No matter what he did, the initial judgments from that first 77 were hard to shake. Even the 66 he shot at Hillview in San Jose was questioned. *San Francisco Chronicle* columnist Art Rosenbaum was one of the spectators and noticed that the foursome would "phenagle around" so that Montague would always have the last putt, and if the hole was already decided his putt would be conceded. This was typical of match play everywhere, but did nothing to define Montague's talents.

"His scores must be taken with a grain of salt," Rosenbaum said. "There is no doubt that he's good, but I'd like to see him in a national open, coming down the last 18 holes, forced to sink every putt, even if it's on the lip of the hole. If he comes through that test of fire, then he deserves superman billing. . . . For the time being, he's still cloaked in mystery."

The tour ended in August 1938, three months after it started. A second, much shorter tour through Texas with Babe Didrikson took place in October. Montague continued to maintain that scores were not important, that his galleries wanted to see him hit trick shots from trouble rather than score birdies. He gave the people what they wanted.

In Fort Worth at the Colonial Country Club, as he and Didrikson both shot 73, the fans even helped him find trouble. Every time he hit a tee shot, someone would kick the ball into the rough or into a divot hole or behind a tree. He was left to work his way out of the predicament.

"Maybe all galleries aren't like that, but mine are," he said. "Over and over I'd hear people say, 'I wish he'd get in the rough and play out of there. So I started going in the rough. It's partly a secret, but sometimes I went in or behind a tree deliberately. That pleased everybody, but hardly helped my scores."

The scores, alas, were all that were reported in the newspapers.

On December 2, 1938, he sailed from Los Angeles on the SS *Matasonia* for Honolulu and points west. He had finally signed with a sponsor, Wilson Sporting Goods, and was off to give a series of exhibitions in Hawaii, the Philippines, and Japan. He was also entered in the Philippines Open, his first professional tournament competition. Wilson reportedly was considering the development of a line of Mysterious Montague oversize clubs if all went well.

The trip seemed to be a perfect way to get things rolling again. Away from the attention of the U.S. press, he could quietly overwhelm the field in the Philippines and put a win on his résumé. He could charm the bosses at Wilson; create a long-term relationship. Away from Hollywood, maybe he could rebuild his golf game and slim down his body. He could get serious.

Oh, yes, and there was one other bit of news. He had gotten married. Maybe that also would help.

Waving good-bye from the dock as the *Matasonia* set sail was Mrs. Esther Plunkett, who had quietly become the woman in his life. Characterized as a "Beverly Hills socialite," the thirty-three-year-old widow had been on the fringe of public events for the past year and a half. She had picked him up when he was first arrested in Los Angeles, met him at the airport when he returned from the trial, discreetly paid many of the bills during his long legal wrangle.

The mother of two children, thirteen-year-old Jack and eight-year-old Faith, she was not a Hollywood glamour queen, but pretty enough, "comely" in one report. Her home on North Bedford Drive was where Montague had returned to live in Beverly Hills, not "with the Kibbees," as he had announced. He had tried to keep her out of the press, mostly succeeded, but still there was speculation about their relationship.

"Are you getting married?" Montague had been asked at the end of the trial.

"Are *you* married?" he replied. "That's personal business."

"Are you getting married?" he was asked when he returned to L.A.

"Who knows what the future holds?" he replied.

Reporters asked Esther Plunkett on the dock again whether she and Montague were engaged or planning to marry, but she refused comment and, according to one report, "blushed and fled." Three weeks later, in the form of Christmas cards signed "Christmas Greetings from the Montagues—Esther and Monty," she finally answered. Yes, they were married.

"We were married some time ago in California," she admitted when called at the Beverly Hills house. "Really, the time or place doesn't mean much now, does it?"

The news at least partially filled in some leftover blanks from the old stories. The economics of Montague's mystery time were more easily explained. The late John H. Plunkett, a printing company executive, had left his wife in solid financial circumstances. (One of her close neighbors was the actress Constance Bennett.) Esther Plunkett was able to help her new man in his various situations. She sold some of her real estate, she later confided to his brother, Harold, to take care of the legal expenses.

Also partially explained, perhaps, was Montague's slow approach to opportunities available to him. He really didn't need the money.

"Mrs. Plunkett gave Montague the polish that made it possible for him to be lionized in Hollywood drawing rooms and at the fashionable Lakeside Country Club," Paul Harrison of the NEA Syndicate speculated. "His golf and her money account for his innumerable fabulous Montague tales of his mystery days."

The newly announced, if not newly wed, husband had nothing to say on the matter. Contacted when he arrived in Manila on Christmas Day, 1938, he refused to answer questions about the announcement in L.A. He said he was there to play golf.

————

The Philippines Open didn't sound like much, and certainly drew little interest in the United States, but it was the oldest tournament on the Asian circuit and had quietly added some muscle in the past few years. The promoters had moved the prize money to five thousand dollars, comparable to what was offered at an average PGA tournament.

The appearance of Montague was a big deal. His story preceded him, complete with bat-shovel-rake specifics. Though Americans had won fourteen of the first sixteen Philippine Opens, a stretch from 1913 to 1928, the winners had all been amateurs who were stationed in Manila for various reasons. Few American pros had visited the country, much less played in the tournament. Montague would have been an attraction even without his press notices.

The defending champion was Norman von Nida, a prickly twenty-four-year-old Australian from Brisbane. Von Nida had made the three-week trip by tramp steamer a year earlier. He complained that the only amusements on the voyage were "drinking and smoking," neither of which was one of his personal vices. (There were no complaints from Montague about the smoking and drinking.)

Slender and small, no more than five feet six, von Nida was the opposite of Montague on the golf course. He relied on accuracy more than distance, though his hands and wrists were remarkably strong from a boyhood job in an abattoir cracking open the skulls of sheep. He had been convinced to try professional golf after he beat the touring Gene Sarazen in a money match in Brisbane. If he could beat Sarazen, then why couldn't he beat other golfers? He was off, starting on a career that eventually would find great success in Europe.

The local favorite was Manila native Larry Montes. He had already won the tournament four times and was the most famous golfer in Asia. Emperor Hirohito of Japan, a golf enthusiast, had summoned him to live in the Imperial Palace and provide personal lessons. Montes was the only foreigner ever allowed to live in the palace. He used a Bobby Jones Calamity Jane—model putter, inscribed with the words, in English, LARRY MONTES NEVER MISSES on the blade. It was a nice touch for lessons in the Imperial Palace.

Montes's initial win, in 1929, the first in the tournament for a Filipino, changed the course of the sport in his country. Membership at the Manila Golf Club, site of the tournament, was restricted to foreigners, so Montes, after he received his trophy, was not allowed to stay for the victory dinner. This outraged an American, Bill Shaw, who embarked on an effort to build a new country club open to all residents, all races.

The result, opened in 1935, was the Wack Wack Golf and Country Club, carved out of the jungle on the outskirts of Manila. Wack Wack (named after the sound of a local bird, the uwak) had become the preeminent course in the country, the home of the Philippines Open. The field now was filled with Filipinos, plus a large group of emerging Japanese golfers.

Montague had to wonder where he had landed. He was a long way from Burnet Park in Syracuse, a long way from the

Lakeside Golf Club. This was a tournament debut on the moon. Once again, he was not prepared for what he had to face. Once again, he was a flop.

"It was on this trip that I met the famous mystery golfer John Montague," von Nida later remembered with writer Ben Robertson in *The Von: Stories and Suggestions from Australian Golf's Little Master*. "Montague was supposed to have burned up all the American courses and by all accounts was able to play as well with a baseball bat, a rake or a shovel as an ordinary person would with a golf club. . . .

"I was as keen as anyone to see Montague's form, but sadly it didn't eventuate and he finished 12 shots behind me when I won the title again. Personally I thought Montague was all talk, better at drinking scotch and big-noting himself than playing golf."

The tournament came down to von Nida and Chin Seisui, best of the Japanese golfers. They were tied with two holes to play. Seisui duck-hooked his drive off the 17th tee, landing in a stretch of tall jungle rough. His caddie plunged into the rough, followed immediately by von Nida's caddie, who pulled out a machete. The machete was not produced to cut down the rough, but as a warning to Seisui's caddie not to try to substitute a new ball for his client's lost old ball. Von Nida proceeded along to the win.

Montague finished in a tie for seventh, back in the pack, despondent, behind von Nida, Seisui, Montes, and three more Japanese golfers. The tournament was barely mentioned in the United States, his failure unnoticed, but he knew how badly he had played. If he couldn't beat these unknown golfers, whom could he beat?

"I was not so good," he lamented to sportswriters when he returned to L.A. on February 8, 1939. "I was just an also-ran, even in the Philippines. I didn't seem to be able to hit 'em the way I should."

The job with Wilson was gone. The advice of Johnny Dawson to the folks at Spalding apparently had been solid. Montague's exploits and his expense account, coupled with his seventh-place finish, were enough to doom the relationship.

An example: Before the trip, he had asked the company for four gunnysacks of Wilson golf balls to bring with him. He had spent much of his time on the ship pitching the balls into the smokestacks. In the harbor at Tokyo, he had pounded them at other ships. The captain of a Japanese warship came out and wanted to know what John Montague was shooting at.

Wilson Sporting Goods didn't need to be part of any international incidents.

The trip did what none of his many advisers could do: it shook Montague into action. He gave up drinking. He lost some weight. He tried at last to find the golfer who had been at the core of the wonder stories. For the next three months in Hollywood, he made a belated attempt to get into shape and reclaim control of his future. Opportunities gone, squandered, dead after his failure with Wilson, he tried to create some new ones.

He entered the 1939 U.S. Open.

"I'm leveling this time," he told Henry McLemore in May, a week before the Open qualifications. "I'm dead serious. I haven't been playing much, as you know—maybe twelve or fifteen rounds in a year—but I've been in training and physically

I'm great. Down from 236 pounds to 216, which is about my best weight, and I'm not only on the wagon, I'm driving it. Haven't played a scotch foursome, and you know the kind of scotch foursome I mean, for months.

"I'm playing a lot better. I broke par with a 70 yesterday and might have been better with a little luck. My woods still aren't what I'd like them to be, but I'm willing to sacrifice distance to get back accuracy."

He chose to make his attempt at Medinah Country Club, outside of Chicago. After playing a short series of exhibitions across the Midwest, he went to Medinah for the one-day, 36-hole sectional qualification event for the Open on May 22, 1939. Twelve slots were open to a field of 112 golfers.

Medinah seemed a perfect spot for him. Built in the early twenties by the Shriners of Chicago, opened in 1925, three separate courses were part of a 640-acre resort the fraternal group hoped would be known as the best golf facility in North America. The Byzantine-inspired clubhouse, resembling an Arab mosque, was an attraction by itself. The Depression had hit the operation hard, the familiar story for country clubs in the thirties, with memberships at Medinah even opened to non-Shriners, but financial solvency had returned and the courses offered long, hard tests for top-flight players. Montague would benefit from the length if he could make his oversize driver perform.

The stakes were obvious.

"Montague won't aim his brassie shots at sparrows on telephone wires during these 36 holes, or play any of his pitches to the green with a baseball bat," Henry McLemore wrote. "Because they hold the key to his future as a golfer. If he plays them badly you may safely write him off the golfing book. If he plays them well he will get a crack at the Open title and who knows that the skill that once was his will return?"

The largest gallery of the day gathered to follow him in the morning on Course 1, the public still intrigued enough by the old stories to take a look. The question was how long Montague could keep his crowd. A march of attrition had begun.

For nine holes he was solid enough, two over par at the turn. After 15 holes, not so bad, he was four over. After 18, seven over on the final three holes, he was cooked. He finished with an 81, eleven over par.

In the afternoon, on Course 2, he continued to struggle in front of a smaller and smaller group. He had a 39 after nine, his woods taking him to strange places, putter ineffective. He limped home, simply picking up his ball on the 18th green and walking away, his round unfinished. Even he couldn't watch the end. If he'd made the putt, he would have shot an 83 and finished nine strokes behind the lowest qualifier.

The United Press reported that he had "fizzled miserably." The Associated Press said he "exploded for once and all the super-golfer legend which grew up about him two years ago when he was known to few in the golfing public." The last vestiges of mystery and glamour were gone.

In 1940, to much less fanfare, heavy again, drinking again, he tried again. The result, surprisingly, was better. He qualified this time at Flintridge Country Club in Los Angeles, taking one of three sectional spots available for the Open nine days later at the Canterbury Country Club in Cleveland. A 77 in the morning put him in peril, but he withstood a double-bogey six on the 16th in the afternoon to finish with a one-over-par 73 and a 150 total to make the field by three shots. No one seemed overly excited. Montague was eight shots behind Flintridge medalist Willie Goggin.

"Imbedded deep in the story about the 100-odd pros and amateurs who qualified for the National Open was a single line that John Montague won one of the three places open in the Los Angeles district . . . ," Bob Considine wrote in the *New York Daily Mirror.* "Two years ago that would have been headline news. For Montague was a great name in sport, a name full of mystery and hocus-pocus. The tales of his prowess had grown in fabulous descriptions. Today his qualification makes only a line.

"No guy ever fell out of the sports pages quite as quickly as Montague."

He was listed as a 30-to-1 shot at Canterbury. Grantland Rice wrote an entire U.S. Open preview story without mentioning Montague's name. Much of his golf in the year since his failure at Medinah had been gimmick exhibitions, playing with a baseball bat, shovel, and rake against Walter Hagen, the aging champion and late-night rambler, now forty-seven years old. The exhibitions and travel had been good fun—the time in Breezy Point, Minnesota, when the groundskeeper quit and the caddies refused to carry for someone playing with a bat, rake, and shovel; the time in Philadelphia when Montague, upset that a piano player in the cocktail lounge wouldn't play his song, went across the room, picked up the piano, and brought it to his table—but no titles had been won, no scores posted that would indicate a great jump in performance.

On a sunny, windless day in Cleveland, June 5, 1940, he finally played in the Open. He was another of those obscure names that moved in the backwash of the celebrated pros like Sammy Snead and Ben Hogan, Byron Nelson and Gene Sarazen.

He was no different from the club pros or solid amateurs who had put together a one-day, once-in-a-lifetime two rounds to qualify, a character to be noticed only if he could post some startling numbers on the leader board. This did not happen. A workmanlike round of golf, four over par after 17 holes, was destroyed on the final tee when he pounded two drives out of bounds. He finished with an 80.

The twenty-eight-year-old Snead, the emerging figure in the sport, now tapped as the next "best golfer in the world," shot a 67, a record for a first-round score at an Open. Thirty-eight-year-old Bobby Jones, the longtime "best golfer in the world," retired for a decade from competition with health problems, watched from the side.

"How're you playing?" he was asked by a sportswriter, casual duffer conversation, a wonder if the famous man played any golf at all now.

"I stopped worrying about my golf the day the Germans invaded Holland," he replied.

The thirty-six-year-old visitor from Beverly Hills, once mentioned in those "best golfer in the world" conversations, also could stop worrying. The conversations were done.

"John Montague, the mystery man, bore out his title in his first appearance in the Open," Bob Considine wrote, far down in his story of the first day. "But the almost nonexistent gallery which followed him decided that the only mystery about rugged John is how he managed to qualify."

He shot an 82 the next day, missing the cut by nine shots. He never played again in a major championship.

A five-page article about "Mr. Moore of Syracuse" was published in the December 7, 1940, issue of *The New Yorker.* The
details of his saga—the robbery in Jay, New York, the golf in
Hollywood, the discovery, the trial in Elizabethtown—filled
most of the text, but the writer, Robert Lewis Taylor, also brought
the tale up to date. He described the domestic situation of the
"somewhat portly" Montague and Esther and her two children
in their "comfortable, but by no means large" eleven-room
home in Beverly Hills.

Houseguests often included Oliver Hardy, Guy Kibbee,
Andy Devine, William Frawley, George Von Elm, and Al Jolson.
The man of the house had ditched the flashier clothes of his earlier days for more conservative, custom-made suits. He seemed
happy enough. He declined to discuss how he made money, but
Esther said he had "business connections." He could still do
some amazing things.

"He continues to enjoy demonstrating that he is a strong
man, and if his stunts are occasionally lacking in finesse, they at
least are to the point," Taylor wrote. "Not long ago he joined
some friends on a yachting trip to Santa Catalina Island and, en
route, someone in the party bet him he couldn't wrench a wash-
basin from its moorings. Montague led the way to the wash-
room, seized the basin, and ripped it loose, together with a part
of the wall. While he was receiving congratulations on this accomplishment, a member of the crew rushed into the room to
report that a couple of pipes had been broken below deck and
that the captain was putting in to shore for emergency repairs."

Montague's failures in the 1939 and 1940 U.S. Opens were
chronicled, along with his "trouble with his short game" and his
complaints about "frequent trouble with his back." He had made

"practically nothing" from golf since the trial in Elizabethtown "unless he had been lucky in betting."

Taylor, the author, wrote: "His subsequent activities make it appear likely that he is better fitted for an easy-going country club life, in which he can impress a small circle of friends with his special talent for trick shots than for tournament play."

The title for the article, stretched across page 92 of the magazine, was "Where Are They Now?" Three years, one month, and eleven days had passed since Elizabethtown.

CHAPTER TWELVE

HOLLYWOOD

1941—72

The basic story of John (the Mysterious) Montague was done. No more big tests would be taken over well-mown hill and dale. No more disappointing results would be recorded. The hollow ending after all of the hoopla, the important questions still unanswered, was the only ending there would be.

A true Hollywood production would have scripted one last stand. A kid, a dog, a dying relative would have been involved, an entry into some important tournament on a whim, four days of spectacular par-busting golf pulled from the air, a trophy presentation as tears rolled down assorted cheeks. There you go, Timmy. That's what Uncle John had inside him.

This was not a movie. The word-of-mouth legend of the secretive man who could do magical things on a golf course was left the same way it was created, unproven by science or numbers or certifiable results in front of a skeptical public. Faith was a necessary component for belief.

The celebrity of John Montague would never totally leave, of course, because a little bit of the adhesive for fame, once applied, always remains, no matter what happens next. He was off into that half-light of leftover public recognition, touched by something notable that had happened in his past, a name seen every once in a while in those little filler items that appear at the bottom of a printed page, a curious note in a column of many notes. He lived in the perfect place for this existence, a town of forty-watt celebrities like himself, Sunset Boulevard characters who had once danced with the truly glamorous, had spoken some lines in an Academy Award production, married So-and-So, played first trumpet in Someone's big band. He was a semi-identifiable face in the Hollywood crowd.

"Montague..."

"Beat Bing Crosby with a baseball bat, shovel, and rake. Once knocked a bird off a telephone wire...."

"Yes, yes, I remember now."

He was around. He played in some California tournaments, played in the Cal Open, finished sixth in 1941, but never won anything of note. He played some exhibitions with Babe Didrikson, with Walter Hagen, with George Von Elm, but now was a trick-shot curiosity more than a star in the making. His personal life, unchanged, roared forward. He still attacked the night better than he attacked the golf course.

"Montague and I and Johnny Weissmuller were invited to play in an invitational in Santa Barbara," professional wrestler

George Zaharias, who married Babe Didrikson, reported. "They gave us a big dormitory room with three double beds.

"We were out having drinks and so forth and I wasn't feeling very good so I came home around midnight. Johnny came home around two and Montague came in around three. He walked over to Johnny Weissmuller's bed and just flipped the mattress and sprawled Johnny all over the floor. He then came over to my bed and I said, 'John, I don't feel very good. I don't want you trying that.'

"It didn't look like he was going to pay any attention to me, so I sat up on the bed and when he came over I grabbed him, spun him around and took him by the nap of the neck and the seat of the pants and picked him off the ground. There was a great big double window and I took him over to it and held him outside. And I told him, 'If you ever try that again, I'll drop you.' "

Babe Ruth called him to Detroit to play in an exhibition against Ty Cobb and Hagen on July 29, 1941. He shot a 70, best score in the foursome, but it didn't matter. Cobb shot a 78 to beat Ruth's 81 and win an invented title of best has-been golf champion. That was the competition that counted. Montague was a small part of the show. No doubt there were cocktails in the night.

He played in some USO exhibitions with Bob Hope during World War II, local events, not the traveling shows to the front. He shot a 67 in a Red Cross exhibition in 1943 at Recreation Park in Long Beach, following a 65 at an exhibition a week earlier, which caused Darsie L. Darsie to write in the *Los Angeles Times* that "all of which revives hope that one of these days 'Mysterious Montague' may again play the golf and the shots he did in those years when he was the 'talk of the world.' " This was nostalgia, not promise.

In the middle of the war, Montague took a job and then a piece of the action as the home professional at the California Country Club, an operation that included Weissmuller, John Wayne, and Fred MacMurray as investors. He was an advertised public asset, his picture taken as he showed movie stars how to putt or hit a sand wedge. When the investment turned sour, he wound up suing Wayne and MacMurray and the more famous partners, but won only a two-thousand-dollar judgment.

In 1947, his wife, Esther Plunkett Montague, died young after a fight with cancer. Montague did not handle this well. He never had been close to her two children. Indeed, her son, Jack, later said he "hated" his stepfather for blowing through all of his mother's money. Alone now, family life done, Montague had few last restraints.

The troubles of a drinking man soon started to land. He was arrested on a drunkenness charge in the back of a pickup truck behind the Beverly Wilshire Hotel in 1948. He had a heart attack in Fresno on the eve of the 1949 California Open. He was hospitalized with an undisclosed stomach ailment in 1954. He was injured in 1955 when he drove into two parked cars and a tree on Hollywood Boulevard after midnight.

The time he spent at the racetracks, Del Mar and Santa Anita, increased with age. The time at the golf course decreased. He talked of fortunes won and fortunes lost, a large man full of bluster, always tied to the next big thing, which never really materialized. He actually filmed some golf shorts, demonstrating the proper use of the shovel, rake, and baseball bat in 1954, but they didn't create great interest.

His only trip back to Syracuse came in 1955, when his father was dying. Matthew Moore had wanted to see "my baby boy" one more time. Montague stayed for a while, known now to his nieces as "Uncle John." His brother, Harold, and one of his sisters, Mary, had visited him in California in the aftermath of the trial and came home with stories of meeting William Frawley and Oliver Hardy and other famous people, but now they were wary when phone calls came from the West Coast. Uncle John was often looking for money to help finance the next best thing. He didn't return to Syracuse in 1957, when his mother died.

His invented life was his real life. His invented name—changed legally a few months after his return from the trial—was his real name. There was no question.

His true home was Hollywood. He went to Florida now and again, followed the sun and the golf ball and the horses, but he always returned to Hollywood. He fit in the movie capital, the land of the deal, hustling with the hustlers, dreaming with the dreamers, lining up a putt, seated in the restaurant, giving opinions at the end of the bar, another former somebody. He was around.

The legend fared worse than the man. The small group of people who had seen John Montague do wondrous things at the Lakeside Golf Club began to disappear. Oliver Hardy finally found a happy marriage. Bing Crosby became the busiest man on the planet. George Von Elm eventually moved to Pocatello, Idaho. W. C. Fields was dead by 1948. The late, late nights in the men's bar at Lakeside were populated by other fast runners like Forrest Tucker and Phil Harris and Mickey Rooney for a while, then vanished altogether.

No new voices were around to repeat the words to the stories. The old voices, once gone, spoke no more.

The biggest loss was Grantland Rice. He never wavered. He wrote a column on April 24, 1954, that contained much of the old material, but also this: "A great many will tell you that Montague, originally a Syracuse boy, was overplayed. This isn't true." Three months later, after typing an appreciation of the talents of twenty-three-year-old Willie Mays, the dean of American sportswriters suffered a stroke and died at the age of seventy-three.

In *The Tumult and the Shouting,* an autobiography released after his death, he called Montague "perhaps the strongest man I ever knew." He told a story about playing in a foursome with Montague, Ty Cobb, and P. Hal Sims, the bridge player. He said, "Montague, of course, could spot us ten strokes each and murder us."

Rice was the heart of the legend. He had brought Westbrook Pegler, Henry McLemore, Alex Morrison, *Time* magazine, and the whole country into the game. His opinion that he had seen "the greatest golfer in the world" in a succession of five-dollar Nassaus at Lakeside was the foundation of all that followed.

His disappointment at Montague's public failures—even though he saw them coming—had to be large. He was the baseball scout who had predicted greatness for the phenom from the sandlots, the editor who signed up the next best-seller that would rock the world. The desired result simply never arrived.

The difference between what Rice saw in 1933 and 1934 and what everyone else saw in 1937 and beyond was about fifty yards. The young Montague had found a technological secret with his oversize driver and had the strength to control it. He was fifty, sixty, seventy years ahead of his time, hitting the ball 300, 350 yards, always farther than everyone else.

This was not illusion. Rice saw what he saw, knew what he knew, not only as a sportswriter, but also as a very good golfer. He had played with the greats of this evolving game, covered them in their big moments, walked next to them when they made history. None of them played the way the young Montague played. This was the future—hit the ball long on the first shot, hit the ball high on the second shot, putt for the birdie. The development of new, lighter materials and bigger and bigger clubs would bring the game this way. Future stars like Jack Nicklaus and Tiger Woods would move the game in this direction. The young Montague was a first step.

Only no one else except Grantland Rice and the celebrated duffers of Lakeside Golf Club ever saw it. That was the shame.

"I hope Montague amazes everyone with his ability," sportswriter Jack Cuddy wrote in the *Washington Post* on the eve of that big exhibition with Babe Ruth and Babe Didrikson on Long Island in November 1937. "I hope he knocks birdies off telephone wires as friends say he can do and I hope he registers a flock of birdies as the cow-pasture circus treks from hole to hole. I hope he emerges from Fresh Meadow as a mighty new sports hero. It's always so tragic and futile to see a legend destroyed."

Destruction, alas, was the result.

The public flop canceled out all of the stories, even the ones told by the country's most eminent sports storyteller. How could the greatest golfer who ever lived never win a tournament? Without proof, without pictures hung on a museum wall, the great artist cannot be considered great. When the moment finally came for Montague, he was too old, too heavy, ordinary.

Not bad, but ordinary. The extra fifty yards that separated him from everyone else were gone. He was back with the pack, back with everyone else.

When Rice died, preceded and followed shortly by his contemporaries, the legend pretty much died. It was replaced by believe-it-or-not kitsch, factoids, the tale of the one-hole match with Crosby, the bird on the wire, the trial. No one made the case that Rice had made. No one saw what he had seen because it was no longer there.

Montague was characterized now as a gadabout and schemer. He sued *Life* magazine in 1956 for an article titled "Larceny on the Links: How Golf's Con Men Take the Sucker," which called him "the first great hustler to take advantage of the palefaces." He didn't have a chance of making money for damages. The bettor, the hustler, had become his role in golf history. He was comic relief, a supporting actor on the side of the serious business.

A sweet story of Art Rogers's appeared on the outdoors pages of the *Los Angeles Times* on February 12, 1960. Montague was hunting with some members of the Greenhead Duck Hunting Club at Santa Ynez. The discussion rolled around to his feat of nailing the bird—the sparrow, whatever it was—on the telephone wire. He was challenged, first, to hit a duck. Then one of the members said that hitting a sitting duck was easy. Hitting a duck in flight, well, that would be doing something.

Montague pulled out a five-wood and a half dozen balls. He said he'd give it a shot.

"I figure these birds come in at about 70 miles per hour," he said. "A well-hit golf ball goes about 140. If the duck flies a straight line, the only problem is timing the drive so the ball reaches the collision point the same time the duck does."

He missed badly on the first two attempts. Everyone laughed. He missed a duck by five feet and the laughing stopped. He missed again by twenty feet. The laughs resumed. On his fifth try the duck was one hundred yards away from Montague as he started to swing, and was sixty yards away when the golf ball went within two inches of its bill. The duck stopped in midair with a squawk.

It was a moment.

In the summer of 1963, Montague wrote a long letter to Bobby Jones from Room 309 at John Wesley Hospital at 2826 South Hope Street in Los Angeles. He was fifty-nine years old now, a few weeks short of his sixtieth birthday, had been in Room 309 for seven months, and the view from his hospital bed was pretty much a good look at his own mortality. He wanted to get things down on paper, the same way Jones and Walter Hagen had in as-told-to autobiographies that had been best-sellers in the past few years.

The pretext for the letter was some public comments by seventy-three-year-old golfer Chick Evans in a two-part Associated Press series. Cantankerous as ever, the first man to win both the U.S. Open and U.S. Amateur in the same year (1916), Evans had leveled the modern golfers like Jack Nicklaus and Arnold Palmer ("They buy their game in the golf shop. Back in the old days when you were playing with seven or eight clubs, you had to develop skill. You had to have a sense of touch"), the modern golf courses ("fairways that look like front lawns...a rough that looks like a crewcut...velvet greens"), and just about anything else he saw in front of him. His biggest target was the golfing sainthood that had been conferred on Bobby Jones.

Evans claimed that Jones was a professional when he completed the Grand Slam by winning the U.S. Amateur in 1930 because he already had accepted $25,000 from studio head Jack Warner for doing those filmed golf shorts at Lakeside. He also said Jones was an unpleasant adversary, a pompous stickler for rules that didn't matter, and finished by saying that Jones was far from the best golfer who had ever played.

"Perhaps the best part of his game was his ability to sink a long putt," Evans said. "He had to be good at that because from 50 yards out he was pitiful."

Montague opened his letter with his opinions of Evans and Evans's comments, not good, then soon moved into his own hospital predicament, his hopes and frustrations. He ultimately looked for help on the book project, one aging golfer to another. Jones was now sixty-one years old, also beset with physical problems. The degenerative spinal condition, cervical spondylosis, which had ended his golf career so early, now had driven him to a wheelchair. He was in daily pain.

Dear Bobby,
Have delayed writing you due to my hospitalization that dates back to Dec. 1962. Will touch on that later. Read the highly unwarranted and derogatory article the informer Chick Evans coughed up to the wire service. Chick must be slipping with old age, "too bad," and one can only attribute such fallacy to jealousy. You won the "Grand Slam" and he

didn't. Played golf with him around Chicago and while I never had occasion to put the acid test to him I'm sure I never would have wanted him to be on my jury. He should turn back the pages to his early life history, check on a few things and start all over again from scratch. When a guy has to resort to such cheapness and unsportsmanlike tactics, a rest home is in view where he can finish the closing chapters of his life's biography. Oddly enough, those around Chicago called him "Chicken," (a pet name) and at this writing it appears he was appropriately nicknamed. Too bad the sinless hacker can't go to the finish line without carrying the burden of an uncalled for wrong done to a right guy. Anyway, it isn't too late to send the ex milkman a policeman's badge, cap and whistle—he might make "Dick Tracey's team."

Watched the Masters on TV, saw you with the boys after the finish and you looked quite well. The present crop of golfers score all right, but they've got a long way to go to match the color and showmanship you, Hagen and the rest of the golfing personalities gave the public.

Since my hospital confinement I've had ample time to think about the near future. Was rushed to the hospital after my fall of 25 feet from a ladder trying to fix a TV antenna. The X-rays revealed I had a broken hip, broken pelvis, fractured coccyx bone, plus multiple body bruises. What a combo!! I've parlayed my action with God's help against time and hope to come out a winner and right now I'm "in the stretch." It's a tough shot, but I've got a club for it and will make it. I was paralyzed from the hips down and only six weeks ago I was allowed to sit up in a wheelchair. I was as tickled as a kid with a new hot rod. My biggest problem was mounting a bedpan in bed. Shoemaker couldn't mount it. Have a hip orderly who wheels me the scenic route over to the Physiotherapy cave where they jiggle me around for an hour three days a week. After the action, I am allowed to sit outside in the sun, which is a pleasure indeed, and I have an excellent view of the exit gate I hope to crash through very soon.

Bobby, I consider myself lucky to survive my misfortune and I'm grateful to the guy upstairs for my recovery. All my bone breaks have healed wonderfully well and I'll be walking without an aid soon. Boy, when people enjoy good health they're millionaires and should thank the Almighty for such a blessing bestowed on them.

Prior to my accident I had something of real merit going for me and when they discharge me from the warehouse, I hope to resume where I left off. A series of golf shorts with Desilu is in the making and I plan to do a master pilot first, then go from there. This is something along with a golf book and biography I sidelined for many years due to my wife's illness (cancer). Now that she has passed on, I am going to do what our dear friend Granny Rice wanted me to do for years. It was too bad he had to go; he was a wonderful man. I was with him on his last visit to the Coast. A lot of the boys (our kind) like Babe Hardy, Frank Borza, Kibbee, Gable and the others have passed on, but they have left pleasant memories to those who knew them. Most of the Lakeside gang have spread out to other clubs and retirement, but some like your friend George Marshall, Davis and other Wilshire CC cronies congregate every day (not working) for bridge and gin rummy sessions.

Have done considerable format work for shorts and quite a bit of my life story while confined here. While I know quite a few literary agents, etc., I would appreciate an expression from you on what might be the best course to proceed. Sometime back, Simon and Schuster, AS Barnes and Doubleday were interested to the extent of publishing books for me. And Granny, if he had lived, intended doing such. Also, Gene Fowler.

Have read yours and the Haig's and I somehow feel, along with others who are interested in me, that following your pattern would be a successful one. So many people I know enjoyed reading you, including Bob Young and Jimmy Dunn. If you feel so inclined to drop me a note touching on the above mentioned, I'll sure appreciate it.

Will sign off for now, Bobby, trusting all is well by you and wishing you the very best of everything in life. Take care and God bless.

Your friend,
John Montague

The letter was handwritten with Palmer Method precision, tight and straight across unlined paper, the trained result of a Catholic education with its assorted raps with a wooden ruler across the knuckles of an unsteady hand. A sense of desperation lurked in the breezy content. The words were too familiar, invoked too many names, made too many nudges, allusions to experiences that probably weren't shared by both parties the same way. This was the letter of a man who was trying too hard.

The reply from Jones was typed. Dictated to secretary Jean Marshall and typed. The words mostly were quick and efficient.

Not unpleasant, but efficient. No names or anecdotes were included. No nonsense.

Dear Monty:

I am terribly sorry to learn that you have been so badly banged up. Fortunately, you are a tough guy and able to take it as well as anybody I can think of.

With reference to your forthcoming book, I would suggest that you avoid the instructional angle completely. We have already had far too much of the same sort of stuff written by professional writers who merely glean ideas from past literature.

On the other hand, you have had a colorful life, which could make an interesting story, and yet is probably one that could be told best in the third person.

The best advice I can give you is to try to hook up with a really able writer and then sell the rights to your story to some publisher. I should think you should get a larger share of the total sales price than the man who merely sets down the words.

I do hope that you will be back in circulation soon and in as good shape as ever. With all good wishes,

> Most sincerely,
> Bob Jones

RTJ:jsm

A letter from a mortgage company, announcing that it sadly could not grant the loan for the requested amount, would have had the same tone. Busy here. Good luck on your future endeavors. Be well. Montague was looking for an introduction, a favor. None was delivered. A door was closed politely but forcefully. Bobby Jones wanted no part of John Montague's troubles. He had his own troubles.

No doubt the man from Hollywood had found similar closed doors in his recent past.

He was out of the hospital and had recovered enough by March 1964 to tell his brother, Harold, in a letter that he had broken par on a pitch-and-putt course and was now looking forward to getting back to regulation golf. He said he thought his distance off the tee would be "satisfactory" once he started playing again.

His business hope of the moment was "the Montescope," a foldable magnifying-glass contraption that could be used to both determine distance from the green and help search for lost balls. He sent along a prototype in a leather carrying case. A holdup in production in Japan probably meant that the Montescope would not be ready to be sold at the Indianapolis 500 in May, which had been the plan, but he hoped it would be available sometime during the second half of the one-year run of the World's Fair in New York, which would open in April.

The remainder of his life would be a succession of enterprises like the Montescope, spins on the carnival wheel in search of the fast fortune that would not come. His health would never be good, rumors floated time and again that he had died or was near death, only to be disproved when he appeared, bigger than ever, still on the move. In his letter to Harold, his optimism over the Montescope was balanced subtly by his return address. He told his brother to reply to John Montague, c/o Whitney Investment Company, 186 No. Canon Drive, Beverly Hills, California, "until further notified." No home address was given.

A new associate was Arthur Abrams, a *Los Angeles Examiner* typesetter by trade, a dreamer by nature. Abrams was another guy who always had a half dozen projects in various stages of gestation. He was an amateur photographer of note, a good storyteller, a big man with a broken nose, friend to everyone he met. He met Montague at a club he had formed, "Cauliflower Alley," a weekly gathering of retired wrestlers and boxers, other big men with broken noses, at Baron's Castle, a restaurant owned by former wrestler Mike Mazurki in the Los Angeles Elks Club building. Also an actor and once the bodyguard for Mae West, Mazurki was the broken-nose president of Cauliflower Alley, former boxer Lou Nova was vice president, and Abrams was the spiritual force.

"We weren't much of a religious family, but every Passover we'd do a dinner," Abrams's son Ira said. "All of these wrestlers would be there. Some old-time actors, too, like Broderick Crawford. It was a different kind of Passover."

Montague fit well into this group. He had the same robust sensibilities. He also fit well with Abrams. They heard the same kind of music, those great symphonies of possibility that ultimately went nowhere.

The typesetter had a plan during World War II to make cheap, three-wheeled jeeps, based on bumper-car technology from amusement parks. Never materialized. A plan for "boatels," houseboats used as hotels, also went nowhere. A pretty good plan for public housing in Mexico—ship down the insides of house trailers, only the insides, and build adobe walls around them—showed promise, but in the end, alas, also never materialized.

"My dad always had great ideas," his son said. "But he wasn't a finisher. He couldn't finish any of them."

Montague became a part of the unfinished dreams. He posed next to the three-wheeled jeep. The Montescope—never materialized, never happened—was a dream. The golfer's fading notoriety was a calling card, an entry to the next round of meetings for the next plan. He posed next to Abrams and the grandson of Geronimo, the Indian chief, after some meeting about doing something big in the desert. There was always something.

A basic dream involved telling Montague's life story. He and Abrams talked often about that. Abrams took pictures of the aging Montague in action with the shovel, rake, and baseball bat. He listened to Montague's melodrama with its many twists. A screenplay—the ultimate Hollywood dream, created in the basement of every dreamer in the town—was written. The hope was that Jackie Gleason, a wonder in *The Hustler* in 1961 as Minnesota Fats, would play the lead role. Gleason was a golfer. Gleason would be perfect.

Never materialized.

Never happened.

On May 25, 1972, still full of dreams, John Montague died. He suffered a heart attack in his room at a residence motel at 1181 Ventura Boulevard in Studio City, where he lived on welfare checks and Social Security. He was sixty-eight years old. The death certificate listed his "Last Occupation" as "Golf Player." His "Kind of Industry" or "Business" was "Professional Sports." He was "Self Employed."

His body was taken to Utter-McKinley's Valley Mortuary on Lankesham Boulevard, where it rested for a week, unclaimed. The Public Administrator's office could uncover no family for this John Montague. That was the final liability of an invented name and an invented life. A plan was made to have the body cremated, ashes spread into the Pacific Ocean or buried in Potter's Field.

Arthur Abrams came forward. He signed for the remains of his business associate and friend and planned a service. An article about all this appeared in the *Los Angeles Times*.

"Some called him the world's greatest strong man," reporter Dwight Chapin wrote. "Some called him a con man."

"He made and lost a million dollars—several times," Arthur Abrams told the reporter.

The article was long, replayed the entire tale, jumped from the front sports page to the middle of the section. An Arthur Abrams picture of an older, balding Montague, lining up a putt with a garden rake, illustrated the text.

Mary Moore, the youngest of Harold's daughters from Syracuse, Montague's niece, was a graduate student at UCLA. Her father had cautioned her to stay away from Uncle John and certainly never to give him money. She had followed the advice, never made contact, but had talked about him, told as much as she knew about the celebrity story to her new L.A. friends.

One of them slipped a copy of the *Times* article under her door. The question "Isn't this your uncle?" was written across the top.

Mary Moore became the family representative at the funeral. She called home, broke the news, and the family contacted Arthur Abrams about paying for the arrangements. She went with her friend, the one who had slipped the newspaper under her door, to the service for the uncle she didn't know.

They were struck by the Hollywood quality of the proceedings, far, far from the Catholic rituals of the old churches in Syracuse. They saw someone, they didn't know who the person was, arrive in a limousine, chauffeur waiting at the door. They saw other people sort of amble in, golf shirts and old pants, as if they were stopping on the way to the supermarket. Only twenty-nine people, Mary Moore and her friend included, were in attendance. Three large pictures of her uncle were against a wall, flanked by three funeral bouquets.

The eulogy was delivered by Richard Arlen, the old friend, the messenger boy turned actor, discovered when he crashed his motorcycle at the studio gate, the golfer who had brought John Montague to the Lakeside Golf Club. Strangely, he talked a lot about Montague's troubles with the law.

Arlen had many of his facts wrong. He seemed to think Montague had gone to trial for killing a Chinese man who "came at him with a meat cleaver." Arlen called it self-defense. He repeated the phrase "Chinese man with a meat cleaver" again and again in his story. People began to smile.

Mary Moore went to the graveside, did her job, and never talked much about her uncle with her family. He seemed to be a forbidden subject. Her father and her aunts seldom talked about him, and when they did the conversation was muffled and brief. He was the black sheep, best forgotten. That generation of the family, her parents and aunts, eventually passed away, and Mary Moore still thought that Uncle John had murdered someone, probably the Chinese man with the meat cleaver.

Not until years later—not long ago—did her sister, Joan D'Aiuto, provide her with the proper details. Joan D'Aiuto had done some research, pulled up some articles from the past. She showed them to her sister. No, Uncle John had never murdered anyone. There had been this robbery, see, golf clubs left in the car. . . .

John Montague is buried in Holy Cross Cemetery in Culver City, California. Holy Cross is the major Catholic cemetery for Hollywood. Bela Lugosi is buried there. Mary Astor, Rita Hayworth, and Jackie Coogan are there. Lawrence Welk is there. Sharon Tate. Mario Lanza. Ray Bolger. John Candy is there. Jimmy Durante. Rosalind Russell. Loretta Young.

A number of the members of the Lakeside Golf Club are there. Mack Sennett. Henry King, the director. Fred MacMurray. Richard Arlen followed John Montague there on March 31, 1976. He died in a nursing home, age seventy-five, from emphysema. On October 14, 1977, Harry Lillis (Bing) Crosby died in Madrid, Spain, at the La Moraleja Golf Course. He had completed eighteen holes and was twenty yards from the clubhouse when he was dropped by a heart attack. The other members of his foursome said he had shot an 85. His body was brought back to Hollywood for a simple service. He was buried on the side of a hill at Holy Cross Cemetery.

There are possibilities.

ACKNOWLEDGMENTS

Thanks to Esther Newberg, my agent. Thanks to Jason Kaufman, my editor, and his assistant, Rob Bloom. Thanks to Bill Thomas and everyone at Doubleday.

Thanks to Joan D'Aiuto, Terri Petersen, Dr. Mary Moore, and John Curtin. Thanks to Suzy Doolittle, Chris Wagner, Ira Abrams, Harriet Hodges, and Lois Laurel Hawes. Thanks to Doug Stark and Patty Moran at Golf House in Far Hills, New Jersey. Thanks to the librarians in the microfilm rooms at the New York, Boston, and Los Angeles public libraries. Thanks to the research librarians at the various academic libraries where I followed many blind roads. Thanks to anyone who answered the phone or returned a call.

Thanks to Charlie Costanzo, Paul Doyle, the rest of the Garden Street Athletic Club, Mark Linehan, Ian Thomson, Jackie MacMullan, Kevin Connolly, Brian Shutt, Tim Murphy, Clark

Booth, Tommy and Suzanne Strempek Shea, and John Schulian.
Thanks to Leigh Alan Montville, and to Robin and Douglas and
Jackson Moleux.

Special thanks to Linda Finkel, first reader and boon companion.

NOTES*† ON SOURCES

CHAPTER 1

The framework for the story of the robbery came from extensive un-bylined reports in both the *Essex County Republican* and the *Adirondack Record–Elizabethtown Post*. Details were added from the testimony of all the principals at the trial seven years later. An interview with Harriet Hodges, one of the Hana children, provided information about family life and operation of the restaurant.

Rum Across the Border: The Prohibition Era in Northern New

---

*Numerous back issues of newspapers used throughout this book were found through the Web service ProQuest, for major U.S. dailies, and Newspaper Archives, for smaller dailies. The unseen stars of any look back at twentieth-century events are the nameless correspondents for the wire services, who recorded history as it happened.

†Numerous Web sites were used to check facts, dates, and spellings.

York, by Allan S. Everest, describes the time and environment. A quote from an unnamed farmer was used from this book.

"Mystery Montague: Was Hollywood's Gift to Golf an Adirondack Felon?" by Suzy Colt (aka Suzy Doolittle) in the June 2004 issue of *Adirondack Life* tells the basic John Montague story. Ms. Doolittle, a researcher at the Essex County History Center, also provided clippings and background information about Elizabethtown and the surrounding area.

CHAPTER 2

The Lakeside Golf Club of Hollywood 50th Anniversary Book, written in 1974 by member Norman Blackburn, contains quotes and anecdotes I used about the club. Published in a limited edition of 1,156 copies for Lakeside members, the book is filled with the reminiscences of and about famous Hollywood people. The copy used here was No. 313, originally owned by Indianapolis 500 racing great Peter DePaolo, purchased online.

Interviews with Allene Gates, the fourth wife of Johnny Weissmuller, and Eddie Gannon, longtime Lakeside employee, answered questions about Lakeside and John Montague in the thirties. An interview with Richard Arlen's daughter, Rose Marie Mauer, added detail to his story.

Golf in Hollywood: Where the Stars Come Out to Play by Robert Z. Chew and David J. Pavoni and *Win 90% of Your Golf Bets* by "Action Al" Williams contain more quotes and anecdotes and retell the basic Montague story in Hollywood.

Stories by Darsie L. Darsie for the *Los Angeles Herald* and assorted other papers and Braven Dyer for the *Los Angeles Times* and

Golf magazine followed Montague's unfolding saga. Both men were friends of the golfer, their work providing many anecdotes.

A Pocketful of Dreams: Bing Crosby, the Early Years, 1903–1940 by Gary Giddins, *Tarzan, My Father* by Johnny Weissmuller Jr., *Stan and Ollie* by Simon Louvish, and *Babe: The Life of Oliver Hardy* by John McCabe give background on some of these famous characters. An interview with Hardy historian Robert J. Wilson led to contact with other folk from *Sons of the Desert,* the thriving Laurel and Hardy fan club.

The WPA Guide to California is a classic look at the state of the state during the thirties. *The Campaign of the Century: Upton Sinclair's Race for Governor of California and the Birth of Media Politics* by Greg Mitchell describes the political and cultural forces at work. *The Book of Hollywood Quotes,* compiled by Gary Herman, was a source for at least three quotes about the town.

CHAPTER 3

Sportswriter: The Life and Times of Grantland Rice by Charles Fountain tells the story of the famous writer. Phone conversations with Fountain provided more details. *How You Played the Game: The Life of Grantland Rice* by William A. Harper was another source. *The Tumult and the Shouting* by Grantland Rice tells the writer's story in his own words.

Pegler: Angry Man of the Press by Oliver Platt describes the life of Westbrook Pegler. Pegler's columns about Montague were distributed by the Scripps-Howard syndicate.

A quote from Fred Russell about Grantland Rice came from interviews for *No Cheering in the Press Box,* by Jerome Holtzman. The book is a classic look at both sport and sportswriting during the thirties.

The columns by Grantland Rice were found in the New York Public Library's microfilm room. Most of his stories about Montague originally appeared in the now-defunct *New York Sun* and were distributed by the North American News Alliance.

The *Time* magazine article of January 25, 1937, that opened Montague to prosecution is available in the *Time* archives online. *Henry R. Luce and the Rise of the American News Media* by James L. Baughman describes the beginning years of the magazine.

CHAPTER 4

"Phantom of the Fairways" by Chris Wagner, in the May 5, 2006, Golf Guide of the *Syracuse Post-Standard,* tells Montague's life from a Syracuse perspective. Wagner provided gracious assistance with background information and a tour of Syracuse, pointing out the places where Montague roamed.

Joe Ganley, late golf writer for the *Syracuse Herald-Journal,* had a lifelong interest in Montague. Ganley's sporadic columns on the subject, plus the letters he received from his readers, provided anecdotes and quotes.

Interviews with Joan D'Aiuto, Terri Petersen, and Dr. Mary Moore, nieces of John Montague, described the family background. John Curtin, a relative by marriage, shared his research on the family genealogy.

Interviews with former mayor William Francis Walsh, David Haynes, and Tony Langan helped sketch the pictures of both Montague and Syracuse in the thirties. Paul Grondahl and Joe Layden provided information about Albany and New York state.

CHAPTER 5

The Jerry Giesler Story by Jerry Giesler (as told to Pete Martin) contains the anecdotes about his legal career. Newspaper reports at the time of Montague's arrest also described the flamboyant lawyer.

The legend of "Death Valley Scotty" is told on the desertusa.com Web site and in assorted newspaper clippings of the time. The legend of Titanic Thompson is well chronicled in many places, notably in the book *The Unsinkable Titanic Thompson* by Carlton Stowers.

CHAPTER 6

The visit of John Brown's body to Elizabethtown is described on the Web site of the Essex County Historical Society, adkhistorycenter.org.

CHAPTER 7

The Henry McLemore stories are contained in four columns he wrote between September 7 and September 21, 1937, for the United Press. They are probably the best up-close accounts of Montague's feats, made better by the fact that they were written by a skeptic. Anecdotes about McLemore's life are contained in *One of Us Is Wrong*, his autobiographical look at his journalistic career.

CHAPTERS 8 and 9

No official transcript of the trial was ever printed since the verdict was an acquittal and there was no chance of a retrial. The testimony is taken from at least six different daily newspaper accounts, especially the *New York Times*, the *Daily Mirror*, the Associated Press, and United Press. The accounts vary, with different emphases on different lines of questioning, and the result in this book is a composite of all of them. The stories by Meyer Berger of the *New York Times* and Bob Considine of the *Daily Mirror* are both comprehensive and colorful indications of the grand journalistic careers that followed.

Interviews with the sons of lawyer James M. Noonan and District Attorney Joseph McDonald provided details about their fathers' lives. An interview with Spencer Egglefield, nephew of Percy Egglefield, provided details about the sheriff's life.

CHAPTER 10

The tale of Babe Didrikson's first round of golf with Grantland Rice is told in *This Life I've Lived*, which she wrote under her married name of Babe Zaharias.

The first mention I ever saw of Mysterious Montague was in *Babe: The Legend Comes to Life* by Robert Creamer. Creamer gives a small account of the famed golf match that included Ruth, Didrikson, Montague, and Sylvia Annenberg. The event was well covered by every newspaper in New York.

CHAPTER 11

The anecdotes about Norman von Nida are included in his memoir *The Von: Stories and Suggestions from Australia's Little Golf Master*, written with Ben Robertson. The anecdotes about Larry Montes come from "Golfing Philippines" by Robin Moyer and Buddy Resurreccion, an article that appeared on golfingphilippines.com.

CHAPTER 12

The letters exchanged between Montague and Bobby Jones are included in the Bob Jones Collection in the USGA Library at Golf House in Far Hills, New Jersey. A printed interview with Gene Andrews, which described Johnny Dawson's meeting with Montague in chapter 11, is also at Golf House. Back issues of *American Golfer*, important in chapter 3, were found at Golf House.

An interview with Arthur Abrams's son, Ira, provided information about the relationship between Abrams and Montague. Details about the Cauliflower Alley Club came from its Web site, cauliflower alley.org.

BIBLIOGRAPHY

Baughman, James L. *Henry R. Luce and the Rise of the American News Media.* Boston: G. K. Hall, 1987.

Baxter, John. *Hollywood in the Thirties.* New York: A. S. Barnes, 1968.

Berger, Meyer. *Meyer Berger's New York: A Great Reporter's Love Affair with a City.* New York: Fordham University Press, 2004.

Blackburn, Norman. *Lakeside Golf Club of Hollywood 50th Anniversary Book.* Burbank, CA: Cal-Ad Company, 1974.

Butts, Edward. *Outlaws of the Lakes: Bootlegging and Smuggling from Colonial Times to Prohibition.* Holt, MI: Thunder Bay Press, 2004.

Chew, Robert Z., and David D. Pavoni. *Golf in Hollywood: Where the Stars Come Out to Play.* Santa Monica, CA: Angel City Press, 1998.

Clavin, Tim. *Sir Walter: Walter Hagen and the Invention of Professional Golf.* New York: Simon & Schuster, 2005.

Corum, Bill. *Off and Running: The Autobiography of Bill Corum.* New York: Henry Holt, 1959.

Everest, Allan S. *Rum Across the Border: The Prohibition Era in Northern New York.* Syracuse, NY: Syracuse University Press, 1978.

Federal Writers' Project of the Works Progress Administration for the State of California. *The WPA Guide to California.* New York: Pantheon Books, 1939.

Fountain, Charles. *Sportswriter: The Life and Times of Grantland Rice.* New York: Oxford University Press, 1993.

Fowler, Gene. *Skyline: A Reporter's Reminiscence of the 1920s.* New York: Viking Press, 1961.

Friedrich, Otto. *City of Nets: A Portrait of Hollywood in the 1940's.* New York: Harper and Row, 1986.

Giddins, Gary. *A Pocketful of Dreams: Bing Crosby, the Early Years, 1903–1940.* Boston: Back Bay Books, 2001.

Giesler, Jerry (as told to Pete Martin). *The Jerry Giesler Story.* New York: Simon & Schuster, 1960.

Hagen, Walter. *The Walter Hagen Story.* New York: Simon & Schuster, 1956.

Harper, William A. *How You Played the Game: The Life of Grantland Rice.* Columbia: University of Missouri Press, 1999.

Herman, Gary. *The Book of Hollywood Quotes.* London: Omnibus Press, 1979.

Louvish, Simon. *Stan and Ollie.* New York: St. Martin's Press, 2002.

McCabe, John. *Babe: The Life of Oliver Hardy.* London: Robson Books.

McGilligan, Pat. *Backstory: Interviews with Screenwriters of Hollywood's Golden Age.* Berkeley and Los Angeles: University of California Press, 1986.

McLemore, Henry. *One of Us Is Wrong*. New York: Henry Holt, 1953.

Mitchell, Greg. *The Campaign of the Century: Upton Sinclair's Race for Governor of California and the Birth of Media Politics*. New York: Random House, 1992.

Pilat, Oliver. *Pegler: Angry Man of the Press*. Boston: Beacon Press, 1963.

Rapoport, Ron. *The Immortal Bobby: Bobby Jones and the Golden Age of Golf*. Hoboken, NJ: John Wiley & Sons, 2005.

Rice, Grantland. *The Tumult and the Shouting: My Life in Sport*. New York: A. S. Barnes, 1954.

Sann, Paul. *Kill the Dutchman! The Story of Dutch Schultz*. New Rochelle, NY: Arlington House, 1971.

Stanton, Tom. *Ty and the Babe*. New York: Thomas Dunne Books, 2007.

Starr, Kevin. *Material Dreams: Southern California Through the 1920s*. New York: Oxford University Press, 1990.

Stowers, Carlton. *The Unsinkable Titanic Thompson*. New York: Paper Jacks, 1988.

Terkel, Studs. *Hard Times: An Oral History of the Great Depression*. New York: Pantheon Books, 1970.

Weissmuller, Johnny, Jr., with William Reed and W. Craig Reed. *Tarzan, My Father*. Toronto: ECW Press, 2002.

West, Nathaniel. *The Day of the Locust*. New York: Time-Life Books, 1965.

Wheeler, John. *I've Got News for You*. New York: E. P. Dutton, 1961.

Williams, "Action Al." *Win 90% of Your Golf Bets*. Anaheim, CA: Wyatt/Tyler Books, 1988.

Zaharias, Babe Didrickson. *This Live I've Led*. New York: A. S. Barnes, 1955.

PHOTOGRAPHY CREDITS

THE BIG BAM
The Life and Times of Babe Ruth

He was the Sultan of Swat. The Caliph of Clout. The Wizard of Whack. The Bambino. And, to his teammates, the Big Bam. *The Big Bam* is a thoroughly original, definitively ambitious, and exhilaratingly colorful biography of Babe Ruth, the largest legend ever to loom in baseball. But who was this large, loud, enigmatic man? Based on newly discovered documents and interviews—including pages from Ruth's personal scrapbooks—this intimate and relevatory portrait of the Babe traces Ruth's life from his bleak childhood in Baltimore to his brash entrance into professional baseball, from Boston to New York and into the record books as the world's most explosive slugger and cultural luminary. *The Big Bam* brings back the pure glory days of the game.

Biography/Sports

TED WILLIAMS
The Biography of an American Hero

The Kid. The Splendid Splinter. Teddy Ballgame. One of the greatest figures of his generation, and arguably the greatest baseball hitter of all time. But what made Ted Williams a legend? Still a gangly teenager when he joined the Boston Red Sox in 1939, Williams's boisterous personality and penchant for towering home runs earned him adoring admirers and venomous critics. Then, at the pinnacle of his prime, Williams left Boston to serve as a fighter pilot in World War II, only to return three years later and then leave again. With unmatched verve and passion, and drawing upon hundreds of interviews, acclaimed bestselling author Leigh Montville brings to life Williams's superb triumphs, lonely tragedies, and intensely colorful personality, in a biography that is fitting of an American hero and legend.

Biography/Sports

EVEL

The High-Flying Life of Evel Knievel: American Showman,
Daredevil, and Legend

Evel Knievel, the father of extreme sports, was a high-
flying daredevil. He was the personification of excitement
and danger and showmanship, and represented a unique
slice of American culture and patriotism. But behind the
flash and the frenzy, who was this man in red, white, and
blue? With characteristic flair and insight, Leigh Montville
delves into Knievel's amazing place in pop culture, as well
as his notorious dark side, exploring Knievel's complicated
and often contradictory relationships with his image, the
media, his own family, and his many demons. With this
all-American saga, Montville has delivered another definitive biography of a one-of-a-kind sports legend.

Biography/Sports

ANCHOR BOOKS
Available wherever books are sold.
www.anchorbooks.com

Printed in the United States
by Baker & Taylor Publisher Services